A Study Guide to

The Constitution of

The Universal House of Justice

A Study Guide to
The Constitution of
The Universal House of Justice

by

Guy Sinclair

GR

George Ronald
Oxford

George Ronald, *Publisher*
www.grbooks.com

© Guy Sinclair 2005
All Rights Reserved

A catalogue record for this book is available from the British Library

ISBN 0–85398–474–3

Contents

Acknowledgements

My own efforts to study the Constitution of the Universal House of Justice have been inspired by the example of Mr Hooper Dunbar, who has for many years nurtured Bahá'í scholarship through his regular classes for youth in Haifa, Israel. I am deeply grateful for the assistance I have received from the Universal House of Justice and the Research Department at the Bahá'í World Centre in response to my various queries. I would also like to thank all those who have participated in Internet discussions with me on issues relating to the Constitution and who provided me with encouragement, information and insights – particularly Dr Khazeh Fananapazir, Dr Kishan Manocha, Mr John Vahid Brown, Mr Ismael Velasco, Mr David Bikman, Dr William Collins, Dr Robert Stockman, Dr Rhett Diessner, Mr Aaron Sealy, Dr Peyvand Khaleghian, Dr Iskandar Hai and Mr Steve Cooney.

Lastly, I am ever grateful to my wife, Tina, who has constantly supported, encouraged and assisted me in completing this project.

To those devoted servants of
Bahá'u'lláh and Trustees of God,
the members of the Universal House of Justice

1

Introduction

The Universal House of Justice in the Bahá'í Writings

The Revelation of Bahá'u'lláh spanned a period of almost four decades, from the time of His incarceration in the Síyáh-Chál (Black Pit) of Tehran in 1852 to His passing in 1892. The first two decades of this Revelation – during which time Bahá'u'lláh was banished successively by the Persian and Ottoman governments and sent to Baghdad (in 1853), Constantinople and Adrianople (in 1863) and 'Akká (in 1868) – yielded many of His best-known writings. These writings include His foremost ethical, mystical and doctrinal works – The Hidden Words, The Seven Valleys and The Book of Certitude (Kitáb-i-Íqán) respectively – as well as many of His other famous works, such as The Four Valleys, the Tablet of Aḥmad, the Tablet of the Holy Mariner, the Súriy-i-Haykal (Súrih of the Temple) and His Tablets to the Kings and Rulers of the world.

It was not until the midpoint of His ministry, however, that Bahá'u'lláh revealed His Most Holy Book (Kitáb-i-Aqdas), which set out the basic laws and institutional framework for the community of His followers. This book, in the words of Shoghi Effendi:

... not only preserves for posterity the basic laws and ordinances on which the fabric of His future World Order must rest, but ordains, in addition to the function of interpretation which it confers upon His Successor, the necessary institutions through which the integrity and unity of His Faith can alone be safeguarded.

In this Charter of the future world civilization its Author ... formally ordains the institution of the 'House of Justice', defines its functions, fixes its revenues, and designates its members as the 'Men of Justice', the 'Deputies of God', the 'Trustees of the All-Merciful'...[1]

It is important to note here that Bahá'u'lláh did not explicitly distinguish between different types of House of Justice in the Most Holy Book. It is evident from the text of the Kitáb-i-Aqdas, however, that Bahá'u'lláh expected there to be at least two levels in this institution – the local House of Justice which was to be established in every city,[2] and a more general House of Justice empowered to legislate on matters not covered by Bahá'u'lláh Himself, for example marriage between relatives[3] and penalties for various offences.[4]

Bahá'u'lláh continued to reveal numerous Tablets in the last two decades of His life. In many of the most important of these Tablets – including the Bishárát (Glad-Tidings), the Kalimát-i-Firdawsíyyih (Words of Paradise), the Ishráqát (Splendours) and the Lawh-i-Dunyá (Tablet of the World) – Bahá'u'lláh elaborated on the laws of His dispensation and provided more examples of the types of duties and powers given to the House of Justice. From these writings it becomes even clearer that a Universal House of Justice is envisaged, which would, for example, deal with matters of state,[5] consult on issues not addressed in the Kitáb-i-Aqdas and enforce 'that which is agreeable to them'.[6] In one of His last works, the Lawh-i-Karmil (Tablet of Carmel), Bahá'u'lláh prophesied the establishment of the World Centre of His Faith on Mount Carmel, referring in allegorical terms to God's 'Ark', the sailing of which, according to Shoghi Effendi, 'is a reference to the establishment of the Universal House of Justice, which is indeed the Seat of Legislation, one of the branches of the World Administrative Centre of the Bahá'ís on this Holy Mountain'.[7]

Appointed by Bahá'u'lláh to act as the Head of His Faith and to be the Centre of His Covenant, 'Abdu'l-Bahá was also granted unique authority to interpret His father's Revelation. In His Tablets and talks, 'Abdu'l-Bahá, like Bahá'u'lláh, also referred to the importance of the House of Justice and, moreover, spoke explicitly of a *Universal* House of Justice 'with members elected from all the people'.[8] In His Will and Testament – a short text of less than 25 pages in its English translation, which nevertheless has a place of central importance in creating the framework of the Bahá'í Administrative Order – 'Abdu'l-Bahá returned to the subject of the House of Justice. Bringing into being the Secondary House of Justice (the institution presently known as the National Spiritual Assembly) this text also fixed the mode of election of the Universal House of Justice by the members of Secondary Houses of Justice worldwide.

In the words of Shoghi Effendi, the Will and Testament of 'Abdu'l-Bahá 'may be regarded in some of its features as supplementary to no less weighty a Book than the Kitáb-i-Aqdas'.[9] Together with the Most Holy Book, the Will and Testament 'constitutes the chief depository wherein are enshrined those priceless elements of that Divine Civilization, the establishment of which is the primary mission of the Bahá'í Faith'.[10] It is this key document that 'provides the measures for the election of the International House of Justice, defines its scope and sets forth its relationship to [the Guardianship]'.[11]

In His Will and Testament, 'Abdu'l-Bahá also appointed His grandson Shoghi Effendi to be the Guardian of the Bahá'í Faith and the authorized interpreter of the Bahá'í Revelation after Him. In Shoghi Effendi's own words, the appointment of a Guardian was necessary to enable the Faith to 'take a long, an uninterrupted view over a series of generations', and to continue to provide 'the necessary guidance to define the sphere of the legislative action of its elected representatives'.[12]

Throughout his ministry (1921–57) Shoghi Effendi looked forward to the eventual establishment of the Universal House of Justice, repeatedly describing that auspicious occasion in glowing terms. With every expansion of the Faith, with the election of every new Local or National Spiritual Assembly, he highlighted the significance of these events in laying a foundation for the election of the Universal House of Justice. Thus he explained in a letter dated 27 November 1929 to the Bahá'ís of Persia:

> The National Spiritual Assemblies, like unto pillars, will be gradually and firmly established in every country on the strong and fortified foundations of the Local Assemblies. On these pillars, the mighty edifice, the Universal House of Justice, will be erected, raising high its noble frame above the world of existence . . .
>
> Then will the Throne of Bahá'u'lláh's sovereignty be founded in the promised land and the scales of justice be raised on high. Then will the banner of the independence of the Faith be unfurled, and His Most Great Law be unveiled and rivers of laws and ordinances stream forth from this snow-white spot with all-conquering power and awe-inspiring majesty, the like of which past ages have never seen.[13]

Shoghi Effendi evoked this goal in message after message, constantly lifting the vision of the Bahá'ís to the future. In an early message to the Bahá'ís of the East, the Guardian of the Bahá'í Faith wrote that when the Universal House of Justice is established, 'God's purpose, wisdom, universal truths, mysteries and realities of the Kingdom, which the mystic Revelation of Bahá'u'lláh has deposited within the Will and Testament of 'Abdu'l-Bahá, shall gradually be revealed and made manifest'.[14] Shoghi Effendi clearly envisaged that the Universal House of Justice would be the instrument by which 'the Cause of God will become world-wide and its light will illumine the whole earth'.[15] In another early letter, this time to the Local Spiritual Assembly of Tehran, Shoghi Effendi looked forward to the formation of the Universal House of Justice, promising:

> When that central pivot of the people of Bahá shall be effectively, majestically and firmly established, a new era will dawn, heavenly bounties and graces will pour out from that Source, and the all-encompassing promises will be fulfilled.[16]

When questioned by Bahá'ís about laws or issues that had not been explicitly mentioned in the writings of either Bahá'u'lláh or 'Abdu'l-Bahá, the Guardian repeatedly referred to a future time when the Universal House of Justice had been elected and could rule on issues 'not explicitly revealed in the Sacred Text'.[17] These statements by Shoghi Effendi, together with similar statements by Bahá'u'lláh and 'Abdu'l-Bahá, form the foundation and framework for the functioning of the Universal House of Justice today. They clearly describe, and provide numerous examples, of issues and questions that the Universal House of Justice is empowered to address. The Constitution of the Universal House of Justice represents, to a significant extent, a codification of such statements, as the Universal House of Justice has itself explained:

> There remains the question concerning the authority for the duties and responsibilities outlined for the Universal House of Justice in its constitution. These provisions are a codification of explicit statements found in the sacred texts and the writings of Shoghi Effendi.[18]

One purpose of the annotations in part 4 of this study guide is to highlight and underscore how the powers and duties set out in the Constitution of the Universal House of Justice all derive directly from the writings of Bahá'u'lláh, 'Abdu'l-Bahá and Shoghi Effendi. A study of these annotations will reveal that the Universal House of Justice has been granted broad duties and decision-making powers in relation to a wide variety of subjects, from aspects of individual worship to promotion of the Lesser Peace, from the education of children to the shape of the future world order.

In this connection, a word might be said about the functioning of the Universal House of Justice in the absence of a living Guardian. Three important letters of the Universal House of Justice, dated 9 March 1965,[19] 27 May 1966[20] and 7 December 1969,[21] have addressed this issue in detail and should be studied carefully.[22] It is clear from the comments of the Universal House of Justice in these letters that Shoghi Effendi was unable to appoint a successor before his passing in 1957, that there is now no way for the Universal House of Justice or any other individual or body to appoint a second Guardian while remaining faithful to the Will and Testament of 'Abdu'l-Bahá and that the Universal House of Justice is the recipient of unfailing divine guidance even in the absence of a living Guardian.

The annotations in this study guide to the Declaration of Trust of the Universal House of Justice illustrate just how many statements of Bahá'u'lláh, 'Abdu'l-Bahá and Shoghi Effendi authorize the Universal House of Justice to act without any reference to the Guardian. It should be borne in mind that Bahá'u'lláh made no explicit mention of the Guardianship in any of His writings, and the only text by 'Abdu'l-Bahá to mention the Guardianship is His Will and Testament. The authority of the Universal House of Justice is thus in no way diminished by the absence of a living Guardian. In his own description of the relationship between the Universal House of Justice and the Guardianship, moreover, Shoghi Effendi described these two institutions as sharing a 'common' and 'fundamental object':

. . . to insure the continuity of that divinely-appointed authority which flows from the Source of our Faith, to safeguard the unity of its followers and to maintain the integrity and flexibility of its teachings. Acting in conjunction with each other these two inseparable institutions administer its affairs, cöordinate its activities, promote its interests, execute its laws and defend its subsidiary institutions . . . Far from being incompatible or mutually destructive, they supplement each other's authority and functions, and are permanently and fundamentally united in their aims.[23]

Nevertheless, the writings of Shoghi Effendi, as Guardian of the Bahá'í Faith, continue to play an important role in defining the powers and scope of authority of the Universal House of Justice, as reference to any collection of messages from the House of Justice will abundantly confirm. Indeed, the Constitution of the Universal House of Justice itself states:

The provenance, the authority, the duties, the sphere of action of the Universal House of Justice all derive from the revealed Word of Bahá'u'lláh which, together with the interpretations and expositions of the Centre of the Covenant and of the Guardian of the Cause . . . constitute the binding terms of reference of the Universal House of Justice and are its bedrock foundation.[24]

Formation of the Universal House of Justice

As well as further delineating the functions of the Universal House of Justice, Shoghi Effendi strove throughout his ministry to prepare the way for the actual formation of that institution. 'Abdu'l-Bahá had already during His own ministry arranged for the election of local bodies where possible in Iran and North America – variously called Local Houses of Justice, Local Houses of Spirituality and Local Spiritual Assemblies – and had also established the institutions of the local and national funds.[25] It was left to the Guardian to fashion these rudimentary institutions into a framework upon which the Universal House of Justice could be established.

The first 16 years of Shoghi Effendi's ministry witnessed, in his own words, 'the birth and the primary stages in the erection of the framework of the Administrative Order of the Faith . . . according to the precepts laid down in 'Abdu'l-Bahá's Will and Testament'.[26] Early in his ministry Shoghi Effendi considered the possibility of electing the Universal House of Justice but decided that this would not be possible until a firm foundation of National Spiritual Assemblies had been established.[27] Instead he quickly arranged for the election of a few National Spiritual Assemblies, in accordance with the provisions of the Will and Testament of 'Abdu'l-Bahá, in countries where strong and established Bahá'í communities already existed. The first few National Spiritual Assemblies were thus formed in the British Isles in 1923, in Germany in 1923, in India in 1923, in Egypt (for Egypt and Sudan) in 1924, and in the United States of America (for the United States and Canada) in 1925. Further National Spiritual Assemblies were formed a little later in Iraq (1931), Persia (1934), Sudan (1934) and Australia and New Zealand (1934).

Before more National Assemblies could be formed, however, additional countries needed to be opened to the Faith and Local Spiritual Assemblies had to be elected. Selecting the North American Bahá'í community as his primary instrument in this enterprise, Shoghi Effendi first ensured that that community gained sound experience of Bahá'í administration. He then encouraged that community to form at least one Local Spiritual Assembly in every state in the United States and every province in Canada and directed it to open the countries of Central and South America to the Faith.

Shoghi Effendi had meanwhile been nurturing the administrative institutions in several other national Bahá'í communities, including the United Kingdom, Iran, Germany, India, and Australia and New Zealand. These communities, like that of North America, were gradually given teaching plans by their Guardian, some requiring the collaboration of a few national communities. Finally, in 1953, Shoghi Effendi launched the first of what he expected to be a series of global

8

Plans – the Ten Year Crusade. This new Plan aimed at a massive expansion of the Bahá'í world community, opening up numerous virgin territories and forming many more Local and National Spiritual Assemblies.

Tragically, Shoghi Effendi never lived to see the completion of the Ten Year Crusade. He passed away in 1957, barely halfway into the Plan, with no successor to take up the mantle of the Guardianship. A detailed history of the testing effects of this shocking event and the heroism of the Bahá'í world in overcoming its grief and pressing on unitedly to attain the goals set for them by their Guardian has not yet been written and is certainly beyond the scope of this short essay. The best summary of this period can be found in the Introduction to *The Ministry of the Custodians*, written by the widow of Shoghi Effendi, the Hand of the Cause Amatu'l-Bahá Rúḥíyyih Khánum.[28] Suffice it to say that by the end of the Ten Year Crusade, the Bahá'í world comprised 56 National and Regional Spiritual Assemblies (from only 12 in 1953) and was thus in a position to carry out the first election of the Universal House of Justice.

In 1951 Shoghi Effendi had appointed a small group of trusted believers to serve on the first International Bahá'í Council. This institution was initially intended to carry out three functions: forging links with the authorities of the State of Israel, assisting Shoghi Effendi with the erection of the superstructure of the Shrine of the Báb and conducting negotiations with the civil authorities on matters relating to personal status.[29] From the outset, however, Shoghi Effendi had a loftier purpose in mind for the Council.

In his message announcing the appointment of the first International Bahá'í Council, Shoghi Effendi outlined a five-step process of evolution through which it would pass. The first step was the initial appointment of the Council, with the three functions outlined above. The remaining four steps were to be its evolution into an 'officially recognized Bahá'í Court', its 'transformation' into a 'duly elected body', its 'efflorescence

9

into Universal House of Justice' and finally its 'fruition' through the 'erection of manifold auxiliary institutions constituting the World Administrative Centre'.[30] The appointment of this first International Bahá'í Council was of such significance in the estimation of Shoghi Effendi that he described it in these words:

> ... THE GREATEST EVENT SHEDDING LUSTRE UPON SECOND EPOCH OF FORMATIVE AGE OF BAHÁ'Í DISPENSATION POTENTIALLY UNSURPASSED BY ANY ENTERPRISE UNDERTAKEN SINCE INCEPTION OF ADMINISTRATIVE ORDER OF FAITH ON MORROW OF 'ABDU'L-BAHÁ'S ASCENSION, RANKING SECOND ONLY TO GLORIOUS IMMORTAL EVENTS ASSOCIATED WITH MINISTRIES OF THE THREE CENTRAL FIGURES OF FAITH IN COURSE OF FIRST AGE OF MOST GLORIOUS DISPENSATION OF THE FIVE THOUSAND CENTURY BAHÁ'Í CYCLE.[31]

With no Guardian to arrange the election of the Universal House of Justice, this crucial task fell to the Hands of the Cause of God in the Holy Land, who had assumed custodianship of the Bahá'í world until the Ten Year Crusade was successfully completed. In November 1960 the Hands of the Cause arranged for a postal election of the International Bahá'í Council the following April, in accordance with Shoghi Effendi's plans.[32] This provided the Bahá'í world with valuable experience of conducting an international election. Two years later, at the very end of the Ten Year Crusade, those same Hands arranged for the first election of the Universal House of Justice. This event, unimaginably momentous in terms of the development of the Bahá'í community and Administrative Order, took place in the home of 'Abdu'l-Bahá in Haifa on the morning of 21 April 1963 and the Universal House of Justice was brought into existence.

Formulating the Constitution of the Universal House of Justice

At the very start of the first global teaching plan under its direction (the Nine Year Plan, 1964–73), the Universal House of Justice announced the following:

At the World Centre of the Faith the tasks of the Plan include
. . . formulation of the Constitution of the Universal House
of Justice . . .[33]

The process of formulating that Constitution was evidently
long and painstaking. At Riḍván 1967 the House of Justice
wrote again to the Bahá'ís of the world, reporting that 'Work
on the highly important task of formulating the Constitution
of the Universal House of Justice is well advanced'.[34] The following statement by the Universal House of Justice sheds light
on its usual decision-making process:

First, of course, it [the Universal House of Justice] observes
the greatest care in studying the Sacred Texts and the interpretations of the Guardian as well as considering the views
of all the members. After long consultation the process of
drafting a pronouncement is put into effect. During this
process the whole matter may well be reconsidered. As a
result of such reconsideration the final judgement may be
significantly different from the conclusion earlier favoured,
or possibly it may be decided not to legislate at all on that
subject at that time.[35]

This quotation conveys a sense of the careful process that
was followed in preparing the Constitution of the Universal
House of Justice, involving a comprehensive survey of all the
Bahá'í writings in Persian, Arabic and English. It was not until
1972, more than eight years after the project commenced,
that the Constitution was finally completed and signed. On
26 November 1972 the Universal House of Justice cabled all
National Spiritual Assemblies with the news:

WITH GRATEFUL JOYOUS HEARTS ANNOUNCE ENTIRE BAHÁ'Í
WORLD ADOPTION PROFOUNDLY SIGNIFICANT STEP IN UNFOLD-
MENT MISSION SUPREME ORGAN BAHÁ'Í WORLD COMMONWEALTH
THROUGH FORMULATION CONSTITUTION UNIVERSAL HOUSE OF

JUSTICE. AFTER OFFERING HUMBLE PRAYERS GRATITUDE ON DAY COVENANT AT THREE SACRED THRESHOLDS BAHJÍ HAIFA MEMBERS GATHERED COUNCIL CHAMBER PRECINCTS HOUSE BLESSED MASTER APPENDED THEIR SIGNATURES FIXED SEAL ON INSTRUMENT ENVISAGED WRITINGS BELOVED GUARDIAN HAILED BY HIM AS MOST GREAT LAW FAITH BAHÁ'U'LLÁH. FULLY ASSURED MEASURE JUST TAKEN WILL FURTHER REINFORCE TIES BINDING WORLD CENTRE TO NATIONAL LOCAL COMMUNITIES THROUGHOUT WORLD RELEASE FRESH ENERGIES INCREASE ENTHUSIASM CONFIDENCE VALIANT WORKERS HIS DIVINE VINEYARD LABOURING ASSIDUOUSLY BRING MANKIND UNDER SHELTER HIS ALL-GLORIOUS COVENANT.[36]

In its message to the Bahá'ís of the World at Riḍván 1973, the Universal House of Justice again confirmed the completion of this mighty project:

The Constitution of the Universal House of Justice, hailed by Shoghi Effendi as the Most Great Law of the Faith of Bahá'u'lláh, has been formulated and published.[37]

No doubt several considerations led the Universal House of Justice to decide to formulate a written constitution for itself. Most significantly among such considerations must be the fact that Shoghi Effendi had referred to such a constitution more than once during his ministry. Discussing the role of the Guardian of the Faith as head of the Universal House of Justice, he had qualified this authority in some important ways, including this emphatic statement:

He [the Guardian] is debarred from laying down independently the constitution that must govern the organized activities of his fellow-members [on the Universal House of Justice], and from exercising his influence in a manner that would encroach upon the liberty of those whose sacred right is to elect the body of his collaborators.[38]

In another letter, addressed to the Bahá'ís in the East at Riḍván 1948, Shoghi Effendi wrote:

. . . in the course of future years of this Bahá'í Dispensation . . . The Most Great Law, the Constitution of the Highest Legislative Body of the Bahá'í community, will be formulated in the utmost perfection.[39]

During his ministry Shoghi Effendi had encouraged the Bahá'ís of North America to formulate constitutions for their local and national institutions. In 1931 by-laws were drafted for the Spiritual Assembly of the Bahá'ís of the City of New York.[40] As Amatu'l-Bahá Rúḥíyyih Khánum explains in *The Priceless Pearl*, the framing of these by-laws, suitable for any Local Spiritual Assembly in the world, provided a legal basis on which Local Assemblies could become incorporated or registered and thus hold legal title to land and buildings, including local centres.[41] On one occasion, Shoghi Effendi explained to the American National Spiritual Assembly that the purpose of the by-laws was 'to clarify and strengthen the administrative legal functions of a Bahá'í community'.[42]

These by-laws established 'the essentials' of local Bahá'í administration and should not be 'amplified and added to'.[43] To this end the Guardian asked Local Assemblies to conform their by-laws to those developed by the New York Assembly, following that pattern 'as closely as local legal technicalities permit' so as to 'maintain international uniformity in essentials'.[44]

The National Bahá'í Constitution, or 'Declaration of Trust and By-Laws of a National Spiritual Assembly', was originally drawn up by the National Spiritual Assembly of the Bahá'ís of the United States and Canada in 1927.[45] Shoghi Effendi said that this Constitution was 'a model for all national Bahá'í constitutions'[46] and would contribute substantially to 'pave the way for the elaboration of the beginnings of the constitution of the worldwide Bahá'í Community that will form the permanent basis upon which the blest and sanctified edifice of the first

International House of Justice will securely rest and flourish'.[47] As such, he encouraged other National Spiritual Assemblies to adopt the Constitution 'in its entirety and without any alteration'.[48] Anything not specifically mentioned in it, he said, was 'a matter of secondary importance' and was 'left to the full discretion' of every National Spiritual Assembly:

> In fundamentals, however, strict conformity should be maintained throughout the Bahá'í world, and to this category belong all the principles, laws and regulations set down in the text of the national constitution.[49]

The text of the generic Local Spiritual Assembly By-Laws and National Spiritual Assembly Declaration of Trust and By-Laws are reprinted at Appendixes I and II. Any reference in these materials simply to 'the By-Laws' should be taken to mean the By-Laws of the Universal House of Justice, unless the context indicates otherwise.

Shoghi Effendi himself thus established the practice of formulating written constitutions for elected Bahá'í institutions. In *God Passes By* he wrote that 'the drafting and adoption of a Bahá'í National constitution' heralded 'the formulation of the constitution of the future Bahá'í World Community'.[50] In a letter to the National Spiritual Assembly of Persia dated 4 June 1934, moreover, Shoghi Effendi discussed the Declaration of Trust and By-Laws of the National Spiritual Assembly of the Bahá'ís of the United States and, significantly, referred to the Constitution of the Universal House of Justice as the 'Most Great Law':

> The text of this Constitution should, with the greatest meticulousness, faithfulness, and precision, be translated into Persian, for it comprises the basic administrative guidelines and fundamental principles of the Bahá'í Community. This Constitution is the Greater Law [*Namús-i-Akbar*] and the Constitution of the Universal House of Justice, which is supreme over all National Spiritual Assemblies, is the Most

14

Great Law [*Namús-i-A'zam*]. Likewise, in these days, when the friends in that country have undertaken nation-wide elections and established national Bahá'í institutions, it is essential that the compilation of the letters of this servant published in America [*Bahá'í Administration*], which are the basic source of the clauses of the Constitution, and supplement its provisions, should also be translated into Persian. They constitute a statement of the root principles of the administration; all matters not mentioned in them are secondary and subsidiary in nature, and diversity in such secondary matters will not at any time cause confusion in the administration of the Cause of God.[51]

The Form and Significance of the Constitution

The Constitution of the Universal House of Justice is divided into two parts: a Declaration of Trust and By-Laws. The Declaration of Trust provides the context of Bahá'í belief in Bahá'u'lláh, the Manifestation of God for this Day; states the fundamental purpose of His Revelation; describes the means for achieving that purpose provided for by Bahá'u'lláh; and affirms the authority of the Universal House of Justice within the Bahá'í system. The Declaration of Trust then summarizes the powers and duties that have been granted to the Universal House of Justice by the Bahá'í writings, quotes Shoghi Effendi's words of guidance to the members of that institution and describes the election of the first Universal House of Justice. The signatures of all nine of its members in 1972, and the seal of the Universal House of Justice, are fixed to the end of the Declaration of Trust.

The second part of the Constitution of the Universal House of Justice – the By-Laws – sets out the basic elements of the Bahá'í Administrative Order. It opens with a 'Preamble' that briefly describes the Administrative Order, states the criteria for membership in the Bahá'í community (Article I), summarizes the conditions for election and the jurisdictions of both Local and National Spiritual Assemblies (Articles II and III) and states the obligations of the members of Spiritual Assemblies (Article IV).

In a long Article V, headed 'The Universal House of Justice', the By-Laws codify the method of electing the Universal House of Justice that was first outlined by 'Abdu'l-Bahá in His Will and Testament (Section 1), the occasions on which vacancies in its membership may arise (Section 2), when by-elections can be called to fill such vacancies (Section 3) and the process by which its meetings are to be called and conducted (Section 4). Section 5 of Article V describes the signature of the Universal House of Justice and Section 6 addresses the issue of how its decisions are to be recorded and verified.

The By-Laws then describe in general terms the process of Bahá'í elections (Article VI), affirm the right of the Universal House of Justice to review the decisions of any Bahá'í institution (Article VII) and outline the process of appeals in the Bahá'í Administrative Order (Article VIII). Articles IX and X set out some basic details of the functioning of the Boards of Counsellors and the Auxiliary Boards respectively. Finally, Article XI addresses future amendment of the Constitution.

The Declaration of Trust and the By-Laws of the Universal House of Justice do not serve any legal purpose under the laws of Israel. As it explained in a letter dated 4 August 1974 to a National Spiritual Assembly, the Universal House of Justice is not incorporated under the laws of any country:

> The Universal House of Justice, the Head of the Bahá'í Faith and the supreme governing body of the Bahá'í International Community, is not incorporated anywhere in the world because its supranational character precludes such a limitation. As far as Israel is concerned, the Universal House of Justice is recognized by the Government of Israel as the Head of the Bahá'í Faith. This is stated in the Agreement between the Government of Israel and the Bahá'í International Community dated 22 April 1987. Article 1 (A) of the Agreement states:

The Government of Israel . . . confirms that the Bahá'í
World Centre is the world spiritual and administrative
centre of the Bahá'í world community and that the
Universal House of Justice in Haifa is the Head of the
Bahá'í Faith and its Supreme Institution in accordance
with its Constitution.

Recognition of the Universal House of Justice as the Head
of the Bahá'í Faith in Israel had also been granted by the
Attorney-General of Israel in 1976 and a Certificate to that
effect was signed on 2 May 1976.[52]

The purpose and function of the Constitution of the Universal
House of Justice, therefore, is to define the role of the Supreme
Institution of the Bahá'í Faith within the worldwide Bahá'í
community. In a letter dated 8 July 1981 written on its behalf to
an individual believer, the Universal House of Justice stated:

The Constitution of the Universal House of Justice and
those of National and Local Spiritual Assemblies can certainly be regarded as instruments of God's Covenant. The
distinctive characteristic of the Constitution of the Universal
House of Justice is that it formulates the principles governing
the operation of an institution described by the Guardian as
the 'apex of the Bahá'í Administrative Order' and defines its
relationships to the other institutions of that Order.[53]

The version of the Constitution of the Universal House of
Justice that was formulated and published in 1972 does not
necessarily represent the final form this document will take.
The Universal House of Justice has the power under Article
XI of its By-Laws to amend its own Constitution and will no
doubt do so in the future as the Bahá'í Administrative Order
evolves and gains strength. It is worth noting that the current
version of the By-Laws of the Universal House of Justice
makes no reference to the International Teaching Centre or

assistants to Auxiliary Board members. Both institutions were created by the Universal House of Justice in 1973, the year after the Constitution was originally published, the former in order to extend into the future the work of the Hands of the Cause residing in the Holy Land.[54] Similarly, the By-Laws do not mention Regional Bahá'í Councils, which have been formally instituted in several countries since 1996 as intermediate institutions between Local and National Spiritual Assemblies. Finally, it should be noted that the By-Laws currently refer to Spiritual Assemblies at the local and national levels, rather than Houses of Justice. Shoghi Effendi has explained that the 'temporary appellation of Spiritual Assemblies' will 'gradually be superseded by the permanent and more appropriate designation of House of Justice' as the powers, duties and prerogatives of these institutions are expanded.[55] Clearly, such future developments will also necessitate amendments to the Constitution.

* * *

The annotations to the Declaration of Trust and By-Laws in sections 3 and 5 of this study guide are intended to assist the reader in understanding the text of the Constitution of the Universal House of Justice. They provide some cross-references to the Bahá'í writings where such correspondences seem to suggest themselves and they supply some additional context and explanation for statements in the Constitution.

These annotations are organized under short passages from the Constitution, in bold type and without quotation marks. Each quotation from the Declaration of Trust is followed by the number of the relevant paragraph in square brackets. The annotations include quotations from the Bahá'í writings and secondary texts. Unpublished sources are described in as much detail as possible. Some sections of quotations have been printed in bold type to highlight similarities between the quotation and the particular passage in the Constitution to which the note relates.

In chapter 3 of this study guide is a compilation of passages from the Bahá'í writings regarding the station of the Universal House of Justice and the divine guidance vouchsafed to that institution. Shoghi Effendi's description of the Constitution of the Universal House of Justice as the 'Most Great Law' gives us some sense of the significance of this document, and in an email sent on its behalf to the author, the Universal House of Justice referred to its Constitution as a 'charter'. Finally, in a letter dated 30 June 1995 written on its behalf to an individual who had inquired about suggestions for improving the Bahá'í administrative system, the Universal House of Justice explained:

> The believers' own study of the writings, especially those of Shoghi Effendi and including the Constitution of the Universal House of Justice, should enable them to arrive at an ever greater understanding of the essentials of the Administrative Order. The workings of the community . . . are organic in nature and so is its growth. As time passes, the community expands, and conditions change, the House of Justice will make such adjustments and developments as are required. In so doing, the House of Justice takes cognizance of the conditions prevailing in the community and any views presented to it, reserving for itself the right of an unfettered decision in the manner described by Shoghi Effendi in 'The Dispensation of Bahá'u'lláh'. Its first consideration must always be to remain faithful to the revealed purpose of Bahá'u'lláh, as expounded and interpreted by 'Abdu'l-Bahá and the Guardian.

It is sincerely hoped that this study guide will assist the Bahá'í community to 'arrive at an ever greater understanding of the essentials of the Administrative Order', to appreciate better the majesty and uniqueness of the system designed by Bahá'u'lláh and to understand more deeply the role and function in that system of the Universal House of Justice.

2

The Station of the Universal House of Justice

A Compilation

An attempt has been made in this compilation to assemble a few quotations from the Bahá'í writings relating specifically to the station and the promises of divine guidance granted to the Universal House of Justice, rather than its powers and duties or aspects of its functioning, all of which are examined in detail later in this study guide. It is hoped that the student of the Constitution will take time to read and reflect upon these passages and thereby attain a greater appreciation of the unique importance of this supreme Bahá'í institution.

From the Writings of Bahá'u'lláh

The men of God's House of Justice have been charged with the affairs of the people. They, in truth, are the Trustees of God among His servants and the daysprings of authority in His countries.[1]

It is incumbent upon the Trustees of the House of Justice to take counsel together regarding those things which have not outwardly been revealed in the Book, and to enforce that which is agreeable to them. God will verily inspire them with whatsoever He willeth, and He, verily, is the Provider, the Omniscient.[2]

From the Writings and Talks of 'Abdu'l-Bahá

The sacred and youthful branch, the guardian of the Cause of God as well as the Universal House of Justice, to be universally elected and established, are both under the care and protection of the Abhá Beauty, under the shelter and unerring guidance of His Holiness, the Exalted One (may my life be offered up for them both). Whatsoever they decide is of God. Whoso obeyeth him not, neither obeyeth them, hath not obeyed God; whoso rebelleth against him and against them hath rebelled against God; whoso opposeth him hath opposed God; whoso contendeth with them hath contended with God; whoso disputeth with him hath disputed with God; whoso denieth him hath denied God; whoso disbelieveth in him hath disbelieved in God; whoso deviateth, separateth himself and turneth aside from him hath in truth deviated, separated himself and turned aside from God. May the wrath, the fierce indignation, the vengeance of God rest upon him![3]

All must seek guidance and turn unto the Centre of the Cause and the House of Justice. And he that turneth unto whatsoever else is indeed in grievous error.[4]

All must consider themselves to be of the order of subjects, submissive and obedient to the commandments of God and the laws of the House of Justice. Should any deviate by so much as a needle's point from the decrees of the Universal House of Justice, or falter in his compliance therewith, then is he of the outcast and rejected.[5]

To epitomize: essential infallibility belongs especially to the supreme Manifestations, and acquired infallibility is granted to every holy soul. For instance, the Universal House of Justice, if it be established under the necessary conditions – with members elected from all the people – that House of Justice will be under the protection and the unerring guidance of God . . . Now the members of the House of Justice have not, individually, essential infallibility; but the body of the House of Justice is under the protection and unerring guidance of God: this is called conferred infallibility.[6]

Should there be differences of opinion, the Supreme House of Justice would immediately resolve the problems. Whatever will be its decision, by majority vote, shall be the real truth, inasmuch as that House is under the protection, unerring guidance and care of the one true Lord. He shall guard it from error and will protect it under the wing of His sanctity and infallibility. He who opposes it is cast out and will eventually be of the defeated.[7]

Let it not be imagined that the House of Justice will take any decision according to its own concepts and opinions. God forbid! The Supreme House of Justice will take decisions and establish laws through the inspiration and confirmation of the Holy Spirit, because it is in the safekeeping and under the shelter and protection of the Ancient Beauty, and obedience to its decisions is a bounden and essential duty and an absolute obligation, and there is no escape for anyone.

Say, O people: Verily the Supreme House of Justice is under the wings of your Lord, the Compassionate, the All-Merciful, that is, under His protection, His care, and His shelter; for He has commanded the firm believers to obey that blessed, sanctified and all-subduing body, whose sovereignty is divinely ordained and of the Kingdom of Heaven and whose laws are inspired and spiritual.[8]

From the Writings of Shoghi Effendi

. . . as the Bahá'í Faith permeates the masses of the peoples of East and West, and its truth is embraced by the majority of the peoples of a number of the Sovereign States of the world, will the Universal House of Justice attain the plenitude of its power, and exercise, as the supreme organ of the Bahá'í Commonwealth, all the rights, the duties, and responsibilities incumbent upon the world's future super-state.[9]

. . . God's Supreme House of Justice shall be erected and firmly established in the days to come. When this most great edifice shall be reared on such an immovable foundation, God's purpose, wisdom, universal truths, mysteries and realities of the Kingdom, which the mystic Revelation of Bahá'u'lláh has deposited within the Will and Testament of 'Abdu'l-Bahá, shall gradually be revealed and made manifest.[10]

When the Universal House of Justice shall have stepped forth from the realm of hope into that of visible fulfilment and its fame be established in every corner and clime of the world, then that august body – solidly grounded and founded on the firm and unshakeable foundation of the entire Bahá'í community of East and West, and the recipient of the bounties of God and His inspiration – will proceed to devise and carry out important undertakings, world-wide activities and the establishment of glorious institutions. By this means the renown of the Cause of God will become world-wide and its light will illumine the whole earth.[11]

These Spiritual Assemblies have been primarily constituted to carry out these affairs, and secondly to lay a perfect and strong foundation for the establishment of the divine and Universal House of Justice. When that central pivot of the people of Bahá shall be effectively, majestically and firmly established, a new era will dawn, heavenly bounties and graces will pour out from that Source, and the all-encompassing promises will be fulfilled.[12]

The National Spiritual Assemblies, like unto pillars, will be gradually and firmly established in every country on the strong and fortified foundations of the Local Assemblies. On these pillars, the mighty edifice, the Universal House of Justice, will be erected, raising high its noble frame above the world of existence. The unity of the followers of Bahá'u'lláh will thus be realized and fulfilled from one end of the earth to the other. The explicit ordinances of His Most Holy Book will be promulgated, applied and carried out most befittingly in the world of creation, and the living waters of everlasting life will stream forth from that fountain-head of God's World Order upon all the warring nations and peoples of the world, to wash away the evils and iniquities of the realm of dust, and heal man's age-old ills and ailments. Then will the visible sovereignty of the Most Great Name shake the foundations of the countries and nations of the world, strike fear and remorse in the hearts of some of the traditional ecclesiastical divines of various creeds and nations, and cause others to become frustrated, disturbed, vanquished and obliterated . . .[13]

Then will the Throne of Bahá'u'lláh's sovereignty be founded in the promised land and the scales of justice be raised on high. Then will the banner of the independence of the Faith be unfurled, and His Most Great Law be unveiled and rivers of laws and ordinances stream forth from this snow-white spot with all-conquering power and awe-inspiring majesty, the like of which past ages have never seen. Then will appear the truth of what was revealed by the Tongue of Grandeur: 'Call out to Zion, O Carmel, and announce the joyful tidings: He that was hidden from mortal eyes is come! His all-conquering sovereignty is manifest; His all-encompassing splendour is revealed.' '. . . O Carmel . . . Well is it with him that circleth around thee, that proclaimeth the revelation of thy glory, and recounteth that which the bounty of the Lord, thy God, hath showered upon thee . . . Ere long will God sail His Ark upon thee, and will manifest the people of Bahá who have been mentioned in the Book of Names.'

Through it the pillars of the Faith on this earth will be firmly established and its hidden powers be revealed, its signs shine forth, its banners be unfurled and its light be shed upon all peoples.[14]

In this great Tablet [of Carmel] which unveils divine mysteries and heralds the establishment of two mighty, majestic and momentous undertakings – one of which is spiritual and the other administrative, both at the World Centre of the Faith – Bahá'u'lláh refers to an 'Ark', whose dwellers are the men of the Supreme House of Justice . . .[15]

3

Annotations to the Declaration of Trust

IN THE NAME OF GOD, THE ONE, THE INCOMPARABLE, THE ALL-POWERFUL, THE ALL-KNOWING, THE ALL-WISE. [para. 1]

The light that is shed from the heaven of bounty, and the benediction that shineth from the dawning-place of the will of God, the Lord of the Kingdom of Names, rest upon Him Who is the Supreme Mediator, the Most Exalted Pen, Him Whom God hath made the dawning-place of His most excellent names and the dayspring of His most exalted attributes. Through Him the light of unity hath shone forth above the horizon of the world, and the law of oneness hath been revealed amidst the nations, who, with radiant faces, have turned towards the Supreme Horizon, and acknowledged that which the Tongue of Utterance hath spoken in the kingdom of His knowledge: 'Earth and heaven, glory and dominion, are God's, the Omnipotent, the Almighty, the Lord of grace abounding!' [para. 2]

The Universal House of Justice chose to preface its constitution with this passage by Bahá'u'lláh, from His *Epistle to the Son of the Wolf*. Shoghi Effendi describes that book as 'the last outstanding Tablet revealed by the pen of Bahá'u'lláh, in which He calls upon that rapacious priest [Shaykh Muḥammad-Taqí, given by Bahá'u'lláh the surname of 'Ibn-i-Dhi'b' or 'Son of the Wolf'] to repent of his acts, quotes some of the most characteristic and celebrated passages of His own writings, and adduces proofs establishing the validity of His Cause'.[1]

The passage quoted at the start of the Declaration of Trust is the exordium and the second paragraph of the *Epistle*, on pages 1–2. Bahá'u'lláh praises the station of the Manifestation of God, emphasizing that all divine names come from Him, as well as His power to forge unity among the nations of earth. The first paragraph of the *Epistle* (after the exordium), not quoted in the Declaration of Trust, concerns God Himself and reads:

> Praise be to God, the Eternal that perisheth not, the Everlasting that declineth not, the Self-Subsisting that altereth not. He it is Who is transcendent in His sovereignty, Who is manifest through His signs, and is hidden through His mysteries. He it is at Whose bidding the standard of the Most Exalted Word hath been lifted up in the world of creation, and the banner of 'He doeth whatsoever He willeth' raised amidst all peoples. He it is Who hath revealed His Cause for the guidance of His creatures, and sent down His verses to demonstrate His Proof and His Testimony, and embellished the preface of the Book of Man with the ornament of utterance through His saying: 'The God of Mercy hath taught the Qur'án, hath created man, and taught him articulate speech.' No God is there but Him, the One, the Peerless, the Powerful, the Mighty, the Beneficent.[2]

With joyous and thankful hearts we testify to the abundance of God's Mercy, to the perfection of His Justice and to the fulfilment of His Ancient Promise. [para. 3]

The Universal House of Justice here testifies to two distinct attributes of God, mercy and justice. The attributes of justice and mercy are often mentioned together in the Bahá'í writings and contrasted so as to demonstrate that all good qualities belong to and come from God. Shoghi Effendi thus explains:

> As regards the passages in the sacred writings indicating the wrath of God . . . the Divinity has many attributes: He is loving & merciful but also just . . . This is why we read so often in the prayers statements such as 'God do not deal with us with justice, but rather through thy infinite mercy'. The wrath of God is in the administration of His justice, both in this world & in the world to come. A God that is only loving or only just is not a perfect God. The Divinity has to possess both of these aspects . . .[3]

The Universal House of Justice also testifies to the fulfilment of God's 'Ancient Promise'. This refers, no doubt, to the promise recorded in all religious scriptures of attainment to the Day of God, when God Himself shall come to earth and establish His Kingdom. Jesus Christ is thus reported to have prayed: 'Thy kingdom come, Thy will be done in earth, as it is in heaven.'[4] Bahá'ís believe that this promise has been fulfilled with the advent of Bahá'u'lláh.

Bahá'u'lláh, the Revealer of God's Word in this Day, [para. 4]

Bahá'ís believe that Bahá'u'lláh is the Manifestation of God for this Day. As such, His writings are regarded by Bahá'ís as Revelation from God. Revealers of the Word of God in previous religious dispensations, according to Bahá'í belief, have included Moses, Jesus and Muḥammad. The description of Bahá'u'lláh as the Revealer of the Word of God can be found in His own writings. In describing the virgin birth of Jesus in His Kitáb-i-Íqán (Book of Certitude), for example, Bahá'u'lláh writes:

28

And now, take heed, O brother! If such things be revealed in this Dispensation, and such incidents come to pass, at the present time, what would the people do? I swear by Him Who is the true Educator of mankind and **the Revealer of the Word of God** that the people would instantly and unquestionably pronounce Him an infidel and would sentence Him to death.[5]

In a note to paragraph 16 of the Kitáb-i-Aqdas, revealed by Bahá'u'lláh in 1873 in 'Akká, and published in an English translation with copious annotations in 1992, we read: "'Pen of the Most High'", "the Supreme Pen" and "the Most Exalted Pen" are references to Bahá'u'lláh, illustrating His function as Revealer of the Word of God.'[6]

the Source of Authority, [para. 4]

This title of Bahá'u'lláh appears twice in 'Questions and Answers', an appendix to His Most Holy Book, the Kitáb-i-Aqdas. The first instance is in Bahá'u'lláh's answer to a question regarding the giving of a promissory note in place of a dowry (a requirement of Bahá'í marriage that is not yet applicable to Bahá'ís in the West): 'Permission to adopt this practice hath been granted by **the Source of Authority**.'[7]

The second instance of this title is found in the answer to a question about the betrothal of a girl before she has reached maturity: 'This practice hath been pronounced unlawful by **the Source of Authority**, and it is unlawful to announce a marriage earlier than ninety-five days before the wedding.'[8]

Elsewhere in the Bahá'í writings the 'source of authority' is described as being held in the hand or grasp of God; this expresses God's ability to command whatever He pleases. Bahá'u'lláh also emphasizes this in 'Questions and Answers': 'In His hand is **the source of authority**; He ordaineth as He pleaseth.'[9]

The Báb reveals the following in chapter 13 of His *Qayyúmu'l-Asmá* (Commentary on the Súrih of Joseph, in the Qur'án):

'Glorified is He besides Whom there is none other God. In His grasp He holdeth the **source of authority**, and verily God is powerful over all things.'[10]

Finally, Bahá'u'lláh reveals the following in a prayer: 'He is supreme over His servants, and standeth over His creatures. In His hand is **the source of authority** and truth.'[11]

> **the Fountainhead of Justice, the Creator of a new World Order, the Establisher of the Most Great Peace, the Inspirer and Founder of a world civilization, the Judge, the Lawgiver, the Unifier and Redeemer of all mankind,** [para. 4]

These titles of Bahá'u'lláh are all found in the writings of Shoghi Effendi, especially in his monumental history of the first Bahá'í century, *God Passes By*. In chapter 6 of that book, the Guardian describes the birth of the Revelation of Bahá'u'lláh in the Síyáh-Chál (an underground dungeon in Tehran in which Bahá'u'lláh was imprisoned for four months from October 1852). He then introduces several of the most important titles of Bahá'u'lláh:

> He Who in such dramatic circumstances was made to sustain the overpowering weight of so glorious a Mission was none other than the One Whom posterity will acclaim, and Whom innumerable followers already recognize, as **the Judge, the Lawgiver and Redeemer of all mankind,** as the Organizer of the entire planet, as **the Unifier** of the children of men, as the Inaugurator of the long-awaited millennium, as the Originator of a new 'Universal Cycle', as **the Establisher of the Most Great Peace**, as **the Fountain of** the Most Great **Justice**, as the Proclaimer of the coming of age of the entire human race, as **the Creator of a new World Order, and as the Inspirer and Founder of a world civilization.**[12]

Shoghi Effendi repeats several of these titles later in the

same work. Thus he writes of the expulsion of Mírzá Yaḥyá (Bahá'u'lláh's treacherous half-brother) from the Bahá'í community in Adrianople, 'at the bidding and through the power of Him Who is **the Fountain-head of** the Most Great Justice',[13] and describes the author of the Kitáb-i-Aqdas as 'at once **the Judge, the Lawgiver, the Unifier and Redeemer of mankind**'.[14]

has proclaimed the advent of God's Kingdom on earth, has formulated its laws and ordinances, enunciated its principles and ordained its institutions. [para. 4]

Summarizing Bahá'u'lláh's ministry, Shoghi Effendi writes that in less than half a century He had, 'despite successive banishments . . . succeeded in rehabilitating [the] fortunes [of the Faith], in proclaiming its Message, in enacting its **laws and ordinances**, in formulating its **principles** and in **ordaining its institutions**'.[15] The Guardian describes these achievements as successive stages in the unfoldment of a single process:

A dynamic process, divinely propelled, possessed of undreamt-of potentialities, world-embracing in scope, world-transforming in its ultimate consequences, had been set in motion on that memorable night when the Báb communicated the purpose of His mission to Mullá Ḥusayn in an obscure corner of S͟híráz [on the evening of 22 May 1844]. It acquired a tremendous momentum with the first intimations of Bahá'u'lláh's dawning Revelation amidst the darkness of the Síyáh-C͟hál of Ṭihrán [1852–3]. It was further accelerated by the Declaration of His mission on the eve of His banishment from Bag͟hdád [in April 1863]. It moved to a climax with the **proclamation** of that same mission during the tempestuous years of His exile in Adrianople [1863–8]. Its full significance was disclosed when the Author of that Mission issued His historic summonses, appeals and warnings to the kings of the earth and the world's ecclesiastical leaders. It was finally consummated by the **laws and ordinances** which He **formulated**, by the **principles** which He **enunciated** and by the **institutions** which He **ordained** during the concluding years of His ministry in the prison-city of 'Akká [1868–92].[16]

In considering the period of Bahá'u'lláh's exile in 'Akká, in northern Palestine, Shoghi Effendi further writes:

> The writings of Bahá'u'lláh during this period, as we survey the vast field which they embrace, seem to fall into three distinct categories. The first comprises those writings which constitute the sequel to the **proclamation** of His Mission in Adrianople. The second includes the **laws and ordinances** of His Dispensation, which, for the most part, have been recorded in the Kitáb-i-Aqdas, His Most Holy Book. To the third must be assigned those Tablets which partly **enunciate** and partly reaffirm the fundamental tenets and **principles** underlying that Dispensation.[17]

Shoghi Effendi groups together laws and ordinances, principles and institutions as essential elements of Bahá'u'lláh's Revelation in a number of other passages in his writings. In describing the distinctive characteristics of the Bahá'í Revelation as compared with previous dispensations, for example, he writes:

> Unlike the Dispensation of Christ, unlike the Dispensation of Muḥammad, unlike all the Dispensations of the past, the apostles of Bahá'u'lláh in every land, wherever they labour and toil, have before them in clear, in unequivocal and emphatic language, all the **laws**, the regulations, the **principles**, the **institutions**, the guidance, they require for the prosecution and consummation of their task.[18]

Shoghi Effendi makes the same point again in *God Passes By*, assessing the significance of the Most Holy Book as well as the Tablets later revealed by Bahá'u'lláh:

> ... the Kitáb-i-Aqdas, revealed from first to last by the Author of the Dispensation Himself, not only preserves for posterity the basic **laws and ordinances** on which the fabric of His future World Order must rest, but **ordains**, in addition to the function of interpretation which it confers upon His Successor, the necessary **institutions** through which the integrity and unity of His Faith can alone be safeguarded ...[19]

The **formulation** by Bahá'u'lláh, in His Kitáb-i-Aqdas, of the fundamental **laws** of His Dispensation was followed, as His Mission drew to a close, by the **enunciation** of certain precepts and **principles** which lie at the very core of His Faith, by the reaffirmation of truths He had previously proclaimed, by the elaboration and elucidation of some of the laws He had already laid down, by the revelation of further prophecies and warnings, and by the establishment of subsidiary ordinances designed to supplement the provisions of His Most Holy Book.[20]

Chapters 10 and 12 of *God Passes By* describe Bahá'u'lláh's proclamation to the kings and rulers of His Day. Passages from these Tablets translated by Shoghi Effendi are compiled in the book *The Proclamation of Bahá'u'lláh*. For a description of the Kitáb-i-Aqdas, as well as of the Tablets revealed later in the 'Akká period, see chapter 12 of *God Passes By*.

To direct and canalize the forces released by His Revelation He instituted His Covenant, [para. 4]

These words again echo those of Shoghi Effendi, in *God Passes By*, discussing here the forces released by 'the revolution of fifty years of almost uninterrupted Revelation':[21]

To direct and canalize these forces let loose by this Heaven-sent process, and to insure their harmonious and continuous operation after His ascension, an instrument divinely ordained, invested with indisputable authority, organically linked with the Author of the Revelation Himself, was clearly indispensable. That instrument Bahá'u'lláh had expressly provided through **the institution of the Covenant**, an institution which He had firmly established prior to His ascension.[22]

In another passage, the institution by Bahá'u'lláh of His Covenant is linked to the proclamation of His message to the kings and rulers of the world during His exile in Adrianople (1863–8) and to His revelation of laws and principles in the Kitáb-i-Aqdas:

In Adrianople Bahá'u'lláh's Message, the promise of the Bábí as well as of all previous Dispensations, had been proclaimed to mankind, and its challenge voiced to the rulers of the earth in both the East and the West. Behind the walls of the prison-fortress of 'Akká the Bearer of God's newborn Revelation had ordained the laws and formulated the principles that were to constitute the warp and woof of His World Order. He had, moreover, prior to His ascension, **instituted the Covenant** that was to guide and assist in the laying of its foundations and to safeguard the unity of its builders.[23]

whose power has preserved the integrity of His Faith, maintained its unity and stimulated its world-wide expansion throughout the successive ministries of 'Abdu'l-Bahá and Shoghi Effendi. [para. 4]

These three functions of the Covenant of Bahá'u'lláh are described by Shoghi Effendi in the following passage from *God Passes By*, reviewing the achievements of Bahá'u'lláh during His lifetime:

Above all the Covenant that was to perpetuate the influence of that Faith, insure its **integrity**, safeguard it from schism, and **stimulate its world-wide expansion**, had been fixed on an inviolable basis.[24]

The preservation of the unity of the Bahá'í Faith is also linked to the Most Holy Book of the Bahá'í dispensation, in which Bahá'u'lláh appointed His eldest Son, 'Abdu'l-Bahá, to be His successor and thus the Centre of His Covenant:

> . . . the Kitáb-i-Aqdas . . . not only preserves for posterity the basic laws and ordinances on which the fabric of His future World Order must rest, but ordains, in addition to the function of interpretation which it confers upon His Successor, the necessary institutions through which the **integrity** and **unity of His Faith** can alone be **safeguarded**.[25]

Shoghi Effendi elsewhere testifies to the power of the Covenant:

> That divinely instituted Covenant had, shortly after its inception, demonstrated beyond the shadow of a doubt its invincible strength . . . Its high claims had, moreover, been fully vindicated through its ability to safeguard the **unity** and **integrity** of the Faith in both the East and the West.[26]

It continues to fulfil its life-giving purpose [para. 4]

Shoghi Effendi explicitly states that the Covenant has a 'life-giving' quality. Writing of the British Bahá'í community, he says that it shares with France the distinction of being the first community 'to be quickened by the **life-giving** influences generated by the newly-established Covenant of Bahá'u'lláh in the Holy Land'.[27] Other passages in his writings highlight the life-giving qualities of the Revelation of Bahá'u'lláh generally. For example, he writes of the '**life-giving** principles'[28] of the Bahá'í Faith and of its 'life-giving Message'.[29]

through the agency of the Universal House of Justice whose fundamental object, as one of the twin successors of Bahá'u'lláh and 'Abdu'l-Bahá [para. 4]

Shoghi Effendi repeatedly emphasizes that there are *two* successors to Bahá'u'lláh and 'Abdu'l-Bahá: the Guardianship and the Universal House of Justice. The following passage demonstrates the emphasis he places on this point:

> For Bahá'u'lláh, we should readily recognize, has not only imbued mankind with a new and regenerating Spirit . . . He, as well as 'Abdu'l-Bahá after Him, has, unlike the Dispensations of the past, clearly and specifically laid down a set of Laws, established definite institutions, and provided for the essentials of a Divine Economy . . . They have also, in unequivocal and emphatic language, appointed those **twin** institutions of the House of Justice and of the Guardianship as their chosen **Successors**, destined to apply the principles, promulgate the laws, protect the institutions, adapt loyally and intelligently the Faith to the requirements of progressive society, and consummate the incorruptible inheritance which the Founders of the Faith have bequeathed to the world.[30]

Shoghi Effendi also often refers to the Guardianship and the Universal House of Justice as 'twin institutions'[31] and as the 'twin pillars' of the Bahá'í Administrative Order.[32]

whose fundamental object, as one of the twin successors of Bahá'u'lláh and 'Abdu'l-Bahá, is to ensure the continuity of that divinely-appointed authority which flows from the Source of the Faith, to safeguard the unity of its followers, and to maintain the integrity and flexibility of its teachings. [para. 4]

This passage repeats, almost verbatim, the words of Shoghi Effendi:

> It should be stated, at the very outset, in clear and unambiguous language, that these twin institutions of the Administrative Order of Bahá'u'lláh should be regarded as divine in origin, essential in their functions and complementary in their aim and purpose. Their common, their **fundamental object is to insure the continuity of that divinely-appointed authority which flows from the Source of our Faith, to safeguard the unity of its followers and to maintain the integrity and flexibility of its teachings**.[33]

These, then, are the purposes that the Guardianship and the Universal House of Justice share in common. Regarding the authority of the Universal House of Justice to 'safeguard the unity' of the 'followers' of the Bahá'í Faith and 'maintain the integrity and flexibility of its teachings', 'Abdu'l-Bahá writes:

> . . . from the conclusions and endorsements of the body of the House of Justice whose members are elected by and known to the worldwide Bahá'í community, no differences will arise; whereas the conclusions of individual divines and scholars would definitely lead to differences, and result in schism, division, and dispersion. The oneness of the Word would be destroyed, the unity of the Faith would disappear, and the edifice of the Faith of God would be shaken.[34]

'The fundamental purpose animating the Faith of God and His Religion', declares Bahá'u'lláh, 'is to safeguard the interests and promote the unity of the human race, and to foster the spirit of love and fellowship amongst men. Suffer it not to become a source of dissension and discord, of hate and enmity. This is the straight Path, the fixed and immovable foundation. Whatsoever is raised on this foundation, the

changes and chances of the world can never impair its strength, nor will the revolution of countless centuries undermine its structure.' [para. 5]

This passage is from the Lawḥ-i-Maqṣúd (Tablet to Mírzá Maqṣúd).[35] Here Bahá'u'lláh states that unity is the central aim of His Revelation.

'Unto the Most Holy Book', 'Abdu'l-Bahá declares in His Will and Testament, 'every one must turn, and all that is not expressly recorded therein must be referred to the Universal House of Justice.' [para. 6]

These words are from Part Two of the Will and Testament of 'Abdu'l-Bahá.[36] The Most Holy Book referred to here is Bahá'u'lláh's Kitáb-i-Aqdas.

The provenance, the authority, the duties, the sphere of action of the Universal House of Justice all derive from the revealed Word of Bahá'u'lláh [para. 7]

The Administrative Order of the Bahá'í Faith is founded on the writings of the Manifestation of God Himself. This fact is emphasized time and again by Shoghi Effendi. For example:

Both in the administrative provisions of the Bahá'í Dispensation, and in the matter of succession, as embodied in the twin institutions of the House of Justice and of the Guardianship, the followers of Bahá'u'lláh can summon to their aid such irrefutable evidences of Divine Guidance that none can resist, that none can belittle or ignore. Therein lies the distinguishing feature of the Bahá'í Revelation. Therein lies the strength of the unity of the Faith, of the validity of a Revelation that claims not to destroy or belittle previous Revelations, but to connect, unify, and fulfil them. This is the reason why Bahá'u'lláh and 'Abdu'l-Bahá have both revealed and even insisted upon certain details in connection with the Divine Economy which they have bequeathed to us, their followers. This is why such an emphasis has been placed in their Will and Testament upon the powers and prerogatives of the ministers of their Faith.[37]

More specifically, Shoghi Effendi writes that 'the local as well as the international Houses of Justice have been expressly enjoined by the Kitáb-i-Aqdas'[38] and that 'the institutions of the International and Local Houses of Justice are specifically designated and formally established' in the Tablets of Bahá'u'lláh.[39] As we proceed with our study, we shall see just how many of the duties and prerogatives of the Universal House of Justice are specified by Bahá'u'lláh Himself.

which, together with the interpretations and exposi-tions of the Centre of the Covenant [para. 7]

'Centre of the Covenant' is one of the titles of 'Abdu'l-Bahá, who was designated by Bahá'u'lláh as His successor. Shoghi Effendi states that 'Abdu'l-Bahá had been made by Bahá'u'lláh the 'sole Interpreter'[40] of the Bahá'í writings. The following passage from Shoghi Effendi's important letter to the Bahá'ís of the West, 'The Dispensation of Bahá'u'lláh', summarizes the titles and explains the station of 'Abdu'l-Bahá, including His interpretive function:

He is, and should for all time be regarded, first and fore-most, as the Centre and Pivot of Bahá'u'lláh's peerless and all-enfolding Covenant, His most exalted handiwork, the stainless Mirror of His light, the perfect Exemplar of His teachings, the unerring Interpreter of His Word, the embod-iment of every Bahá'í ideal, the incarnation of every Bahá'í virtue, the Most Mighty Branch sprung from the Ancient Root, the Limb of the Law of God, the Being 'round Whom all names revolve', the Mainspring of the Oneness of

Humanity, the Ensign of the Most Great Peace, the Moon of the Central Orb of this most holy Dispensation – styles and titles that are implicit and find their truest, their highest and fairest expression in the magic name 'Abdu'l-Bahá. He is, above and beyond these appellations, the 'Mystery of God' – an expression by which Bahá'u'lláh Himself has chosen to designate Him, and which, while it does not by any means justify us to assign to Him the station of Prophethood, indicates how in the person of 'Abdu'l-Bahá the incompatible characteristics of a human nature and superhuman knowledge and perfection have been blended and are completely harmonized.[41]

and of the Guardian of the Cause – who, after 'Abdu'l-Bahá, is the sole authority in the interpretation of Bahá'í Scripture [para. 7]

The authority to interpret the Bahá'í writings is explicitly conferred upon Shoghi Effendi in the first part of the Will and Testament of 'Abdu'l-Bahá:

O my loving friends! After the passing away of this wronged one, it is incumbent upon the Aghsán (Branches) [the male descendants of Bahá'u'lláh], the Afnán (Twigs) [the descendants of the family of the Báb] of the Sacred Lote-Tree, the Hands (pillars) of the Cause of God and the loved ones of the Abhá Beauty [Bahá'u'lláh] to turn unto Shoghi Effendi – the youthful branch branched from the two hallowed and sacred Lote-Trees and the fruit grown from the union of the two offshoots of the Tree of Holiness, – as he is the sign of God, the chosen branch, the guardian of the Cause of God, he unto whom all the Aghsán, the Afnán, the Hands of the Cause of God and His loved ones must turn. He is the **expounder of the words of God** and after him will succeed the first-born of his lineal descendents [*sic*].[42]

Shoghi Effendi has elucidated the role of the Guardian in a number of places. In 'The Dispensation of Bahá'u'lláh', in particular, he clearly delineates the sphere of authority of the Guardianship:

> . . . it is made indubitably clear and evident that the Guardian of the Faith has been made the Interpreter of the Word . . . The interpretation of the Guardian, functioning within his own sphere, is as authoritative and binding as the enactments of the International House of Justice . . .[43]

Shoghi Effendi has described his own role as Guardian as being 'overshadowed by the unfailing, the unerring protection of Bahá'u'lláh and of the Báb, and . . . [sharing] with 'Abdu'l-Bahá the right and obligation to interpret the Bahá'í teachings'.[44] The 'right of interpretation' with which Bahá'u'lláh has invested the Guardian, he says, is one of the factors which 'must and will, in a manner unparalleled in any previous religion, safeguard from schism the Faith from which it has sprung'.[45]

Anyone who reads the Bahá'í scriptures also interprets them in discovering their meaning. However, only 'Abdu'l-Bahá and Shoghi Effendi were able to *authoritatively* interpret the writings for the Bahá'í community; no other individual or institution may do so. The Guardian thus advised the Bahá'ís:

> I feel that regarding such interpretations (of verses from the Scriptures) no one has the right to impose his view or opinion and require his listeners to believe in his particular interpretation of the sacred and prophetic writings. I have no objection to your interpretations and inferences so long as they are represented as your own personal observations and reflections.[46]

Shoghi Effendi has stated that his own infallibility as Guardian 'is confined to matters which are related strictly to the Cause and interpretation of the teachings; he is not an infallible authority on other subjects, such as economics, science, etc.'.[47]

The Guardian's infallibility covers interpretation of the Revealed Word and its application. Likewise any instructions he may issue having to do with the protection of the Faith, or its well being must be closely obeyed, as he is infallible in the protection of the Faith.[48]

constitute the binding terms of reference of the Universal House of Justice and are its bedrock foundation. [para. 7]

The terms of reference of the Universal House of Justice are set out in the writings of Bahá'u'lláh and in the authoritative interpretations of 'Abdu'l-Bahá and Shoghi Effendi. In 'The Dispensation of Bahá'u'lláh', Shoghi Effendi explains that one of the Guardian's functions is to assist in defining the sphere of the legislative action of the House of Justice.[49] The Universal House of Justice has further elucidated the relationship between the Word and its own sphere of jurisdiction:

As the sphere of jurisdiction of the Universal House of Justice in matters of legislation extends to whatever is not explicitly revealed in the Sacred Text, it is clear that the Book itself is the highest authority and delimits the sphere of action of the House of Justice. Likewise, the Interpreter of the Book must also have the authority to define the sphere of the legislative action of the elected representatives of the Cause. The writings of the Guardian and the advice given by him over the thirty-six years of his Guardianship show the way in which he exercised this function in relation to the Universal House of Justice as well as to National and Local Spiritual Assemblies.[50]

The House of Justice has also stated that:

. . . the application of Bahá'í laws, the elucidation and extension of basic administrative principles, and the all-important function of legislating on matters not explicitly recorded in our teachings are dependent upon a careful study by the Universal House of Justice of the revealed and pertinent words of Bahá'u'lláh and 'Abdu'l-Bahá, as well as the illuminating interpretations and directions of Shoghi Effendi.[51]

The authority of these Texts is absolute and immutable [para. 7]

Shoghi Effendi draws a distinction between the Word of God, the fixed and inherent meaning of which the authorized interpreters (that is, 'Abdu'l-Bahá and the Guardian himself) explain, and the more flexible legislative role of the House of Justice. He concludes:

> Such is the **immutability** of His revealed Word. Such is the elasticity which characterizes the functions of His appointed ministers. The first preserves the identity of His Faith, and guards the integrity of His law. The second enables it, even as a living organism, to expand and adapt itself to the needs and requirements of an ever-changing society.[52]

until such time as Almighty God shall reveal His new Manifestation to Whom will belong all authority and power. [para. 7]

Bahá'u'lláh repeatedly affirms that each and every Manifestation of God is endowed with the authority to do what He wills:

> . . . they Who are the Luminaries of truth and the Mirrors reflecting the light of divine Unity, in whatever age and cycle they are sent down from their invisible habitations of ancient glory unto this world, to educate the souls of men and endue with grace all created things, are invariably endowed with an all-compelling **power**, and invested with invincible sovereignty.[53]

43

Shoghi Effendi refers to the Central Figures of the Bahá'í Faith as 'the appointed Channels and Embodiments of Divine **authority and power**'.[54] He elsewhere identifies as a 'fundamental verity' the doctrine that the Báb 'is fully entitled to rank as one of the self-sufficient Manifestations of God, that He has been invested with sovereign **power and authority**, and exercises all the rights and prerogatives of independent Prophethood'.[55]

Bahá'u'lláh writes in the Kitáb-i-Aqdas that the next Manifestation of God will not appear before 'the expiration of a full thousand years' from His own Revelation.[56] In the notes to this verse, we find the following comment:

> Bahá'u'lláh cautions against ascribing to 'this verse' anything other than its 'obvious meaning', and in one of His Tablets, He specifies that 'each year' of this thousand year period consists of 'twelve months according to the Qur'án, and of nineteen months of nineteen days each, according to the Bayán'.
>
> The intimation of His Revelation to Bahá'u'lláh in the Síyáh-Chál of Tihrán, in October 1852, marks the birth of His Prophetic Mission and hence the commencement of the one thousand years or more that must elapse before the appearance of the next Manifestation of God.[57]

'Abdu'l-Bahá has authoritatively interpreted Bahá'u'lláh's statement in the Kitáb-i-Aqdas as follows:

> The meaning of this is that any individual who, before the expiry of a full thousand years – years known and clearly established by common usage and requiring no interpretation – should lay claim to a Revelation direct from God, even though he should reveal certain signs, that man is assuredly false and an impostor.
>
> This is not a reference to the Universal Manifestation, for it is clearly set forth in the Holy Writings that centuries,

nay thousands of years, must pass on to completion, before a Manifestation like unto this Manifestation shall appear again.

It is possible, however, that after the completion of a full thousand years, certain Holy Beings will be empowered to deliver a Revelation: this, however, will not be through a Universal Manifestation. Wherefore every day of the cycle of the Blessed Beauty is in reality equal to one year, and every year of it is equal to a thousand years.[58]

And further:

My purpose is this, that ere the expiration of a thousand years, no one has the right to utter a single word, even to claim the station of Guardianship. The Most Holy Book is the Book to which all peoples shall refer, and in it the Laws of God have been revealed. Laws not mentioned in the Book should be referred to the decision of the Universal House of Justice. There will be no grounds for difference . . . Beware, beware lest anyone create a rift or stir up sedition. Should there be differences of opinion, the Supreme House of Justice would immediately resolve the problems. Whatever will be its decision, by majority vote, shall be the real truth, inasmuch as that House is under the protection, unerring guidance and care of the one true Lord. He shall guard it from error and will protect it under the wing of His sanctity and infallibility. He who opposes it is cast out and will eventually be of the defeated.[59]

Shoghi Effendi, in a letter written on his behalf, confirms that future Manifestations of God will be empowered to legislate and even abrogate the laws of Bahá'u'lláh:

After Bahá'u'lláh many Prophets will, no doubt, appear but they will be under His Shadow. Although they may abrogate the laws of this Dispensation in accordance with the needs and requirements of the age in which they appear, they nevertheless draw their spiritual force from this mighty Revelation . . . Whatever progress may be achieved, in later ages, after the unification of the whole human race is achieved, will be but improvement in the machinery of the world. For the machinery itself has been already created by Bahá'u'lláh. The task of continually improving and perfecting this machinery is one which later Prophets will be called upon to achieve. They will thus move and work within the orbit of the Bahá'í Cycle.[60]

There being no successor to Shoghi Effendi as Guardian of the Cause of God, [para. 8]

On 6 October 1963 the Universal House of Justice shared the following decision with the Bahá'í world:

After prayerful and careful study of the Holy Texts bearing upon the question of the appointment of the successor to Shoghi Effendi as Guardian of the Cause of God, and after prolonged consultation which included consideration of the views of the Hands of the Cause of God residing in the Holy Land, the Universal House of Justice finds that there is no way to appoint or to legislate to make it possible to appoint a second Guardian to succeed Shoghi Effendi.[61]

This decision was further explained by the Universal House of Justice in a letter of 9 March 1965 to the National Spiritual Assembly of the Netherlands:

At the time of our beloved Shoghi Effendi's death it was evident, from the circumstances and from the explicit requirements of the Holy Texts, that it had been impossible for him to appoint a successor in accordance with the provisions of the Will and Testament of 'Abdu'l-Bahá. This situation, in which the Guardian died without being able to appoint a successor, presented an obscure question not covered by the explicit Holy Text, and had to be referred to the Universal House of Justice. The friends should clearly understand that before the election of the Universal House of Justice there was no knowledge that there would be no Guardian. There could not have been any such foreknowledge, whatever opinions individual believers may have held. Neither the Hands of the Cause of God, nor the International Bahá'í Council, nor any other existing body could make a decision upon this all-important matter. Only the House of Justice had authority to pronounce upon it. This was one urgent reason for calling the election of the Universal House of Justice as soon as possible.[62]

Again, in a letter to an individual Bahá'í on 27 May 1966, the Universal House of Justice wrote:

There is no doubt at all that in the Will and Testament of 'Abdu'l-Bahá, Shoghi Effendi was the authority designated to appoint his successor, but he had no children and all the surviving Aghṣán had broken the Covenant. Thus, as the Hands of the Cause stated in 1957, it is clear that there was no one he could have appointed in accordance with the provisions of the Will. To have made an appointment outside the clear and specific provisions of the Master's Will and Testament would obviously have been an impossible and unthinkable course of action for the Guardian, the divinely appointed upholder and defender of the Covenant. Moreover, that same Will had provided a clear means for the confirmation of the Guardian's appointment of his successor, as you are aware. The nine Hands to be elected by the body of the Hands were to give their assent by secret ballot to the Guardian's choice. In 1957 the entire body of the Hands, after fully investigating the matter, announced that Shoghi Effendi had appointed no successor and left no will. This is documented and established.

The fact that Shoghi Effendi did not leave a will cannot be adduced as evidence of his failure to obey Bahá'u'lláh – rather should we acknowledge that in his very silence there is a wisdom and a sign of his infallible guidance. We should ponder deeply the writings that we have, and seek to understand the multitudinous significances that they contain. Do not forget that Shoghi Effendi said two things were necessary for a growing understanding of the World Order of Bahá'u'lláh: the passage of time and the guidance of the Universal House of Justice.[63]

the Universal House of Justice is the Head of the Faith and its supreme institution, [para. 8]

During his ministry as Guardian of the Bahá'í Faith (1921–57), Shoghi Effendi was, in his own words, 'the **supreme** spiritual **head** of the community'.[64] That function is now performed by the Universal House of Justice.

In preparation for the formation of three National Spiritual Assemblies in Canada and the republics of Latin America during the course of the second Seven Year Plan of the American Bahá'í community (1946–53), Shoghi Effendi wrote:

The erection of these three pillars, raising to eleven the number of existing National Spiritual Assemblies, which are to be designated in future as Secondary Houses of Justice, and are designed to support the highest legislative body in the administrative hierarchy of the Faith, will, as the Divine Plan continues to unfold, be supplemented by the formation of similar bodies which, as they multiply, will, of necessity, broaden the basis and reinforce the representative character, of the **supreme** elective **institution** which, in conjunction with the institution of Guardianship, must direct and coordinate the activities of a world-encircling Faith.[65]

In 1951 Shoghi Effendi cabled the Bahá'í world with news of

his decision to form an International Bahá'í Council, which he called the 'forerunner of **supreme** administrative **institution** destined to emerge' in the world spiritual centre of the Bahá'í Faith.[66] In other messages the Guardian clearly indicates the supremacy of the Universal House of Justice, calling it the 'Supreme Body'.[67]

to which all must turn, [para. 8]

Authority for the statement that 'all must turn' to the Universal House of Justice comes from the Will and Testament of 'Abdu'l-Bahá. This passage is in Part Two:

> To none is given the right to put forth his own opinion or express his particular conviction. **All must** seek guidance and **turn** unto the Centre of the Cause and the House of Justice. And he that turneth unto whatsoever else is indeed in grievous error.[68]

In Part One of that document 'Abdu'l-Bahá writes that 'Unto this body [the Universal House of Justice] all things must be referred.'[69]

More fundamentally, this function of the Universal House of Justice is derived from the Words of Bahá'u'lláh Himself. This is from the Tablet of Bishárát ('Glad Tidings'):

> Inasmuch as for each day there is a new problem and for every problem an expedient solution, such affairs should be referred to the Ministers of the House of Justice that they may act according to the needs and requirements of the time.[70]

The Universal House of Justice has explained that the House of Justice is one of two centres to which all Bahá'ís must turn:

> In the Bahá'í Faith there are two authoritative centres appointed to which the believers must turn . . . one centre is

49

the Book with its Interpreter, and the other is the Universal House of Justice guided by God to decide on whatever is not explicitly revealed in the Book. This pattern of centres and their relationships is apparent at every stage in the unfoldment of the Cause.[71]

and on it rests the ultimate responsibility for ensuring the unity and progress of the Cause of God. [para. 8]

The Universal House of Justice here repeats the wording it had used previously in a letter to an individual Bahá'í in 1966 in answer to questions about the functioning of the House of Justice in the absence of a living Guardian:

The Universal House of Justice, which the Guardian said would be regarded by posterity as 'the last refuge of a tottering civilization', is now, in the absence of the Guardian, the sole infallibly guided institution in the world to which all must turn, and on it rests the **responsibility for ensuring the unity and progress of the Cause of God** in accordance with the revealed Word. There are statements from the Master and the Guardian indicating that the Universal House of Justice, in addition to being the Highest Legislative Body of the Faith, is also the body to which all must turn, and is the 'apex' of the Bahá'í Administrative Order, as well as the 'supreme organ of the Bahá'í Commonwealth'. The Guardian has in his writings specified for the House of Justice such fundamental functions as the formulation of future worldwide teaching plans, the conduct of the administrative affairs of the Faith, and the guidance, organization, and unification of the affairs of the Cause throughout the world.[72]

The Universal House of Justice further explains how it has been designed to fulfil this responsibility, quoting the words of Shoghi Effendi:

In a letter written on 14 March 1927 to the Spiritual Assembly of the Bahá'ís of Istanbul, the Guardian's Secretary explained, on his behalf, the principle in the Cause of action by majority vote. He pointed out how, in the past, it was certain individuals who 'accounted themselves as superior in knowledge and elevated in position' who caused division, and that it was those 'who pretended to be the most distinguished of all' who 'always proved themselves to be the source of contention'. 'But praise be to God', he continued, 'that the Pen of Glory has done away with the unyielding and dictatorial views of the learned and the wise, dismissed the assertions of individuals as an authoritative criterion, even though they were recognized as the most accomplished and learned among men and ordained that all matters be referred to authorized centres and specified Assemblies. Even so, no Assembly has been invested with the absolute authority to deal with such general matters as affect the interests of nations. Nay rather, He has brought all the assemblies together under the shadow of one House of Justice, one divinely appointed Centre, so that there would be only one Centre and all the rest integrated into a single body, revolving around one expressly designated Pivot, thus making them all proof against schism and division.'[73]

Further, there devolve upon it the duties of directing and coordinating the work of the Hands of the Cause, of ensuring the continuing discharge of the functions of protection and propagation vested in that institution, and of providing for the receipt and disbursement of the Ḥuqúqu'lláh. [para. 8]

Ḥuqúqu'lláh (the Right of God) is an institution established by Bahá'u'lláh in the Kitáb-i-Aqdas, according to which Bahá'ís voluntarily offer a fixed portion of their possessions to the Head of the Faith, 'used for the promotion of the Faith of God and its interests as well as for various philanthropic purposes'.[74] In

Part One of His Will and Testament, 'Abdu'l-Bahá states that the Ḥuqúqu'lláh should be 'offered through the guardian of the Cause of God, that it may be expended for the diffusion of the Fragrances of God and the exaltation of His Word, for benevolent pursuits and for the common weal'.[75] He also made the Hands of the Cause of God responsible to the Guardian in that same document.[76]

In 1966, the Universal House of Justice explained that it would have to assume certain functions of the Guardian in his absence:

> As the Universal House of Justice has already announced, it cannot legislate to make possible the appointment of a successor to Shoghi Effendi, nor can it legislate to make possible the appointment of any more Hands of the Cause, but it must do everything within its power to ensure the performance of all those functions which it shares with these two mighty Institutions. **It must make provision for the proper discharge in future of the functions of protection and propagation**, which the administrative bodies share with the Guardianship and the Hands of the Cause; it must, in the absence of the Guardian, **receive and disburse the Ḥuqúqu'lláh**, in accordance with the following statement of 'Abdu'l-Bahá: 'Disposition of the Ḥuqúq, wholly or partly, is permissible, but this should be done by permission of the authority in the Cause to whom all must turn.'[77]

As we have seen above, one of two authorities 'to whom all must turn' is the Universal House of Justice.[78]

Among the powers and duties with which the Universal House of Justice has been invested are: [para. 9]

The significance and extent of the powers and duties of the Universal House of Justice are suggested in certain passages in the writings of Shoghi Effendi, such as this:

. . . as the Bahá'í Faith permeates the masses of the peoples of East and West, and its truth is embraced by the majority of the peoples of a number of the Sovereign States of the world, will the Universal House of Justice attain the plenitude of its power, and exercise, as the supreme organ of the Bahá'í Commonwealth, all the rights, the duties, and responsibilities incumbent upon the world's future super-state.[79]

To ensure the preservation of the Sacred Texts and to safeguard their inviolability; [para. 10]

This duty was taken up immediately upon the election of the Universal House of Justice in 1963. Some background is provided in a letter from the Universal House of Justice to all National Spiritual Assemblies in December 1967:

> We have already pointed out to the friends on several occasions that the application of Bahá'í laws, the elucidation and extension of basic administrative principles, and the all-important function of legislating on matters not explicitly recorded in our teachings are dependent upon a careful study by the Universal House of Justice of the revealed and pertinent words of Bahá'u'lláh and 'Abdu'l-Bahá, as well as the illuminating interpretations and directions of Shoghi Effendi.
>
> Through the labours of the beloved Guardian himself, and the collaboration of the National Spiritual Assembly of Persia, great strides have already been taken to collate the Writings of Bahá'u'lláh and 'Abdu'l-Bahá. Even up to the present time, a special National Committee in Persia is assiduously and regularly engaged in classifying the Holy Texts of the Founder of our Faith, and the Centre of the Covenant in fulfilment of the goal of the Nine Year Plan . . .[80]

The Universal House of Justice wrote again to all National Spiritual Assemblies on 26 August 1984, on the subject of 'Safeguarding the Letters of Shoghi Effendi'.[81]

to analyse, classify, and coordinate the Writings;
[para. 10]

This is another, related duty of which the Universal House of Justice was highly conscious from the outset, making it its 'primary concern':

> Since the Universal House of Justice came into being in 1963, its primary concern at the World Centre of the Faith has been with . . . collating the Sacred Texts and the letters of Shoghi Effendi and indexing them . . .[82]

This was made a goal of the first plan executed under the headship of the House, the Nine Year Plan, 1964–73:

> At the World Centre of the Faith the tasks of the Plan include . . . continued collation and **classification** of the Bahá'í Sacred Scriptures as well as of the writings of Shoghi Effendi . . .[83]

It was also made a goal of the Five Year Plan (1974–9)[84] and of the Seven Year Plan (1979–86). This is from a message of the Universal House of Justice on the occasion of Naw-Rúz in 1979:

> Work will be continued on the collation and **classification** of the Sacred Texts and a series of compilations gleaned and translated from the writings of the Faith will be sent out to the Bahá'í world to help in deepening the friends in their understanding of the fundamentals of the Faith, enriching their spiritual lives, and reinforcing their efforts to teach the Cause.[85]

A statement from the Universal House of Justice indicates one scheme of classification currently used by the Bahá'í World Centre:

The Archival collection held at the World Centre is divided into three categories, and between these three groups there are varying degrees of overlap They are as follows:

Authenticated items: Originals or reproductions of Tablets and letters as dispatched to or received by their addressees.

Transcribed items: Secondary copies of Tablets or letters, copied by scribes of varying degrees of reliability, sometimes copied from an authenticated item, sometimes copied from another transcribed item.

Draft copies or Working copies: These include copies prepared by a scribe/secretary for checking prior to preparing the final copy, copies kept by the scribe/secretary or by Shoghi Effendi for later reference.

In light of the information provided above, we are able to inform you that there are some 7,169 original and photocopies of original Tablets of Bahá'u'lláh, 15,815 by 'Abdu'l-Bahá, and 17,118 letters of Shoghi Effendi. In addition, there are some 98,000 copies of other such Tablets and letters, many of which have not as yet been authenticated.

With regard to the Writings of the Báb, the Archival collection holds approximately 135 original Tablets, and 55 photocopies.[86]

and to defend and protect the Cause of God and emancipate it from the fetters of repression and persecution; [para. 10]

Shoghi Effendi, describing the common purposes of the Guardianship and the Universal House of Justice, writes:

Acting in conjunction with each other these two inseparable

institutions administer its affairs, coordinate its activities, promote its interests, execute its laws and **defend** its subsidiary institutions.[87]

Shoghi Effendi has written that the Bahá'í Faith will pass through certain stages of obscurity, repression, recognition, establishment and so on. The stage mentioned here in the Declaration of Trust is 'emancipation'. These various stages are described in a number of places in the Guardian's writings. The clearest description is this, written at the start of the Ten Year Crusade (1953–63):

This present Crusade, on the threshold of which we now stand, will, moreover, by virtue of the dynamic forces it will release and its wide repercussions over the entire surface of the globe, contribute effectually to the acceleration of yet another process of tremendous significance which will carry the steadily evolving Faith of Bahá'u'lláh through its present stages of obscurity, of repression, of **emancipation** and of recognition – stages one or another of which Bahá'í national communities in various parts of the world now find themselves in – to the stage of establishment, the stage at which the Faith of Bahá'u'lláh will be recognized by the civil authorities as the state religion, similar to that which Christianity entered in the years following the death of the Emperor Constantine, a stage which must later be followed by the emergence of the Bahá'í state itself, functioning, in all religious and civil matters, in strict accordance with the laws and ordinances of the Kitáb-i-Aqdas, the Most Holy, the Mother-Book of the Bahá'í Revelation, a stage which, in the fullness of time, will culminate in the establishment of the World Bahá'í Commonwealth, functioning in the plenitude of its powers, and which will signalize the long-awaited advent of the Christ-promised Kingdom of God on earth – the Kingdom of Bahá'u'lláh – mirroring however faintly upon this humble handful of dust the glories of the Abhá Kingdom.[88]

The Universal House of Justice took up the task of defending the Cause early on in its ministry:

> At the World Centre of the Faith the tasks of the [Nine Year] Plan include . . . continued efforts directed towards the emancipation of the Faith from the fetters of religious orthodoxy and its recognition as an independent religion . . .[89]

The Bahá'í community is still unemancipated in a number of countries. In some places the Bahá'í community is actively persecuted (most notably in Iran), while in others (such as several other Middle Eastern countries) the Faith is generally repressed. The Universal House of Justice continues to coordinate the external affairs efforts of national Bahá'í communities worldwide in order to secure the emancipation of the Bahá'í Faith in these countries.

To advance the interests of the Faith of God; [para. 11]

This duty encompasses several others discussed both above and below, and recalls this expression of the Guardian, describing the elected members of Bahá'í Assemblies: 'those whose priceless privilege is to guard over, administer the affairs, and **advance the interests** of these Bahá'í institutions'.[90]

to proclaim, propagate and teach its Message; [para. 11]

This duty is related intimately to that of advancing the interests of the Faith of God (above), and guiding, organizing, coordinating and unifying its activities (below). Several passages in the writings of Shoghi Effendi indicate that the administrative institutions of the Bahá'í Faith must be concerned with propagating (teaching, promoting) the Bahá'í message. For example, he states that the 'present administration' is 'endeavouring to propagate' the 'faithful application of the spiritual principles' of the Bahá'í Faith)[91] and that these institutions are in fact 'designed to propagate'[92] the Faith of God.

More specifically, Shoghi Effendi, writing of the teaching plan in Africa undertaken by the British, American, Iranian and Egyptian National Spiritual Assemblies (1951–3), looked forward to the initiation of global plans, which would in turn pave the way for the 'ultimate organic union [of] these assemblies' through the 'formation' of the 'International House [of] Justice destined [to] launch enterprises embracing whole Bahá'í world'.[93] Again he forecast the same development:

> On the success of this enterprise, unprecedented in its scope, unique in its character and immense in its spiritual potentialities, must depend the initiation, at a later period in the Formative Age of the Faith, of undertakings embracing within their range all National Assemblies functioning throughout the Bahá'í World, undertakings constituting in themselves a prelude to the launching of world-wide enterprises destined to be embarked upon, in future epochs of that same Age, by the Universal House of Justice . . .[94]

The Universal House of Justice has affirmed its own role in propagating the Bahá'í message:

> Above all, it must, with perfect faith in Bahá'u'lláh, **proclaim** His Cause and enforce His law so that the Most Great Peace shall be firmly established in this world and the foundations of the Kingdom of God on earth shall be accomplished.[95]

Since its first election in 1963 the Universal House of Justice has coordinated the teaching and proclamation work of the Cause. With regard to proclamation, the House of Justice used the occasion of the 1968 centenary of Bahá'u'lláh's own proclamation of His mission to issue a volume of key passages from His writings (*The Proclamation of Bahá'u'lláh*) and to deliver this message itself to 'the heads of all states'.[96] This proclamation was extended with the publication of a major communication addressed by the Universal House of Justice to the peoples of the world in 1985, *The Promise of World Peace*,[97] and with numerous public happenings and initiatives in the course of the Holy Year commemorating the centenary of the Ascension of Bahá'u'lláh (1992–3). It was further reinforced in April 2002 when the Universal House of Justice wrote a special message addressed to the world's religious leaders and instructed National Spiritual Assemblies to arrange for its distribution.

In addition, the Universal House of Justice has continued Shoghi Effendi's practice of initiating specific-term plans in the prosecution of the Divine Plan of 'Abdu'l-Bahá, which is the Charter for the worldwide propagation of the Bahá'í Faith.[98] Here is a list of all such plans formulated by the Universal House of Justice:

Nine Year Plan (1964–73)
Five Year Plan (1974–9)
Seven Year Plan (1979–86)
Six Year Plan (1986–92)
Two Year Subsidiary Plan (1990–2)
Three Year Plan (1993–6)
Four Year Plan (1996–2000)
One Year Plan (2000–1)
Five Year Plan (2001–6)

The Universal House of Justice has stated that the latest Five Year Plan is the first in a series of Plans that will continue until 2021.

to expand and consolidate the institutions of its Administrative Order; [para. 11]

This term of reference is obviously related closely to the previous one. It recalls the language used by Shoghi Effendi in relation to the mission of the British Bahá'í community, foreseeing the future development of the Bahá'í administrative institutions in that country:

The Bahá'ís of the British Isles are now, slowly, laboriously and in strict accordance with the principles of a steadily expanding, divinely appointed Administrative Order, building up the essential and primary institutions which are destined to act as the chief and most powerful instruments for the proclamation of the Faith to the masses of their countrymen, at a subsequent stage in the development of the Faith in their land. As these institutions **expand and are consolidated,** the community will find itself equipped, not only to carry the Message of the New Day to the multitudes throughout the length and breadth of its homeland, but prepared and fortified to initiate teaching campaigns beyond the shores of its native land, and in distant territories and various parts of the Empire of which that land is the heart and centre.[99]

The charter for the establishment of the Administrative Order throughout the world is the Will and Testament of 'Abdu'l-Bahá.[100]

to usher in the World Order of Bahá'u'lláh; [para. 11]

Shoghi Effendi has specifically linked this accomplishment with the destiny of the American Bahá'í community. On the occasion of his wedding to Mary Maxwell (Amatu'l-Bahá Rúḥíyyih Khánum), the Guardian wrote:

Institution of Guardianship, head cornerstone of the Administrative Order of the Cause of Bahá'u'lláh, already ennobled through its organic connection with the Persons of Twin Founders of the Bahá'í Faith, is now further reinforced through direct association with West and particularly with the American believers, whose spiritual destiny is to **usher in the World Order of Bahá'u'lláh.**[101]

to promote the attainment of those spiritual qualities

which should characterize Bahá'í life individually and collectively; [para. 11]

This duty may be derived from the following words of Bahá'u-'lláh, charging the Universal House of Justice with promoting the principles of religion:

> The progress of the world, the development of nations, the tranquillity of peoples, and the peace of all who dwell on earth are among the principles and ordinances of God. Religion bestoweth upon man the most precious of all gifts, offereth the cup of prosperity, imparteth eternal life, and showereth imperishable benefits upon mankind. It behoveth the chiefs and rulers of the world, and in particular the Trustees of God's House of Justice, to endeavour to the utmost of their power to safeguard its position, promote its interests and exalt its station in the eyes of the world.[102]

'Abdu'l-Bahá has described the spiritualization of society that will be brought about under the leadership of the Universal House of Justice:

> As to the difference between that material civilization now prevailing, and the divine civilization which will be one of the benefits to derive from the House of Justice, it is this: material civilization, through the power of punitive and retaliatory laws, restraineth the people from criminal acts; and notwithstanding this, while laws to retaliate against and punish a man are continually proliferating, as ye can see, no laws exist to reward him . . .
>
> Divine civilization, however, so traineth every member of society that no one, with the exception of a negligible few, will undertake to commit a crime.[103]

The messages of the Universal House of Justice are full of guidance relating to the attainment of spiritual qualities by

Bahá'í individuals, communities and Assemblies.

to do its utmost for the realization of greater cordiality and comity amongst the nations and for the attainment of universal peace; [para. 11]

The duty of the Universal House of Justice to promote peace, 'cordiality and comity' between nations has been laid down by the Manifestation of God Himself in several places, particularly in the Tablets He revealed after the Kitáb-i-Aqdas. This is from His Lawḥ-i-Dunyá, the 'Tablet of the World':

> It is incumbent upon the ministers of the House of Justice to promote the Lesser **Peace** so that the people of the earth may be relieved from the burden of exorbitant expenditures. This matter is imperative and absolutely essential, inasmuch as hostilities and conflict lie at the root of affliction and calamity.[104]

This is from Bahá'u'lláh's Tablet of Ishráqát ('Splendours'):

> In the abundance of Our grace and loving-kindness We have revealed specially for the rulers and ministers of the world that which is conducive to safety and protection, tranquillity and **peace**; haply the children of men may rest secure from the evils of oppression. He, verily, is the Protector, the Helper, the Giver of victory. It is incumbent upon the men of God's House of Justice to fix their gaze by day and by night upon that which hath shone forth from the Pen of Glory for the training of peoples, the upbuilding of nations, the protection of man and the safeguarding of his honour.[105]

In another passage later in the same Tablet, Bahá'u'lláh discusses the adoption of an international auxiliary language, for the purpose of promoting 'union and concord':

> The sixth Ishráq is union and concord amongst the children

of men. From the beginning of time the light of unity hath shed its divine radiance upon the world, and the greatest means for the promotion of that unity is for the peoples of the world to understand one another's writing and speech. In former Epistles We have enjoined upon the Trustees of the House of Justice either to choose one language from among those now existing or to adopt a new one, and in like manner to select a common script, both of which should be taught in all the schools of the world. Thus will the earth be regarded as one country and one home.[106]

In a letter written on his behalf to the National Spiritual Assembly of the United States and Canada on 14 March 1939, Shoghi Effendi explains the role of the Universal House of Justice in bringing about the Most Great Peace:

With reference to the question you have asked concerning the time and means through which the Lesser and Most Great Peace, referred to by Bahá'u'lláh, will be established, following the coming World War: Your view that the Lesser Peace will come about through the political efforts of the states and nations of the world, and independently of any direct Bahá'í plan or effort, and the Most Great Peace be established through the instrumentality of the believers, and by the direct operation of the laws and principles revealed by Bahá'u'lláh and the functioning of the Universal House of Justice as the supreme organ of the Bahá'í superstate – your view on this subject is quite correct and in full accord with the pronouncements of the Guardian as embodied in 'The Unfoldment of World Civilization'.[107]

In 1985, designated by the United Nations an International Year of Peace, the Universal House of Justice instructed all national communities to undertake programmes to promote the Lesser Peace.[108] In the same year, the House of Justice itself issued a statement addressed to the peoples of the world on the subject of peace, and arranged for its presentation to Heads of State and governments throughout the world.[109]

and to foster that which is conducive to the enlightenment and illumination of the souls of men and the advancement and betterment of the world; [para. 11]

The duty to promote human enlightenment is linked to several other duties mentioned above, such as propagating the message of Bahá'u'lláh and promoting the acquisition of spiritual qualities. It can also be inferred from specific statements of Bahá'u'lláh. For example, He makes the House of Justice secondarily responsible for the education of children. This probably relates more specifically to the local House of Justice (Local Spiritual Assembly) but also has implications for the secondary and international Houses of Justice:

> Unto every father hath been enjoined the instruction of his son and daughter in the art of reading and writing and in all that hath been laid down in the Holy Tablet. He that putteth away that which is commanded unto him, the Trustees are then to take from him that which is required for their instruction, if he be wealthy, and if not the matter devolveth upon the House of Justice. Verily, have We made it a shelter for the poor and needy.[110]

This injunction is reinforced by 'Abdu'l-Bahá:

> Among the divine Texts as set forth in the Most Holy Book and also in other Tablets is this: it is incumbent upon the father and mother to train their children both in good conduct and the study of books; study, that is, to the degree required, so that no child, whether girl or boy, will remain illiterate. Should the father fail in his duty he must be compelled to discharge his responsibility, and should he be unable to comply, let the House of Justice take over the education

of the children; in no case is a child to be left without an education.[111]

To enact laws and ordinances not expressly recorded in the Sacred Texts; [para. 12]

This duty and prerogative of the Universal House of Justice is expressed by Bahá'u'lláh Himself in general terms in the Kalimát-i-Firdawsíyyih ('Words of Paradise'):

> It is incumbent upon the Trustees of the House of Justice to take counsel together regarding those things which have not outwardly been revealed in the Book, and to enforce that which is agreeable to them. God will verily inspire them with whatsoever He willeth, and He, verily, is the Provider, the Omniscient.[112]

In the annex to His Most Holy Book, entitled 'Questions and Answers', Bahá'u'lláh states that certain supplementary laws should be legislated by the House of Justice. These include, for example, the penalties for 'adultery, sodomy, and theft, and the degrees thereof'[113] and 'the legitimacy or otherwise of marrying one's relatives'.[114] In the Tablet of Ishráqát ('Splendours'), Bahá'u'lláh permits the charging of 'interest and profit on gold and silver' and states that 'the conduct of these affairs hath been entrusted to the men of the House of Justice that they may enforce them according to the exigencies of the time and the dictates of wisdom'.[115]

The notes to the Aqdas also suggest further areas for legislation, such as the details of criminal law:

> The details of the Bahá'í law of punishment for murder and arson, a law designed for a future state of society, were not specified by Bahá'u'lláh. The various details of the law, such as degrees of offence, whether extenuating circumstances are to be taken into account, and which of the two prescribed

punishments is to be the norm are left to the Universal House of Justice to decide in light of prevailing conditions when the law is to be in operation. The manner in which the punishment is to be carried out is also left to the Universal House of Justice to decide.[116]

The Islamic law of Zakát (a regular charity binding upon Muslims) has been extended into the Bahá'í dispensation by Bahá'u'lláh,[117] although this law is not yet in force. The details of this law are left to the Universal House of Justice:

> Bahá'u'lláh states that the Bahá'í law of Zakát follows 'what hath been revealed in the Qur'án' (Q&A 107). Since such issues as the limits for exemption, the categories of income concerned, the frequency of payments, and the scale of rates for the various categories of Zakát are not mentioned in the Qur'án, these matters will have to be set forth in the future by the Universal House of Justice. Shoghi Effendi has indicated that pending such legislation the believers should, according to their means and possibilities, make regular contributions to the Bahá'í Fund.[118]

The details of laws relating to marriage also appear to be left to the Universal House of Justice to legislate upon:

> 'Abdu'l-Bahá, in one of His Tablets, summarized some of the provisions for determining the level of the dowry . . . In this same Tablet, 'Abdu'l-Bahá encouraged the believers to refer questions concerning the application of this law to the Universal House of Justice, which has 'the authority to legislate'. He stressed that 'it is this body which will enact laws and legislate upon secondary matters which are not explicit in the Holy Text'.[119]

'Abdu'l-Bahá repeatedly emphasizes the Universal House of Justice's legislative function in His Will and Testament. This passage is from Part One of that document: 'It [Universal House of Justice] enacteth all ordinances and regulations that are not to be found in the explicit Holy Text.'[120]

These passages are from Part Two of the Will and Testament:

> Unto the Most Holy Book every one must turn and all that is **not expressly recorded** therein must be referred to the Universal House of Justice. That which this body, whether unanimously or by a majority doth carry, that is verily the Truth and the Purpose of God Himself. Whoso doth deviate therefrom is verily of them that love discord, hath shown forth malice, and turned away from the Lord of the Covenant.[121]

> It is incumbent upon these members (of the Universal House of Justice) to gather in a certain place and deliberate upon all problems which have caused difference, questions that are obscure and matters that are **not expressly recorded** in the Book. Whatsoever they decide has the same effect as the Text itself . . . this House of Justice hath power to enact laws that are **not expressly recorded** in the Book and bear upon daily transactions . . .[122]

'Abdu'l-Bahá discusses this subject in *Some Answered Questions* in the course of explaining the meanings of infallibility:

> . . . the Universal House of Justice, if it be established under the necessary conditions – with members elected from all the people – that House of Justice will be under the protection and the unerring guidance of God. If that House of Justice shall decide unanimously, or by a majority, upon any question not mentioned in the Book, that decision and command will be guarded from mistake.[123]

Another Tablet by 'Abdu'l-Bahá bears on the same point:

My purpose is this, that ere the expiration of a thousand years, no one has the right to utter a single word, even to claim the station of Guardianship. The Most Holy Book is the Book to which all peoples shall refer, and in it the Laws of God have been revealed. Laws not mentioned in the Book should be referred to the decision of the Universal House of Justice. There will be no grounds for difference . . .[124]

A further Tablet by 'Abdu'l-Bahá relating to this subject is quoted by the Universal House of Justice in a letter to an individual in 1966. That passage is worth repeating here in full as it explains the wisdom of investing the Universal House of Justice with the power of legislation:

Those matters of major importance which constitute the foundation of the Law of God are **explicitly recorded in the Text**, but subsidiary laws are left to the House of Justice. The wisdom of this is that the times never remain the same, for change is a necessary quality and an essential attribute of this world, and of time and place. Therefore the House of Justice will take action accordingly.

Let it not be imagined that the House of Justice will take any decision according to its own concepts and opinions. God forbid! The Supreme House of Justice will take decisions and establish laws through the inspiration and confirmation of the Holy Spirit, because it is in the safekeeping and under the shelter and protection of the Ancient Beauty, and obedience to its decisions is a bounden and essential duty and an absolute obligation, and there is no escape for anyone.

Say, O people: Verily the Supreme House of Justice is under the wings of your Lord, the Compassionate, the All-Merciful, that is, under His protection, His care, and His shelter; for He has commanded the firm believers to obey that blessed, sanctified, and all-subduing body, whose sovereignty is divinely ordained and of the Kingdom of Heaven and whose laws are inspired and spiritual.

Briefly, this is the wisdom of referring the laws of society to the House of Justice. In the religion of Islam, similarly, not every ordinance was explicitly revealed; nay not a tenth part of a tenth part was included in the Text; although all matters of major importance were specifically referred to, there were undoubtedly thousands of laws which were unspecified. These were devised by the divines of a later age according to the laws of Islamic jurisprudence, and individual divines made conflicting deductions from the original revealed ordinances. All these were enforced. Today this process of deduction is the right of the body of the House of Justice, and the deductions and conclusions of individual learned men have no authority, unless they are endorsed by the House of Justice. The difference is precisely this, that from the conclusions and endorsements of the body of the House of Justice whose members are elected by and known to the worldwide Bahá'í community, no differences will arise; whereas the conclusions of individual divines and scholars would definitely lead to differences, and result in schism, division, and dispersion. The oneness of the Word would be destroyed, the unity of the Faith would disappear, and the edifice of the Faith of God would be shaken.[125]

Shoghi Effendi has also stressed the legislative function of the Universal House of Justice. In a letter to the Bahá'ís of the East, dated Naw-Rúz 1954, he explains the symbolism of the Tablet of Carmel and mentions the 'Supreme House of Justice, which, in conformity with the exact provisions of the Will and Testament of the Centre of the Mighty Covenant, is the body which should lay down **laws not explicitly revealed in the Text**'.[126] In *God Passes By*, Shoghi Effendi again refers to 'the powers and prerogatives of the Universal House of Justice, possessing the exclusive right to legislate on matters **not explicitly revealed** in the Most Holy Book'.[127]

Early in his ministry, Shoghi Effendi explained that the House of Justice would be responsible for elaborating Bahá'í administrative policy:

In connection with the fundamental questions of general policy referred to in your letter, I feel that the basic principles, laid down but briefly stated in my past letters, which must guide the administration of the affairs of the Bahá'í Movement, pending the definite formation of the first authoritative Universal House of Justice, must be further affirmed, elucidated, and explained in greater detail, for the complete knowledge of all the individual members of the vast and growing community of the believers in America.[128]

Again, in detailing the difference between the Bahá'í system and older forms of secular and religious government, Shoghi Effendi highlighted this power of the Universal House of Justice:

Nor can the Bahá'í Administrative Order be dismissed as a hard and rigid system of unmitigated autocracy or as an idle imitation of any form of absolutistic ecclesiastical government, whether it be the Papacy, the Imamate or any other similar institution, for the obvious reason that upon the international elected representatives of the followers of Bahá'u'lláh [i.e. the members of the Universal House of Justice] has been conferred the exclusive right of legislating on matters **not expressly revealed** in the Bahá'í writings. Neither the Guardian of the Faith nor any institution apart from the International House of Justice can ever usurp this vital and essential power or encroach upon that sacred right.[129]

Summarizing the contents of those Tablets revealed by Bahá'u'lláh after the Kitáb-i-Aqdas, Shoghi Effendi writes:

To the trustees of the House of Justice He assigns the duty of legislating on matters **not expressly provided** in His writings, and promises that God will 'inspire them with whatsoever He willeth'.[130]

In a letter written on his behalf, Shoghi Effendi also explains the relationship between the revealed Law of Bahá'u'lláh and the laws created by the Universal House of Justice:

> ... the Laws revealed by Bahá'u'lláh in the Aqdas are, whenever practical and not in direct conflict with the Civil laws of the land, absolutely binding on every believer or Bahá'í institution whether in the East or in the West. Certain laws, such as fasting, obligatory prayers, the consent of the parents before marriage, avoidance of alcoholic drinks, monogamy, should be regarded by all believers as universally and vitally applicable at the present time. Others have been formulated in anticipation of a state of society destined to emerge from the chaotic conditions that prevail today.
>
> When the Aqdas is published, this matter will be further explained and elucidated. What has not been formulated in the Aqdas, in addition to matters of detail and of secondary importance arising out of the application of the laws already formulated by Bahá'u'lláh, will have to be enacted by the Universal House of Justice. This body can supplement but never invalidate or modify in the least degree what has already been formulated by Bahá'u'lláh.[131]

In the course of his ministry Shoghi Effendi identified specific topics and areas that have been left for the Universal House of Justice to legislate upon. These include:

a) The titles of Bahá'í institutions

> As to the title to be adopted for letterheads, I would suggest, pending the formation of the Universal House of Justice, the phrase 'The National Spiritual Assembly of the Bahá'ís of the United States and Canada', retaining the word 'spiritual' and restricting the meaning of the term 'assembly' to be applied only to the body of nine elected by the friends whether for local or national purposes.[132]

b) The constitutions of Bahá'í Assemblies

This document [the Declaration of Trust developed by the National Spiritual Assembly of the Bahá'ís of the United States and Canada], when correlated and combined with the set of by-laws which I trust are soon forthcoming, will serve as a pattern to every National Bahá'í Assembly, be it in the East or in the West, which aspires to conform, pending the formation of the first Universal House of Justice, with the spirit and letter of the world-order ushered in by Bahá'u'lláh.[133]

c) The method of electing Bahá'í Assemblies

In connection with the best and most practical methods of procedure to be adopted for the election of Bahá'í Spiritual Assemblies, I feel that in view of the fact that definite and detailed regulations defining the manner and character of Bahá'í elections have neither been expressly revealed by Bahá'u'lláh nor laid down in the Will and Testament of 'Abdu'l-Bahá, it devolves upon the members of the Universal House of Justice to formulate and apply such system of laws as would be in conformity with the essentials and requisites expressly provided by the Author and Interpreter of the Faith for the conduct of Bahá'í administration.[134]

d) The frequency and timing of elections

This National Spiritual Assembly, which, pending the establishment of the Universal House of Justice, will have to be re-elected once a year . . .[135]

Pending its [the Universal House of Justice] establishment, and to insure uniformity throughout the East and throughout the West, all local Assemblies will have to be re-elected once a year, during the first day of Riḍván, and the result of polling, if possible, be declared on that day.[136]

72

e) The membership and election of the Universal House of Justice

The membership of the Universal House of Justice is confined to men. Fixing the number of the members, the procedures for election and the term of membership will be known later, as these are not explicitly revealed in the Holy Text.[137]

f) 'Ground organization'

There is nothing about 'ground organization'. These details are left for future legislation.[138]

g) Prohibited substances

Concerning the use of alcoholic drinks and drugs the Guardian wishes you to know that they have been explicitly forbidden in the 'Kitáb-i-Aqdas'. Opium is, undoubtedly, prohibited. But smoking, though allowed, is discouraged. Various other points which may be raised in this connection and which have not been explained in the Holy Writings have to be carefully considered and acted upon by the future International House of Justice which is the body empowered by Bahá'u'lláh to legislate in all matters which have not been explicitly revealed in the Sacred Writings of the Faith.[139]

h) Bahá'í anniversaries and calendar

Concerning the date of the anniversary of the Báb's declaration the Guardian feels that it would be preferable to postpone the consideration of this problem until the Universal House of Justice is established. In the meantime he would advise you to follow the system actually in use in the Bahá'í world (i.e. year 9) even in Germany. According to this system the hundredth anniversary of the declaration of the Faith should be celebrated in May of the year 101, that is when we enter the second Bahá'í century. By year 90 we should not mean that 90 years have elapsed since the declaration of the Báb but that we are in the 9th [*sic*] year. But whether it is preferable to adopt this system or that suggested by you and which, you remark, is in use among Christians and Moslems, the future House of Justice has to decide.[140]

Regarding Naw-Rúz: If the vernal equinox falls on the 21st of March before sunset, it is celebrated on that day. If at any time after sunset, Naw-Rúz will then, as stated by Bahá'u'lláh, fall on the 22nd. As to which spot should be regarded as the standard, this is a matter which the Universal House of Justice will have to decide.[141]

The Guardian instructs that in Samoa all of the Holy Days should be celebrated in accordance with the Solar calendar, in accordance with the practice of the Western Bahá'ís. The Guardian of course has in mind that the Bahá'ís in the East follow the Lunar calendar, for certain of the Holy Days. He has in mind especially the instructions in the *Aqdas* with regard to the Twin festivals. However as the Faith develops around the world there are many problems involved in the observance of certain of the Holy Days, particularly the Twin festivals according to the Lunar Calendar.

In the future, no doubt all of the Holy Days will follow the Solar calendar, and provisions be made as to how the Twin Festivals will be celebrated universally.

As indicated above, there are many problems involved in the application of the statements concerning the Twin Festivals, which will have to be worked out by the House of Justice.[142]

i) Vivisection

As there is no definite and conclusive statement on vivisection in the Bahá'í teachings, this is a matter which the International House of Justice will have to pass upon in the future.[143]

As regards the question the Auckland Assembly has asked about vivisection, there is nothing on this subject in the

Bahá'í teachings. At a future date such matters will no doubt be taken up by the International House of Justice.[144]

j) Capital punishment

Regarding the question of capital punishment, provision is made for it in the Aqdas, but this is not the time to go into details. When the Aqdas is promulgated and the House of Justice comes into being will be the time to go into these matters in greater detail. For the present they should be given no publicity.[145]

The question of whether capital punishment should be inflicted on the criminally insane is one for the Universal House of Justice to decide. Such people, however, not being responsible for their actions, will not suffer any spiritual effect from acts committed while mentally deranged.[146]

k) Marriage

There is no specific minimum age mentioned in the Bahá'í teachings at which girls may marry. In the future, this and other questions unspecified will be dealt with by the International House of Justice. In the meantime, we must not be too strict in enforcing our opinions on peoples still living in primitive social orders.[147]

l) Obligatory prayers

First, with regard to your questions concerning the obligatory prayers, the Aqdas does not give detailed instructions about them. The Universal House of Justice, however, will have to define the exact time for their recital, and lay down, if required, other detailed instructions concerning their use. One of the three obligatory prayers should be recited. This is an obligation. But individual believers are absolutely free to choose any one of them. There is no particular time of day fixed for the reading of the long prayer. The use of the Greatest Name 95 times a day is not absolutely binding.[148] This and other similar matters will be clearly and fully explained when the Aqdas is published. At present, however, the friends should be careful not to lay an undue emphasis upon them.[149]

m) Abortion

Regarding the practice of abortion: as no specific reference has been made to the subject in the Writings of Bahá'u'lláh, it devolves upon the International House of Justice to definitely pronounce upon it. There can be no doubt, however, that this practice, involving as it does the destruction of human life, is to be strongly deprecated.[150]

As there is nothing specific in the Bahá'í Writings on the subject of abortion, it will consequently have to be dealt with by the Universal House of Justice, when that Body is formed.[151]

n) Euthanasia

Regarding 'mercy killings' or legalized euthanasia; this is also a matter which the Universal House of Justice will have to legislate upon.[152]

o) Sterilization

As regards the sterilization of the mentally deficient or the physically unfit; the Teachings bear no direct reference to the subject, and it therefore devolves on the Universal House of Justice to decide and legislate on this matter.[153]

p) Age of retirement

With reference to Bahá'u'lláh's command concerning the engagement of the believers in some sort of profession; the teachings are most emphatic on this matter, particularly the statement in the Aqdas to this effect which makes it quite clear that idle people who lack the desire to work can have no place in the new World Order. As a corollary of this principle, Bahá'u'lláh further states that mendicity should not only be discouraged but entirely wiped out from the face of society. It is the duty of those who are in charge of the organization of society to give every individual the opportunity of acquiring the necessary talent in some kind of profession, and also the means of utilizing such a talent, both for its own sake and for the sake of earning the means of his livelihood. Every individual, no matter how handicapped and limited he may be, is under the obligation of engaging in some work or profession, for work, especially when performed in the spirit of service, is according to Bahá'u'lláh, a form of worship. It has not only a utilitarian purpose, but has a value in itself, because it draws us nearer to God, and enables us to better grasp His purpose for us in this world. It is obvious, therefore, that the inheritance of wealth cannot make anyone immune from daily work. As to the question of retirement from work for individuals who have reached a certain age, this is a matter on which the International House of Justice will have to legislate as there are no provisions in the Aqdas concerning it.[154]

Rather than strictly defining and limiting the powers of the Universal House of Justice, it is suggested that these quotations should be taken as indicative of some of the broad areas in which it is empowered to legislate. Issues on which the Universal House of Justice has specifically declined to legislate *for the present* include euthanasia,[155] the circumstances in which an abortion would be justifiable[156] and the use of flavoured extracts in foods.[157]

The Universal House of Justice has explained why it has so far refrained from over-exercising its power of legislation:

The Universal House of Justice does not feel that the time has come for it to provide detailed legislation on subjects such as abortion, homosexuality and other moral issues. The principles pertaining to these issues are available in the book 'Lights of Guidance' and elsewhere. In studying these principles, it should be noted that in most areas of human behaviour there are acts which are clearly contrary to the law of God and others which are clearly approved or permissible; between these there is often a grey area where it is not immediately apparent what should be done. It has been a human tendency to wish to eliminate these grey areas so that every aspect of life is clearly prescribed. A result of this tendency has been the tremendous accretion of interpretation and subsidiary legislation which has smothered the spirit of certain of the older religions. In the Bahá'í Faith moderation, which is so strongly upheld by Bahá'u'lláh, is applied here also. Provision is made for supplementary legislation by the Universal House of Justice – legislation which it can itself abrogate and amend as conditions change. There is also a clear pattern already established in the Sacred Scriptures, in the interpretations made by 'Abdu'l-Bahá and Shoghi Effendi, and in the decisions so far made by the Universal House of Justice, whereby an area of the application of the laws is intentionally left to the conscience of each individual believer. This is the age in which mankind must attain maturity, and one aspect of this is the assumption by individuals of the responsibility for deciding, with the assistance of consultation, their own course of action in areas which are left open by the law of God.

It should also be noted that it is neither possible nor desirable for the Universal House of Justice to set forth a set of rules covering every situation. Rather is it the task of the individual believer to determine, according to his own prayerful understanding of the Writings, precisely what his course of conduct should be in relation to situations which he encounters in his daily life. If he is to fulfil his true mission in life as a follower of the Blessed Perfection, he will pattern his life according to the Teachings. The believer cannot attain this objective merely by living according to a set of rigid regulations. When his life is oriented towards service to Bahá'u'lláh, and when every conscious act is performed within this frame of reference, he will not fail to achieve the true purpose of his life.

Therefore, every believer must continually study the Sacred Writings and the instructions of the beloved Guardian, striving always to attain a new and better understanding of their import to him and to his society. He should pray fervently for divine guidance, wisdom and strength to do what is pleasing to God, and to serve Him at all times and to the best of his ability.[158]

Summary Table: Topics for Legislation by the Universal House of Justice

Areas	Sources
General: laws and other matters not expressly revealed in the Bahá'í writings	Bahá'u'lláh, *Tablets*, p. 68; 'Abdu'l-Bahá, *Will*, paras. 14, 38; *Some Answered Questions*, p. 172; *Compilation*, vol. 1, pp. 322, 341; Universal House of Justice, *Messages*, p. 85; Shoghi Effendi, *World Order*, pp. 153–4; *God Passes By*, pp. 218–19, 326.
'matters of detail and of secondary importance arising out of the application of the laws' formulated by Bahá'u'lláh	Shoghi Effendi, *Directives*, p. 4.
Penalties for adultery, sodomy and theft	Bahá'u'lláh, *Kitáb-i-Aqdas*, p. 121.
Marriage laws	Bahá'u'lláh, *Kitáb-i-Aqdas*, p. 122. Shoghi Effendi, *Unfolding Destiny*, p. 334
Details relating to the charging of interest (usury)	Bahá'u'lláh, *Tablets*, pp. 133–4.
Details of the law of punishment for murder and arson	Bahá'u'lláh, *Kitáb-i-Aqdas*, p. 204.
Details of the law of Zakát (a regular charity)	Bahá'u'lláh, *Kitáb-i-Aqdas*, pp. 234–5.

Areas	Sources
Application of the law relating to dowry	Bahá'u'lláh, *Kitáb-i-Aqdas*, p. 209.
Elaboration of Bahá'í administrative policy	Shoghi Effendi, *Bahá'í Administration*, p. 78.
Titles of Bahá'í institutions	Shoghi Effendi, *Bahá'í Administration*, pp. 82–3.
Constitutions of Bahá'í Assemblies	Shoghi Effendi, *Bahá'í Administration*, pp. 134–5.
Method of electing Bahá'í Assemblies	Shoghi Effendi, *Bahá'í Administration*, pp. 135–6.
Frequency and timing of elections	Shoghi Effendi, *Bahá'í Administration*, pp. 40, 41
Membership and election of the House of Justice	Letter written on behalf of Shoghi Effendi to an individual, 27 May 1940.
'Ground organization'	Shoghi Effendi, *Divine Guidance*, vol. 2, p. 82.
Prohibited substances	Shoghi Effendi, *Dawn*, pp. 196–7.
Bahá'í anniversaries and calendar	Shoghi Effendi, *Divine Guidance*, vol. 2, pp. 49–50; *Directives*, p. 30; *Canada*, pp. 230–1.
Vivisection	Shoghi Effendi, *Antipodes*, pp. 397, 411.
Capital punishment	Shoghi Effendi, *Antipodes*, p. 412; *Canada*, p. 66.
Detailed instructions about obligatory prayers	Letter written on behalf of Shoghi Effendi to an individual, 10 October 1936.
Abortion	Letters written on behalf of Shoghi Effendi to individuals, 13 November 1940 and 20 October 1953.
Euthanasia	Shoghi Effendi, *Canada*, p. 66.
Sterilization	Shoghi Effendi, *Canada*, p. 67.
Age of retirement	Shoghi Effendi, *Directives*, p. 83.

to abrogate, according to the changes and requirements of the time, its own enactments; [para. 12]

This wording derives from statements of Shoghi Effendi such as the following, and ultimately from the Will and Testament of 'Abdu'l-Bahá:

> Not only has the House of Justice been invested by Bahá'u'lláh with the authority to legislate whatsoever has not been explicitly and outwardly recorded in His holy Writ, upon it has also been conferred by the Will and Testament of 'Abdu'l-Bahá the right and power **to abrogate, according to the changes and requirements of the time, whatever has been already enacted and enforced by a preceding House of Justice.** In this connection, He revealed the following in His Will: 'And inasmuch as the House of Justice hath power to enact laws that are not expressly recorded in the Book and bear upon daily transactions, so also it hath power to repeal the same. Thus for example, the House of Justice enacteth today a certain law and enforceth it, and a hundred years hence, circumstances having profoundly changed and the conditions having altered, another House of Justice will then have power, according to the exigencies of the time, to alter that law. This it can do because that law formeth no part of the divine explicit text. The House of Justice is both the initiator and the abrogator of its own laws.'[159] Such is the immutability of His revealed Word. Such is the elasticity which characterizes the functions of His appointed ministers. The first preserves the identity of His Faith, and guards the integrity of His law. The second enables it, even as a living organism, to expand and adapt itself to the needs and requirements of an ever-changing society.[160]

Elsewhere, after citing words of Bahá'u'lláh that guarantee divine inspiration to the House of Justice, Shoghi Effendi writes:

Not only does 'Abdu'l-Bahá confirm in His Will Bahá'u'lláh's above-quoted statement, but invests this body with the additional right and power **to abrogate, according to the exigencies of time, its own enactments**, as well as those of a preceding House of Justice.[161]

Communicating through his secretary, Shoghi Effendi responded to the questions of an individual believer, explaining that the power of abrogation ensures that the Universal House of Justice maintains an essential element of flexibility:

. . . one of the reasons God has given us the institution of Guardianship is to prevent men from crystallizing the Cause of God into a rigid system. Your questions are mostly along the line of trying to lay down a fixed pattern for future society, long before the time for such a pattern is ripe. Remember that Bahá'u'lláh says what is not already revealed, the International House of Justice must in the future legislate, and it can make, and abrogate if necessary, its own laws. This means not fixity in guiding society, but fluidity![162]

Examples of the Universal House of Justice abrogating its own laws according to the exigencies of time might include:

- its various rulings on the number, areas, boards and terms of Continental Counsellors[163]
- its decisions during the Five Year Plan (1974–9) to allow certain Local Spiritual Assemblies to be re-elected at any time during the Riḍván Festival and to allow first time elections of Local Spiritual Assemblies to take place at any point during the year; and its abrogation of those rulings at the start of the Four Year Plan (1996–2000)[164]

to deliberate and decide upon all problems which have caused difference; to elucidate questions that are obscure; [para. 12]

These broad powers are conferred upon the Universal House of Justice in Part One of the Will and Testament of 'Abdu'l-Bahá: 'By this body all the difficult **problems** are to be resolved . . .'[165] The actual wording of this part of the Declaration of Trust, however, comes from Part Two:

> It is incumbent upon these members (of the Universal House of Justice) to gather in a certain place and **deliberate upon all problems which have caused difference, questions that are obscure** and matters that are not expressly recorded in the Book. Whatsoever they decide has the same effect as the Text itself.[166]

The same duties are affirmed in other Tablets of 'Abdu'l-Bahá, such as this:

> The greatness of the Cause will clear away these differences and may be compared to health in the body of man which, when established, cureth all disease and weakness . . .
> Praise be to God, all such doors are closed in the Cause of Bahá'u'lláh for a special authoritative Centre hath been appointed – a Centre that solveth all difficulties and wardeth off all differences. The Universal House of Justice, likewise, wardeth off all **differences** and whatever it prescribeth must be accepted and he who transgresseth is rejected.[167]

Shoghi Effendi has provided at least two examples of the kinds of questions which the Universal House of Justice is empowered to elucidate. The first example relates to the 'new world order' outlined in the Will and Testament of 'Abdu'l-Bahá:

> And as we make an effort to demonstrate that love to the world may we also clear our minds of any lingering trace of unhappy misunderstandings that might obscure our clear conception of the exact purpose and methods of this new world order, so challenging and complex, yet so consummate

and wise. We are called upon by our beloved Master in His Will and Testament not only to adopt it unreservedly, but to unveil its merit to all the world. To attempt to estimate its full value, and grasp its exact significance after so short a time since its inception would be premature and presumptuous on our part. We must trust to time, and the guidance of God's Universal House of Justice, to obtain a clearer and fuller understanding of its provisions and implications . . .

Pending the establishment of the Universal House of Justice, whose function it is to lay more definitely the broad lines that must guide the future activities and administration of the Movement, it is clearly our duty to strive to obtain as clear a view as possible of the manner in which to conduct the affairs of the Cause, and then arise with single-mindedness and determination to adopt and maintain it in all our activities and labours. [168]

The second example relates to questions regarding international institutions:

Touching the point raised in the Secretary's letter regarding the nature and scope of the Universal Court of Arbitration, this and other similar matters will have to be explained and **elucidated** by the Universal House of Justice, to which, according to the Master's explicit instructions, all important and fundamental questions must be referred. At present the exact implication and full significance of the provisions of the Master's Will are as yet imperfectly understood, and time will serve to reveal the wisdom and the far-reaching effects of His words. [169]

Early in its ministry, in 1965, the Universal House of Justice found it necessary to distinguish its own elucidations from the Guardian's authoritative interpretations of scripture:

There is a profound difference between the interpretations

of the Guardian and the elucidations of the House of Justice in exercise of its function to deliberate upon all problems which have caused difference, questions that are obscure and matters that are not expressly recorded in the Book'. The Guardian reveals what the Scripture means; his interpretation is a statement of truth which cannot be varied. Upon the Universal House of Justice, in the words of the Guardian, 'has been conferred the exclusive right of legislating on matters not expressly revealed in the Bahá'í Writings'. Its pronouncements, which are susceptible of amendment or abrogation by the House of Justice itself, serve to supplement and apply the Law of God. Although not invested with the function of interpretation, the House of Justice is in a position to do everything necessary to establish the World Order of Bahá'u'lláh on this earth. Unity of doctrine is maintained by the existence of the authentic texts of Scripture and the voluminous interpretations of 'Abdu'l-Bahá and Shoghi Effendi, together with the absolute prohibition against anyone propounding 'authoritative' or 'inspired' interpretations or usurping the function of the Guardian. Unity of administration is assured by the authority of the Universal House of Justice.[170]

This letter continues, first quoting from the Persian writings of Shoghi Effendi:

'As to the order and the management of the spiritual affairs of the friends, that which is very important now is the consolidation of the Spiritual Assemblies in every centre, because, on these fortified and unshakable foundations, God's Supreme House of Justice shall be erected and firmly established in the days to come. When this most great Edifice shall be reared on such an immovable foundation, God's purpose, wisdom, universal truths, mysteries and realities of the Kingdom, which the mystic revelation of Bahá'u'lláh has deposited within the Will and Testament of 'Abdu'l-Bahá, shall gradually be revealed and made manifest.' (Letter dated 19 December 1923 – translated from the Persian)

Statements such as these indicate that the full meaning of the Will and Testament of 'Abdu'l-Bahá, as well as an understanding of the implications of the World Order ushered in by that remarkable document, can be revealed only gradually to men's eyes, and after the Universal House of Justice has come into being. The friends are called upon to trust to time and to await the guidance of the Universal House of Justice, which, as circumstances require, will make pronouncements that will resolve and clarify obscure matters.[171]

The House of Justice returned again to this subject two decades later, specifying in a letter to an individual Bahá'í on 25 October 1984 one of the areas in which it exercises its power of elucidation:

In a letter dated 9 March 1965, the Universal House of Justice stresses the 'profound difference' that exists between the 'interpretations of the Guardian and the elucidations of the House of Justice in exercise of its function to "deliberate upon all problems which have caused difference, questions that are obscure, and matters that are not expressly recorded in the Book"'. Among these is the outlining of such steps as are necessary to establish the World Order of Bahá'u'lláh on this earth. The elucidations of the Universal House of Justice stem from its legislative function, while the interpretations of the Guardian represent the true intent inherent in the Sacred Texts. The major distinction between the two functions is that legislation with its resultant outcome of elucidation is susceptible of amendment by the House of Justice itself, whereas the Guardian's interpretation is a statement of truth which cannot be varied.[172]

Again, on 15 December 1994, the Universal House of Justice wrote to an individual:

The elucidations of the Universal House of Justice stem from its legislative function, and as such differ from interpretation. The divinely inspired legislation of the House of Justice does not attempt to say what the revealed Word means – it states what must be done in cases where the revealed Text or its authoritative interpretation is not explicit. It is, therefore, on quite a different level from the sacred Text, and the Universal House of Justice is empowered to abrogate or amend its own legislation whenever it judges the conditions make this desirable.[173]

Letters and memoranda by the Research Department, even if attached to a letter by or on behalf of the Universal House of Justice, are not themselves considered authoritative elucidations of the House of Justice:

> It is also vital that the believers understand clearly that these Research Department statements should be regarded as representing no more than the views of that Department. While such views are very useful as an aid to resolving perplexities or gaining an enhanced understanding of the Bahá'í teachings, they should never be taken to be in the same category as the elucidations and clarifications provided by the House of Justice in the exercise of its assigned functions.[174]

We may improve our understanding of the Universal House of Justice's power of elucidation by examining specific statements which it has itself identified as elucidation of questions that are obscure. These include statements:

- On the impossibility of Shoghi Effendi appointing a successor in accordance with the provisions of the Will and Testament of 'Abdu'l-Bahá: 'This situation, in which the Guardian died without being able to appoint a successor, presented an **obscure** question not covered by the explicit Holy Text, and had to be referred to the Universal House of Justice.'[175]

- On 'the uniqueness of the translations of Shoghi Effendi' in a letter written on behalf of the Universal House of Justice to an individual, 8 September 1964 (identified as elucidation in a letter of 16 September 1992).[176]
- On the registration of children and youth as Bahá'ís: 'In letters replying to questions on the registration of children and youth the Universal House of Justice has attempted to avoid laying down rulings that are universally applicable. However, for the assistance of National Spiritual Assemblies it is now providing the following summary of guidelines and **elucidations** that have been given.'[177]
- On 'the nature of the Institution of the Continental Boards of Counsellors and its relationship to the Institution of the Hands of the Cause': 'we feel it is timely for us to give further **elucidation**'.[178]
- On the relationship between the Guardianship and the Universal House of Justice: 'We hope that these **elucidations** will assist the friends in understanding these relationships more clearly, but we must all remember that we stand too close to the beginnings of the System ordained by Bahá'u'lláh to be able fully to understand its potentialities or the interrelationships of its component parts.'[179]
- On the goals of plans: 'To supplement the message which is being addressed to each of your Communities giving its specific goals under the Five Year Plan, we now share with you a number of **elucidations**.'[180]

The Universal House of Justice has also suggested some topics on which it will provide further elucidation in the future:

- On the World Order of Bahá'u'lláh: 'At this time we have the benefit of many . . . interpretations by Shoghi Effendi and also the initial guidance of the Universal House of Justice, which will continue to **elucidate** aspects of this mighty system as it unfolds.'[181]

- On the laws of the Kitáb-i-Aqdas regarding hunting:

It must be borne in mind that hunting is not forbidden by Bahá'u'lláh. The warning that is given is against excessive hunting, but what constitutes an excess in hunting has to be defined by the House of Justice in the future. Similarly, the laws that prescribe avoiding the eating of game if it is found dead in a trap or net can be applied universally only when the necessary subsidiary details to such laws are decided upon by the House of Justice . . .

In the light of the above, the friends in such areas as . . . may continue their hunting practices as they have been doing over the years, within the latitude allowed by the civil authorities. Only gradually, and as circumstances will permit, will the relevant laws of the Aqdas become applicable to them in the future. At that time these laws will be **elucidated** and supported by supplementary legislation, as may be called for.[182]

- On the law of divorce (year of waiting):

There is a Tablet from 'Abdu'l-Bahá which states that the year of waiting is waived in the case of an unfaithful wife. This aspect of the Bahá'í law of divorce, however, will need **elucidation** and supplementary legislation by the Universal House of Justice. Therefore, at the present time, in divorce cases such as the one you cited, the husband must still observe the year of waiting, which involves payment of the wife's expenses during this period.[183]

Summary Table: Topics for Elucidation by the Universal House of Justice

Area	Sources
General: all the difficult problems	'Abdu'l-Bahá, *Will and Testament*, para. 25.

Area	Sources
General: all problems which have caused difference	'Abdu'l-Bahá, *Will and Testament*, para. 38; *Selections*, p. 15; *Compilation*, vol. 1, p. 322.
General: questions that are obscure	'Abdu'l-Bahá, *Will and Testament*, para. 38.
Provisions and implications of this new world order	Shoghi Effendi, *Bahá'í Administration*, pp. 62–3.
Broad lines that guide the future activities and administration of the Faith	Shoghi Effendi, *Bahá'í Administration*, pp. 62–3.
Nature and scope of the Universal Court of Arbitration	Shoghi Effendi, *Bahá'í Administration*, p. 46.
Impossibility of Shoghi Effendi appointing a successor	Universal House of Justice, *Messages*, p. 50.
Uniqueness of the translations of Shoghi Effendi	Letter of the Universal House of Justice, 8 September 1964.
Registration of children and youth as Bahá'ís	Universal House of Justice, *Messages*, pp. 549–50.
Nature of the Institution of the Continental Boards of Counsellors	Universal House of Justice, *Messages*, p. 214.
Relationship between the Guardianship and the Universal House of Justice	Universal House of Justice, *Messages*, p. 161.
Goals of plans	Universal House of Justice, *Messages*, p. 266.
World Order of Bahá'u'lláh	Letter of the Universal House of Justice, 27 April 1995.
Laws of the Kitáb-i-Aqdas regarding hunting	Letter of the Universal House of Justice, 28 May 1984.
Law of divorce (year of waiting)	Letter of the Universal House of Justice, 17 June 1987.

to safeguard the personal rights, freedom and initiative of individuals; [para 12]

This wording draws on the following passage from the writings of Shoghi Effendi:

> The unity of the human race, as envisaged by Bahá'u'lláh, implies the establishment of a world commonwealth in which all nations, races, creeds and classes are closely and permanently united, and in which the autonomy of its state members and the **personal freedom and initiative of the individuals** that compose them are definitely and completely **safeguarded.**[184]

We can see this obligation expressed in the writings of Bahá'u'lláh, for example in the following quotation from the Kalimát-i-Firdawsíyyih ('Words of Paradise'):

> We exhort the men of the House of Justice and command them to ensure the protection and **safeguarding** of men, women and children. It is incumbent upon them to have the utmost regard for the interests of the people at all times and under all conditions.[185]

And in this, from the Tablet of Ishráqát ('Splendours'):

> In the abundance of Our grace and loving-kindness We have revealed specially for the rulers and ministers of the world that which is conducive to safety and protection, tranquillity and peace; haply the children of men may rest secure from the evils of oppression. He, verily, is the Protector, the Helper, the Giver of victory. It is incumbent upon the men of God's House of Justice to fix their gaze by day and by night upon that which hath shone forth from the Pen of Glory for the training of peoples, the upbuilding of nations, the protection of man and the **safeguarding** of his honour.[186]

and to give attention to the preservation of human honour, to the development of countries and the stability of states; [para. 12]

Bahá'u'lláh states explicitly that the Universal House of Justice should be concerned with matters that affect nations as a whole, not just individuals or Bahá'í communities. State-related subjects to which the Universal House of Justice should give attention can be derived from statements of Bahá'u'lláh Himself:

a) Progress and development

The religion of God and His divine law are the most potent instruments and the surest of all means for the dawning of the light of unity amongst men. The progress of the world, the development of nations, the tranquillity of peoples, and the peace of all who dwell on earth are among the principles and ordinances of God . . . It behoveth the chiefs and rulers of the world, and in particular the Trustees of God's House of Justice, to endeavour to the utmost of their power to safeguard its position, promote its interests and exalt its station in the eyes of the world. In like manner it is incumbent upon them to enquire into the conditions of their subjects and to acquaint themselves with the affairs and activities of the divers communities in their dominions.[187]

b) Matters of state

All matters of State should be referred to the House of Justice, but acts of worship must be observed according to that which God hath revealed in His Book.[188]

c) The Lesser Peace

It is incumbent upon the ministers of the House of Justice to promote the Lesser Peace so that the people of the earth may be relieved from the burden of exorbitant expenditures. This matter is imperative and absolutely essential, inasmuch as hostilities and conflict lie at the root of affliction and calamity.[189]

d) *All affairs*

According to the fundamental laws which We have formerly revealed in the Kitáb-i-Aqdas and other Tablets, all affairs are committed to the care of just kings and presidents and of the Trustees of the House of Justice.[190]

The wide remit of the House of Justice is confirmed by Shoghi Effendi in a letter dated 30 November 1930, written on his behalf:

Regarding the question raised in your letter, Shoghi Effendi believes that for the present the Movement, whether in the East or the West, should be dissociated entirely from politics. This was the explicit injunction of 'Abdu'l-Bahá ... Eventually, however, as you have rightly conceived it, the Movement will, as soon as it is fully developed and recognized, embrace both religious and political issues. In fact Bahá'u'lláh clearly states that affairs of state as well as religious questions are to be referred to the House of Justice into which the Assemblies of the Bahá'ís will eventually evolve.[191]

To promulgate and apply the laws and principles of the Faith; [para. 13]

This wording again comes from Shoghi Effendi, here describing the administrative system devised by Bahá'u'lláh and 'Abdul-Bahá:

They have also, in unequivocal and emphatic language, appointed those twin institutions of the House of Justice and of the Guardianship as their chosen Successors, destined to **apply the principles, promulgate the laws**, protect the institutions, adapt loyally and intelligently the Faith to the requirements of progressive society, and consummate the incorruptible inheritance which the Founders of the Faith have bequeathed to the world.[192]

In a letter of 27 November 1929 to the Bahá'ís of Persia, Shoghi Effendi further indicates that the complete promulgation and application of the laws of the Most Holy Book will take place under the auspices of the Universal House of Justice:

> The National Spiritual Assemblies, like unto pillars, will be gradually and firmly established in every country on the strong and fortified foundations of the Local Assemblies. On these pillars, the mighty edifice, the Universal House of Justice, will be erected, raising high its noble frame above the world of existence. The unity of the followers of Bahá'u'lláh will thus be realized and fulfilled from one end of the earth to the other. The explicit ordinances of His Most Holy Book will be **promulgated, applied** and carried out most befittingly in the world of creation, and the living waters of everlasting life will stream forth from that fountain-head of God's World Order upon all the warring nations and peoples of the world, to wash away the evils and iniquities of the realm of dust, and heal man's age-old ills and ailments.[193]

Shoghi Effendi clearly foresaw the progressive promulgation and application the laws of the Faith, as indicated in his prospective survey of the future at the conclusion of *God Passes By*:

> The codification of the Kitáb-i-Aqdas, the Mother-Book of the Bahá'í Revelation, and the systematic promulgation of its laws and ordinances, are as yet unbegun. The preliminary measures for the institution of Bahá'í courts, invested with the legal right to apply and execute those laws and ordinances, still remain to be undertaken.[194]

Steps in the progressive application of Bahá'í law under the House of Justice include:

- The ongoing application of the law of the Mashriqu'l-Adhkár in the construction of Houses of Worship in Langenhain, Germany, dedicated in 1964; Panama, completed in 1972; New Delhi, India, completed in 1986; Apia, Samoa, completed in 1984; and Santiago, Chile, to commence construction during the Five Year Plan (2001–6).
- The further implementation of the law of the Mashriqu'l-Adhkár by a parallel process of encouraging the establishment of regular devotional gatherings in every community.[195] On 28 December 1999 the Universal House of Justice wrote to the Bahá'ís of the world:

The spiritual growth generated by individual devotions is reinforced by loving association among the friends in every locality, by worship as a community and by service to the Faith and to one's fellow human beings. These communal aspects of the godly life relate to the law of the Mashriqu'l-Adhkár which appears in the Kitáb-i-Aqdas. Although the time has not come for the building of local Mashriqu'l-Adhkárs, the holding of regular meetings for worship open to all and the involvement of Bahá'í communities in projects of humanitarian service are expressions of this element of Bahá'í life and a further step in the implementation of the Law of God.

- The publication of the Synopsis and Codification of the Kitáb-i-Aqdas (1973).
- The publication of an annotated translation of the Kitáb-i-Aqdas (1992).
- The application of the law of Ḥuqúqu'lláh to the Bahá'ís of the world (1992).
- The application to all Bahá'ís of all specifics of the laws of obligatory prayer and fasting, and the recital of 'Alláh-u-Abhá' 95 times each day (1999).

to safeguard and enforce that rectitude of conduct

95

which the Law of God enjoins; [para. 13]

This was described by Shoghi Effendi as the 'highest mission' of the Universal House of Justice:

> It must be made the hallmark of that numerically small, yet intensely dynamic and highly responsible body of the elected national representatives of every Bahá'í community, which constitutes the sustaining pillar, and the sole instrument for the election, in every community, of that Universal House whose very name and title, as ordained by Bahá'u'lláh, symbolizes **that rectitude of conduct** which is its highest mission **to safeguard and enforce.**[196]

to preserve and develop the Spiritual and Administrative Centre of the Bahá'í Faith, permanently fixed in the twin cities of 'Akká and Haifa; [para. 13]

This description of the World Centre of the Bahá'í Faith draws on several statements by Shoghi Effendi. On the decision to form the first International Bahá'í Council, Shoghi Effendi described that body as the 'forerunner of supreme administrative institution destined to emerge in fullness of time within precincts beneath shadow of World **Spiritual Centre of Faith** already established in **twin cities of 'Akká and Haifa'**.[197] He later wrote of the 'assistance of the newly-formed International Council . . . through contact with authorities designed to spread the fame, consolidate the foundations and widen the scope of influence emanating from the **twin spiritual, administrative World Centres permanently fixed in the Holy Land** constituting the midmost heart of the entire planet'.[198]

Later still, Shoghi Effendi described 'the enlargement of the scope of Bahá'í international endowments in **the twin cities of 'Akká and Haifa,** constituting the World Centre of the Faith'.[199] And finally, foreseeing the future glory of the administrative centre on Mount Carmel, he spoke of 'the splendour of the institutions which that triumphant Faith must erect on the slopes of a mountain, destined to be so linked with the city of 'Akká that a single grand metropolis will be formed to enshrine the **spiritual** as well as the **administrative** seats of the future Bahá'í Commonwealth'.[200]

The Charter for 'the development of the institutions of the Faith at its World Centre' is Bahá'u'lláh's Tablet of Carmel.[201] The Shrine of the Báb is situated on the northern slope of that mountain while the Shrine of Bahá'u'lláh is at Bahjí, north of the city of 'Akká.

Development of both the spiritual and the administrative world centres of the Bahá'í Faith was commenced under the Guardianship of Shoghi Effendi. During his ministry the Shrine of the Báb on Mount Carmel in Haifa was extended, a superstructure added and terraces constructed below it. Gardens were designed and constructed around the Shrine of Bahá'u'lláh at Bahjí and both the Shrine and the Mansion of Bahá'u'lláh were renovated. The resting places of the wife (Ásíyih Khánum), daughter (Bahíyyih Khánum) and son (Mírzá Mihdí) of Bahá'u'lláh, as well as of the wife of 'Abdu'l-Bahá (Munírih Khánum), were moved to Mount Carmel and fitting monuments were constructed for them. Shoghi Effendi himself designed gardens in the shape of an arc around these monuments and the first building, an International Archives, was constructed on the western end of that arc.

At the start of its ministry the Universal House of Justice signalled its intention to continue the development of the spiritual and administrative centre of the Bahá'í Faith, initiated during the ministries of 'Abdu'l-Bahá and Shoghi Effendi:

At the World Centre of the Faith the tasks of the [Nine Year] Plan include . . the preparation of a plan for the befitting development and beautification of the entire area of Bahá'í property surrounding the Holy Shrines; extension of the existing gardens on Mount Carmel . . .[202]

The Universal House of Justice has explained the significance of more recent developments on Mount Carmel:

> The Edifices and Terraces now under construction are a manifest expression of the emergence from obscurity of the Faith of Bahá'u'lláh and of the determining role it is ordained to play in the affairs of humankind. When the buildings are completed, they will stand as the visible seat of mighty institutions whose purpose is no other than the spiritualization of humanity and the preservation of justice and unity throughout the world. The future significance of the Terraces is evident from their characterization by Shoghi Effendi as 'the Pathway of the Kings and Rulers of the World'. The beauty and magnificence of the Gardens and Terraces now under development are symbolic of the nature of the transformation which is destined to occur both within the hearts of the world's peoples and in the physical environment of the planet.
>
> The establishment of the World Administrative Centre of the Faith on Mount Carmel at this juncture in the fortunes of mankind is essential to hasten the accomplishment of God's purpose for humanity through the operation of the World Order of Bahá'u'lláh. The believers are called upon to sustain this vast collective enterprise upon which the community of the Most Great Name is now embarked, through a sacrificial outpouring of material resources and through their dedication to the work of the Cause at this time of unprecedented need and opportunity. [203]

Steps taken to preserve and develop the Bahá'í World Centre under the direction of the Universal House of Justice include:

- The acquisition of property adjacent to Bahjí (1969)
- The creation and appointment of the first International Teaching Centre (1973)
- The purchase and subsequent renovation of the House of 'Abdu'lláh Páshá (1975 onwards)

- The construction of the Seat of the Universal House of Justice (inaugurated 1982)
- The development and beautification of Bahá'í property surrounding the Holy Shrines (continuous)
- The construction of the Terraces of the Shrine of the Báb and of three buildings on the Arc: the International Teaching Centre, the Centre for the Study of the Texts and the Archives Extension (1987–2001)

to administer the affairs of the Bahá'í community throughout the world; to guide, organize, coordinate and unify its activities; [para. 13]

These obligations are derived from at least two specific statements of Shoghi Effendi. The first is this reference, from early in his ministry: 'the International House of Justice, that Supreme Council that will **guide, organize and unify the affairs** of the Movement throughout the world'.[204]

The second statement is this, from 'The Dispensation of Bahá'u'lláh':

It should be stated, at the very outset, in clear and unambiguous language, that these twin institutions [the Guardianship and the Universal House of Justice] of the Administrative Order of Bahá'u'lláh should be regarded as divine in origin, essential in their functions and complementary in their aim and purpose. Their common, their fundamental object is to insure the continuity of that divinely-appointed authority which flows from the Source of our Faith, to safeguard the unity of its followers and to maintain the integrity and flexibility of its teachings. Acting in conjunction with each other these two inseparable institutions **administer its affairs, coordinate its activities,** promote its interests, execute its laws and defend its subsidiary institutions.[205]

The Guardian wrote elsewhere of the Universal House of Justice, 'whose function it is to lay more definitely the broad lines that must **guide** the future **activities** and administration of the Movement'[206] and 'that will symbolize the unity and **coordinate and unify the activities** of these National Assemblies'.[207]

to found institutions; [para. 13]

Shoghi Effendi clearly foresaw that the Universal House of Justice would found additional institutions:

> I can only for the moment cite at random certain of these opportunities which stand out preeminently, in any attempt to survey the possibilities of the future: The election of the International House of Justice and its establishment in the Holy Land, the spiritual and administrative centre of the Bahá'í world, together with the formation of its auxiliary branches and subsidiary **institutions** . . .[208]

Describing the evolution of the International Bahá'í Council into the Universal House of Justice, the Guardian wrote of its 'final fruition through erection of manifold auxiliary **institutions** constituting the World Administrative Centre destined to arise and function and remain permanently established in close neighbourhood of Twin Holy Shrines'.[209] Again, he foresaw the development of the Council into a 'properly recognized and independently functioning Bahá'í court, which will attain its consummation in the institution of the Universal House of Justice and the emergence of the auxiliary administrative agencies, revolving around this highest legislative body'.[210]

In a letter to the Bahá'ís of the East in 1924, Shoghi Effendi included the following among the future functions of the Universal House of Justice: 'to devise and carry out important undertakings, world-wide activities and the establishment of glorious **institutions**'.[211] And finally, there is this vision of the future of the Bahá'í Revelation in *God Passes By*:

... a Revelation destined to blossom forth, in a later period into the flourishing institutions of a world-wide administrative System, and to ripen, in the Golden Age as yet unborn, into mighty agencies functioning in consonance with the principles of a world-unifying, world-redeeming Order.[212]

Institutions already formed under this authority include:

- The Continental Boards of Counsellors (1968[213])
- The International Teaching Centre (1973)
- Regional Councils in various countries (from 1997)

In relation to the last of these institutions, the Universal House of Justice has written the following, providing some background and context for this part of its Constitution:

The expansion of the Bahá'í community and the growing complexity of the issues which are facing National Spiritual Assemblies in certain countries have brought the Cause to a new stage in its development. They have caused us in recent years to examine various aspects of the balance between centralization and decentralization. In a few countries we have authorized the National Spiritual Assemblies to establish State Bahá'í Councils or Regional Teaching and Administrative Committees. From the experience gained in the operation of these bodies, and from detailed examination of the principles set forth by Shoghi Effendi, we have reached the conclusion that the time has arrived for us to formalize a new element of Bahá'í administration, between the local and national levels, comprising institutions of a special kind, to be designated as 'Regional Bahá'í Councils'
...
The institutions of the Administrative Order of Bahá'u-'lláh, rooted in the provisions of His Revelation, have emerged gradually and organically, as the Bahá'í community has grown through the power of the divine impulse

imparted to humankind in this age. The characteristics and functions of each of these institutions have evolved, and are still evolving, as are the relationships between them. The writings of the beloved Guardian expound the fundamental elements of this mighty System and make it clear that the Administrative Order, although different in many ways from the World Order which it is the destiny of the Bahá'í Revelation to call into being, is both the 'nucleus' and 'pattern' of that World Order. Thus, the evolution of the institutions of the Administrative Order, while following many variants to meet changing conditions in different times and places, should strictly follow the essential principles of Bahá'í administration which have been laid down in the Sacred Text and in the interpretations provided by 'Abdu'l-Bahá and the Guardian.[214]

to be responsible for ensuring that no body or institution within the Cause abuse its privileges or decline in the exercise of its rights and prerogatives; [para. 13]

This is derived from words of the Guardian regarding the responsibility of National Spiritual Assemblies over their spheres of jurisdiction.[215] The principle expressed by Shoghi Effendi in the following quotation is thus applied by the Universal House of Justice at an international level:

I wish to reaffirm in clear and categorical language, the principle already enunciated upholding the supreme authority of the National Assembly in all matters that affect the interests of the Faith in that land. There can be no conflict of authority, no duality under any form or circumstances in any sphere of Bahá'í jurisdiction whether local, national or international. The National Assembly, however, although the sole interpreter of its Declaration of Trust and By-Laws, is directly and morally responsible if it allows **any body or institution within its jurisdiction to abuse its privi-**

leges or to decline in the exercise of its rights and privileges.[216]

and to provide for the receipt, disposition, adminis-tration and safeguarding of the funds, endowments and other properties that are entrusted to its care; [para. 13]

During His lifetime, funds and endowments were received by the Manifestation of God. In the Kitáb-i-Aqdas Bahá'u'lláh empowers the Universal House of Justice to receive endow-ments on His behalf:

> **Endowments** dedicated to charity revert to God, the Revealer of Signs. None hath the right to dispose of them without leave from Him Who is the Dawning-place of Revel-ation. After Him, this authority shall pass to the Aghṣán, and after them to the House of Justice – should it be established in the world by then – that they may use these endowments for the benefit of the Places which have been exalted in this Cause, and for whatsoever hath been enjoined upon them by Him Who is the God of might and power.[217]

The Universal House of Justice has commented on the appli-cation of this verse:

> The passing of Shoghi Effendi in 1957 precipitated the very situation provided for in this passage, in that the line of Aghṣán ended before the House of Justice had been elected. Although, as is seen, the ending of the line of Aghṣán at some stage was provided for, we must never underestimate the grievous loss that the Faith has suffered.[218]

At present the Universal House of Justice receives contributions to the International Fund, as well as payments of Ḥuqúqu'lláh and other endowments.

To adjudicate disputes falling within its purview; to give judgement in cases of violation of the laws of the Faith and to pronounce sanctions for such violations; [para. 14]

These powers relate to the judicial jurisdiction of the Universal House of Justice. They are implicit in several of the passages from the writings of Bahá'u'lláh, 'Abdu'l-Bahá and Shoghi Effendi cited above. In the Kitáb-i-Aqdas Bahá'u'lláh leaves it to the Universal House of Justice to decide upon the sanctions for sexual offences and theft.[219] The following passage, from the writings of 'Abdu'l-Bahá, appears to relate to the adjudication of disputes:

> Praise be to God, all such doors are closed in the Cause of Bahá'u'lláh for a special authoritative Centre hath been appointed – a Centre that solveth all difficulties and wardeth off all differences. The Universal House of Justice, likewise, wardeth off all differences and whatever it prescribeth must be accepted and he who transgresseth is rejected.[220]

Shoghi Effendi clearly indicated that Local Assemblies could take on the functions of religious courts. This was particularly applicable to the Middle East, where many laws of personal status were administered by religious communities:

> . . . the imposition of sanctions by Bahá'í elective Assemblies, now assuming the duties and functions of religious courts, on recalcitrant members of the community by denying them the right to vote and of membership in these Assemblies and their committees – all these are to be associated with the first stirrings of a community that had erected the fabric of its Administrative Order . . .[221]

Moreover, as we have seen above, Shoghi Effendi described the International Bahá'í Council as developing into an international Bahá'í court before efflorescing into the Universal House of Justice itself.[222] It is unlikely that, having been a court in its embryonic stages, the fully-formed House of Justice would not retain these judicial powers.

Shoghi Effendi has outlined the general principles relating to administrative sanctions for the violation of Bahá'í law. This is from a letter by the Universal House of Justice to a National Spiritual Assembly dated 9 December 1991:

> A survey of the letters written on behalf of the Guardian shows that he advised the National Spiritual Assemblies that they should resort to the severe sanction of deprivation of a believer's administrative rights only for such matters as 'disgraceful conduct, flagrantly contrary to our Teachings', 'seriously injuring the Faith in the eyes of the public through his conduct or flagrantly breaking the laws of God', 'gross immorality and open opposition to the administrative functions of the Faith, and disregard for the laws of personal status', 'conduct which is disgracing the Cause', and 'breaking of laws, such as the consent of parents to marriage', or 'acts of such an immoral character as to damage the good name of the Faith'.
>
> It is clear that the removal of voting rights is a serious action which an Assembly should take reluctantly when the circumstances require that the Bahá'í community or its reputation in the eyes of the public must be protected from the effects of an individual's behaviour, and where the authority of the laws of the Faith must be upheld. It should be the hope and prayer of the Assembly that the believer who has been administratively expelled from membership in the Bahá'í community will come to see that his behaviour is in violation of the teachings, will endeavour to rectify his conduct, and will thus open the way to being welcomed back into the community so that he can lend his support to the vital and glorious task of establishing the World Order of Bahá'u'lláh . . .

In deciding whether or not to remove voting rights, every case should be considered on its merits and in light of the particular circumstances. The purpose of the administrative sanction should be borne clearly in mind in deciding how much weight to give to factors such as the passage of time, the extent to which the individual concerned has experienced an adverse reaction in the Bahá'í community, the degree of suffering and contrition exhibited by the believer whose status is being questioned, his stature in the Bahá'í community or the wider society, and media publicity of his delinquent behaviour. While there is room for compassion, this should not deflect you from giving due consideration to the responsibility you bear to protect the community and its good name, and to uphold the authority of Bahá'í law.[223]

The Universal House of Justice has described what the application of this administrative sanction entails:

. . . One who has lost his voting rights is considered to be a Bahá'í but *not* one in good standing. The following restrictions and limitations apply to such a believer:

He cannot attend Nineteen Day Feasts or other meetings for Bahá'ís only, including International Conferences, and therefore cannot take part in consultation on the affairs of the community.

He cannot contribute to the Bahá'í Fund.

He cannot receive newsletters and other bulletins whose circulation is restricted to Bahá'ís.

He cannot have a Bahá'í marriage ceremony and therefore is not able to marry a Bahá'í.

He may not have a Bahá'í pilgrimage.

Although he is free to teach the Faith on his own behalf, he should not be used as a teacher or speaker in programmes sponsored by Bahá'ís.

He is debarred from participating in administrative matters, including the right to vote in Bahá'í elections.

He cannot hold office or be appointed to a committee.

He should not be given credentials (which imply that he is a Bahá'í in good standing).

. . . Although generally speaking a believer deprived of his voting rights is not restricted except as stated above, the following privileges have been expressly stipulated as not denied:

He may attend the observances of the nine Holy Days.

He may attend any Bahá'í function open to non-Bahá'ís.

He may receive any publication available to non-Bahá'ís.

He is free to teach the Faith as every individual believer has been enjoined by Bahá'u'lláh to teach.

Association with other believers is not forbidden.

He may have the Bahá'í burial service if he or his family requests it, and he may be buried in a Bahá'í cemetery.

Bahá'í charity should not be denied him on the ground that he has lost his voting rights.

Bahá'í institutions may employ him, but should use discretion as to the type of work he is to perform.

He should have access to the Spiritual Assembly.[224]

to provide for the enforcement of its decisions; [para. 14]

This power can be traced to a passage from the writings of Bahá'u'lláh, as Shoghi Effendi testifies:

> It should also be borne in mind that the machinery of the Cause has been so fashioned, that whatever is deemed necessary to incorporate into it in order to keep it in the forefront of all progressive movements, can, according to the provisions made by Bahá'u'lláh, be safely embodied therein. To this testify the words of Bahá'u'lláh, as recorded in the Eighth Leaf of the exalted Paradise: 'It is incumbent upon the Trustees of the House of Justice, to take counsel together regarding those things which have not outwardly been revealed in the Book, and to **enforce** that which is agreeable to them. God will verily inspire them with whatsoever He willeth, and He, verily, is the Provider, the Omniscient.'[225]

The Will and Testament further states that enforcement of the laws of the Universal House of Justice is to be undertaken by governments:

> This House of Justice enacteth the laws and the government **enforceth** them. The legislative body must reinforce the executive, the executive must aid and assist the legislative body . . . [226]

to provide for the arbitration and settlement of disputes arising between peoples; [para. 14]

Disputes between peoples (that is, between states, countries, nations or ethnic groups) are to be settled by the Supreme Tribunal or Universal Court of Arbitration. However, the

House of Justice is empowered to elucidate the role of this institution:

> Touching the point raised in the Secretary's letter regarding the nature and scope of the Universal Court of Arbitration, this and other similar matters will have to be explained and elucidated by the Universal House of Justice, to which, according to the Master's explicit instructions, all important and fundamental questions must be referred. At present the exact implication and full significance of the provisions of the Master's Will are as yet imperfectly understood, and time will serve to reveal the wisdom and the far-reaching effects of His words.[227]

Also see a message written on behalf of the Universal House of Justice to an individual Bahá'í on 31 January 1985 on the subject of the Lesser Peace and the Supreme Tribunal.[228]

> **and to be the exponent and guardian of that Divine Justice which can alone ensure the security of, and establish the reign of law and order in, the world.** [para. 14]

This duty derives from the words of Shoghi Effendi:

> . . . that Universal House of Justice which, as its title implies, is **to be the exponent and guardian of that Divine Justice which can alone insure the security of, and establish the reign of law and order in,** a strangely disordered **world**.[229]

The House of Justice has offered the following comment on the principle of 'Divine Justice':

> The concept of due process, in the sense of a legal principle which may be embodied in a constitution and which requires

the government to treat people fairly, is clearly encompassed by the Bahá'í principle of 'Divine Justice,' a principle characterized as the 'crowning distinction of all Local and National Assemblies'. It is also implicit in the qualities of rectitude of conduct to be manifested 'in every verdict which the elected representatives of the Bahá'í community . . . may be called upon to pronounce'.[230]

The members of the Universal House of Justice, designated by Bahá'u'lláh 'the Men of Justice', [para. 15]

This designation appears in paragraph 52 of the Kitáb-i-Aqdas[231] and is highlighted by Shoghi Effendi in *God Passes By*:

In it [the Kitáb-i-Aqdas] He formally ordains the institution of the 'House of Justice', defines its functions, fixes its revenues, and **designates** its **members** as **the 'Men of Justice'**, the 'Deputies of God', the 'Trustees of the All-Merciful' . . .[232]

Also see Article V of the By-Laws of the Universal House of Justice and annotations, on the membership of the Universal House of Justice.

'the people of Bahá who have been mentioned in the Book of Names', [para. 15]

This title comes from Bahá'u'lláh's Tablet of Carmel, as the Guardian has explained:

For it must be clearly understood, nor can it be sufficiently emphasized, that the conjunction of the resting-place of the Greatest Holy Leaf with those of her brother and mother incalculably reinforces the spiritual potencies of that consecrated Spot which, under the wings of the Báb's overshadowing Sepulchre, and in the vicinity of the future Mashriqu'l-Adhkár, which will be reared on its flank, is destined to evolve into the focal centre of those world-shaking, world-embracing, world-directing administrative institutions, ordained by Bahá'u'lláh and anticipated by 'Abdu'l-Bahá, and which are to function in consonance with the principles that govern the twin institutions of the Guardianship and the Universal House of Justice. Then, and then only, will this momentous prophecy which illuminates the concluding passages of the Tablet of Carmel be fulfilled: 'Ere long will God sail His Ark upon thee (Carmel), and will manifest **the people of Bahá who have been mentioned in the Book of Names.**'[233]

Shoghi Effendi is even more explicit about the meaning of this phrase in a letter to the Bahá'ís of the East in 1954:

In this great Tablet [of Carmel] which unveils divine mysteries and heralds the establishment of two mighty, majestic and momentous undertakings – one of which is spiritual and the other administrative, both at the World Centre of the Faith – Bahá'u'lláh refers to an 'Ark', whose dwellers are the men of the Supreme House of Justice . . .[234]

'the Trustees of God amongst His servants and the daysprings of authority in His countries', [para. 15]

In His Tablet of Ishráqát ('Splendours'), Bahá'u'lláh has revealed a passage which, He says, should be counted 'as part of the Most Holy Book':

The men of God's House of Justice have been charged with the affairs of the people. They, in truth, are **the Trustees of God among His servants and the daysprings of authority in His countries.**[235]

shall in the discharge of their responsibilities ever bear in mind the following standards set forth by

Shoghi Effendi, the Guardian of the Cause of God: [para. 15]

In the conduct of the administrative affairs of the Faith, in the enactment of the legislation necessary to supplement the laws of the Kitáb-i-Aqdas, the members of the Universal House of Justice, it should be borne in mind, are not, as Bahá'u'lláh's utterances clearly imply, responsible to those whom they represent, nor are they allowed to be governed by the feelings, the general opinion, and even the convictions of the mass of the faithful, or of those who directly elect them. They are to follow, in a prayerful attitude, the dictates and promptings of their conscience. They may, indeed they must, acquaint themselves with the conditions prevailing among the community, must weigh dispassionately in their minds the merits of any case presented for their consideration, but must reserve for themselves the right of an unfettered decision. 'God will verily inspire them with whatsoever He willeth', is Bahá'u'lláh's incontrovertible assurance. They, and not the body of those who either directly or indirectly elect them, have thus been made the recipients of the divine guidance which is at once the life-blood and ultimate safeguard of this Revelation. [para. 16][236]

4

Questions and Exercises on the Declaration of Trust

Discussion Questions and Exercises

1. Make a list of titles of Bahá'u'lláh that are used in the Constitution. What other titles for Bahá'u'lláh can you find in the Bahá'í writings?

2. List the different texts that are referred to by name or quoted from in the Declaration of Trust.

3. How does the 'fundamental object' of the Universal House of Justice relate to the 'fundamental purpose' of the religion of God, both described in the Declaration of Trust?

4. Make your own compilation of short quotations from the Bahá'í writings about the importance and station of the Universal House of Justice.

5. Explain the difference between the laws revealed by Bahá'u'lláh and the laws enacted by the Universal House of Justice.

6. In the Will and Testament of 'Abdu'l-Bahá, the Guardian of the Faith was given the duties of directing the Hands of the Cause of God and of receiving and disbursing the Ḥuqúqu'lláh. Why do these duties now fall to the Universal House of Justice?

7. How many of the powers and duties of the Universal House of Justice set out in the Constitution derive from the writings of Bahá'u'lláh? How many from the writings of 'Abdu'l-Bahá? How many derive only from the writings of Shoghi Effendi?

8. Give some actual examples of how each power or duty has been used or carried out by the Universal House of Justice thus far.

9. Choose one of the powers and duties of the Universal House of Justice from the Declaration of Trust. Try to collect as many statements as you can from the writings of Bahá'u'lláh, 'Abdu'l-Bahá and Shoghi Effendi that relate to this power or duty. Repeat this exercise with other powers and duties.

10. Are the duties of the Universal House of Justice limited only to dealing with 'religious' matters? Or do they also have some responsibility for issues usually dealt with by governments? Where in the Bahá'í writings are they given such responsibility?

Self-testing Quiz

1. In which book can you find the passage which is cited in the 'Exordium' at the start of the Declaration of Trust?

2. Through what agency does the Covenant of Bahá'u'lláh continue to fulfil its life-giving purpose?

3. Who/what are the twin successors of Bahá'u'lláh and 'Abdu'l-Bahá?

4. What is the fundamental purpose of the Faith of God, according to Bahá'u'lláh and stated in the Declaration of Trust?

5. From where do the authority, duties and sphere of action of the Universal House of Justice derive?

6. Complete these sentences: '. . . the revealed Word of _ _____ which, together with the interpretations and expositions of the Centre of the _____ and of the Guardian of the Cause . . . constitute the binding terms of _____ of the Universal House of Justice and are its bedrock _____. The authority of these Texts is _____ and _____ until such time as Almighty God shall reveal His new Manifestation to Whom will belong all _____ and power.'

7. Complete this sentence: The members of the Universal House of Justice must 'acquaint themselves with the _____ prevailing among the community, must weigh dispassionately in their minds the merits of any case presented for their _____, but must reserve for themselves the right of an _____ decision'.

8. On what date was the Universal House of Justice first elected?

9. Who called and made arrangements for the first election of the Universal House of Justice?

10. Where and when was the Declaration of Trust formulated and signed by the members of the Universal House of Justice?

11. Compare the text of the Declaration of Trust of the Universal House of Justice and that of the National Spiritual Assembly at appendix III. Highlight or underline passages that appear in both.

5

Annotations to the By-Laws

The Universal House of Justice is the supreme institution of an Administrative Order

This phrase comes from Shoghi Effendi's descriptions of the Universal House of Justice as the '**supreme** administrative **institution** destined to emerge in fullness of time within precincts beneath shadow of World Spiritual Centre of Faith'[1] and 'the **supreme** elective **institution** which, in conjunction with the institution of Guardianship, must direct and coordinate the activities of a world-encircling Faith'.[2]

whose salient features, whose authority and whose principles of operation are clearly enunciated in the Sacred Writings of the Bahá'í Faith and their authorized interpretations.

The annotations to the Declaration of Trust, above, demonstrate that the authority of the Universal House of Justice rests firmly on the writings of Bahá'u'lláh, 'Abdu'l-Bahá and Shoghi Effendi. In his writings, the Guardian repeatedly emphasizes the divine origin of the administrative principles of the Faith, in several places saying that these principles have been 'clearly enunciated'. Referring to the role of the North American Bahá'ís in establishing the framework of the Administrative Order, for example, he writes:

> It is a task which must involve, apart from the immediate obligation of enabling every group to evolve into a local Assembly, the setting up of the entire machinery of the Administrative Order in conformity with the spiritual and administrative principles governing the life and activities of every established Bahá'í community throughout the world. No departure from these cardinal and **clearly enunciated** principles, embodied and preserved in Bahá'í national and local constitutions, common to all Bahá'í communities, can under any circumstances be tolerated.[3]

Elsewhere, Shoghi Effendi describes aspects of the Administrative Order as 'clearly defined' in the writings of Bahá'u'lláh and 'Abdu'l-Bahá. In 'The Dispensation of Bahá'u'lláh', for example, Shoghi Effendi affirms that however difficult it may be for us to comprehend the Bahá'í Administrative Order, as close to it as we are, there are nevertheless 'certain salient features of this scheme which . . . are already so clearly defined' that it would be 'inexcusable to either misconceive or ignore'.[4] Discussing the functions of the Guardianship and of the Universal House of Justice, Shoghi Effendi writes that, considered separately, 'each operates within a clearly defined sphere of jurisdiction'.[5] In another place he contrasts the clarity of the Bahá'í administrative system with the situation pertaining in earlier religious dispensations:

> Where, we may confidently ask, in the recorded sayings of Jesus Christ, whether in the matter of succession or in the provision of a set of specific laws and clearly defined administrative ordinances, as distinguished from purely spiritual principles, can we find anything approaching the

detailed injunctions, laws and warnings that abound in the authenticated utterances of both Bahá'u'lláh and 'Abdu'l-Bahá?[6]

More generally, Shoghi Effendi writes of the Faith that its 'guiding principles are the truths which ['Abdu'l-Bahá] . . . has so **clearly enunciated** in His public addresses throughout the West' and its laws 'are those which have been expressly ordained in the Kitáb-i-Aqdas'.[7] Elsewhere he writes that the 'fundamental laws and cardinal principles' of the Faith were **'clearly enunciated'**.[8]

This Administrative Order consists, on the one hand, of a series of elected councils, universal, secondary and local, in which are vested legislative, executive and judicial powers over the Bahá'í community

The Declaration of Trust of the Universal House of Justice describes powers and duties that fall into each of these three categories. A letter written on behalf of the Universal House of Justice to the National Spiritual Assembly of Grenada in 1985 states that:

> While ultimately the major function of the Universal House of Justice will be that of legislation, it has continuing responsibility for executive and judicial functions of the institution. Therefore it is not accurate to refer to members of the House of Justice as 'legislators', understandable as is the wish to give simple titles rather than complex ones.[9]

The elected councils referred to in this part of the By-Laws are, of course, the Universal House of Justice, National Spiritual Assemblies and Local Spiritual Assemblies respectively. The reference to the National Spiritual Assembly as a 'secondary' council derives from the Will and Testament of 'Abdu'l-Bahá, which states that 'in all countries a secondary House of Justice must be instituted'.[10] In His writings Bahá'u'lláh had ordained local and international (or universal) Houses of Justice but had not mentioned an equivalent national institution. It was therefore left to 'Abdu'l-Bahá to create a 'secondary' House of Justice at the national level. Shoghi Effendi has explained that by 'leaving certain matters unspecified and unregulated in His Book of Laws, Bahá'u'lláh seems to have deliberately left a gap in the general scheme of Bahá'í Dispensation, which the unequivocal provisions of the Master's Will has filled'.[11]

It has not been possible to identify any single, specific statement in the writings of Bahá'u'lláh, 'Abdu'l-Bahá or Shoghi Effendi that explicitly endows the elected Bahá'í institutions with 'legislative, executive and judicial powers over the Bahá'í community'. However, each of the various powers and functions of the Universal House of Justice set out in the Declaration of Trust can be categorized as either legislative, executive or judicial in nature.

and, on the other, of eminent and devoted believers appointed for the specific purposes of protecting and propagating the Faith of Bahá'u'lláh under the guidance of the Head of that Faith.

The 'eminent and devoted believers' referred to here are, in the first place, the Hands of the Cause of God, 'nominated and appointed by the guardian of the Cause of God' under the terms of the Will and Testament of 'Abdu'l-Bahá.[12] Although no more Hands of the Cause can be appointed in the absence of a living Guardian, their functions have been extended into the future through the creation and appointment by the Universal House of Justice of Continental Boards of Counsellors[13] (see Article IX of the By-Laws of the Universal House of Justice and annotations below). The members of the Continental Boards of Counsellors are assisted by Auxiliary Board members, who specialize in either the protection or the propagation of the Faith (see Article X of the By-Laws of the Universal House of Justice and annotations below). These Auxiliary Board members in turn each appoint assistants to help them carry out their functions at a grassroots level.

The Universal House of Justice referred to this part of its By-Laws in a letter to the National Spiritual Assembly of the Bahá'ís of the United States of 19 May 1994:

> As you know, a distinguishing feature of the Administrative Order is the existence of elected institutions, on the one hand, which function corporately with vested legislative, executive and judicial powers, and of appointed, eminent and devoted believers, on the other hand, who function primarily as individuals for the specific purposes of protecting and propagating the Faith under the guidance of the Head of the Faith. The two sets of institutions collaborate in their functions so as to ensure the progress of the Cause.[14]

This Administrative Order is the nucleus and pattern of the World Order adumbrated by Bahá'u'lláh.

This description of the relationship between the Administrative Order of the Faith and the World Order of Bahá'u'lláh again derives from the writings of Shoghi Effendi. Discussing the Administrative Order in 'The Dispensation of Bahá'u'lláh', written at a time when he was strenuously working to establish that Order throughout the Bahá'í world, the Guardian offers this long-term vision of its destiny:

> It will, as its component parts, its organic institutions, begin to function with efficiency and vigour, assert its claim and demonstrate its capacity to be regarded not only as **the nucleus** but the very **pattern** of the New **World Order** destined to embrace in the fullness of time the whole of mankind.[15]

In his Foreword to *God Passes By*, the Guardian outlined four periods in the first Bahá'í century, describing the last (1921–44) as synchronizing with 'the birth of the Formative Age of the Bahá'í Era, with the founding of the Administrative Order of the Faith of Bahá'u'lláh – a system which is at once the harbinger, the **nucleus and pattern** of His **World Order**'.[16] Writing a year later in 1945, Shoghi Effendi urged the North American Bahá'ís to continue their teaching work, encouraging them to share this vision of the Faith:

> A more audacious assertion of the challenging verities of the Faith; a more convincing presentation of its distinguishing truths; a fuller exposition of the character, the aims and the achievements of its rising Administrative system as the **nucleus and pattern** of its future world-embracing **order** . . . these stand out as the paramount tasks summoning to a challenge, during these years of transition and turmoil, the entire body of the American believers.[17]

In 1946 Shoghi Effendi looked forward to the accomplishments of the second Bahá'í century (1944–2044):

> The second century is destined to witness a tremendous deployment and a notable consolidation of the forces working towards the world-wide development of that Order, as well as the first stirrings of that **World Order**, of which the present Administrative System is at once the precursor, the **nucleus and pattern** – an Order which, as it slowly crystallizes and radiates its benign influence over the entire planet, will proclaim at once the coming of age of the whole human race, as well as the maturity of the Faith itself, the progenitor of that Order.[18]

And finally, writing in 1947, Shoghi Effendi reflected on the period 1921 to 1946, which he designated the first epoch of the Formative Age of the Faith:

> The first epoch witnessed the birth and the primary stages in

the erection of the framework of the Administrative Order of the Faith – the **nucleus and pattern** of its **World Order** – according to the precepts laid down in 'Abdu'l-Bahá's Will and Testament, as well as the launching of the initial phase of the world-encompassing Plan bequeathed by Him to the American Bahá'í Community.[19]

In the course of its divinely propelled organic growth its institutions will expand, putting forth auxiliary branches and developing subordinate agencies, multiplying their activities and diversifying their functions, in consonance with the principles and purposes revealed by Bahá'u'lláh for the progress of the human race.

The Universal House of Justice has the power to 'found institutions'.[20] This part of the By-Laws refers to at least one statement by Shoghi Effendi, writing here in 1938 and considering the future prospects of the Bahá'í Faith:

I can only for the moment cite at random certain of these opportunities which stand out preeminently, in any attempt to survey the possibilities of the future: The election of the International House of Justice and its establishment in the Holy Land, the spiritual and administrative centre of the Bahá'í world, together with the formation of its **auxiliary branches** and subsidiary institutions . . .[21]

I. MEMBERSHIP IN THE BAHÁ'Í COMMUNITY

The Bahá'í Community shall consist of all persons recognized by the Universal House of Justice as possessing the qualifications of Bahá'í faith and practice.

In an important early letter Shoghi Effendi outlines 'the qualifications of a true believer', emphasizing 'discretion, caution and tact' in applying these qualifications:

> Regarding the very delicate and complex question of ascertaining the qualifications of a true believer, I cannot in this connection emphasize too strongly the supreme necessity for the exercise of the utmost discretion, caution and tact, whether it be in deciding for ourselves as to who may be regarded a true believer or in disclosing to the outside world such considerations as may serve as a basis for such a decision. I would only venture to state very briefly and as adequately as present circumstances permit the principal factors that must be taken into consideration before deciding whether a person may be regarded a true believer or not. Full recognition of the station of the Forerunner, the Author, and the True Exemplar of the Bahá'í Cause, as set forth in 'Abdu'l-Bahá's Testament; unreserved acceptance of, and submission to, whatsoever has been revealed by their Pen; loyal and steadfast adherence to every clause of our Beloved's sacred Will; and close association with the spirit as well as the form of the present-day Bahá'í administration throughout the world – these I conceive to be the fundamental and primary considerations that must be fairly, discreetly and thoughtfully ascertained before reaching such a vital decision.[22]

The key qualifications listed here are also included in Article II of the By-Laws of the National Spiritual Assembly. In a letter to all National Spiritual Assemblies dated 4 April 2001, the Universal House of Justice clarified why there is sometimes a need to determine an individual's qualifications to enjoy membership in the Bahá'í community:

> One's beliefs are an internal and personal matter; no person or institution has the right to exert compulsion in matters of belief. Since there is a wide range of meanings in the Sacred Scriptures, there are bound to be different ways in

which individuals understand many of the Bahá'í teachings. Nevertheless, it is necessary for the viability of the Bahá'í community that its members share a common understanding of essentials. This implies a commitment by each member to function within the framework established by such an understanding.

This framework includes, for example, cognizance of the existence of a Divine Revelation brought by Bahá'u'lláh, the Manifestation of God for this age, and acceptance of the two primary duties prescribed by God, as expressed in the Kitáb-i-Aqdas, the Most Holy Book of the Bahá'í Revelation. These are: 'recognition of Him Who is the Dayspring of His Revelation and the Fountain of His laws,' and observance of 'every ordinance of Him Who is the Desire of the world. These twin duties,' the Aqdas firmly states, 'are inseparable. Neither is acceptable without the other.'[23]

'Abdu'l-Bahá, appointed by Bahá'u'lláh as the Interpreter of His writings, reaffirms these fundamentals of Bahá'í belief. In His Will and Testament He writes:

This is the foundation of the belief of the people of Bahá (may my life be offered up for them): 'His Holiness, the Exalted One [the Báb], is the Manifestation of the Unity and Oneness of God and the Forerunner of the Ancient Beauty. His Holiness the Abhá Beauty (may my life be a sacrifice for His steadfast friends) is the Supreme Manifestation of God and the Dayspring of His Most Divine Essence. All others are servants unto Him and do His bidding.'[24]

It is within the context of these statements of basic belief and practice that membership in the Bahá'í Faith is determined. The Universal House of Justice then refers to the statement by Shoghi Effendi on the qualifications of believers, cited above.[25]

1. **In order to be eligible to vote and hold elective office, a Bahá'í must have attained the age of twenty-one years.**

This statement reflects Article II of the By-Laws of the National Spiritual Assembly, as well as Article V of the By-Laws of the Local Spiritual Assembly. It codifies a policy established by Shoghi Effendi:

> Regarding the age of fifteen fixed by Bahá'u'lláh: This relates only to purely spiritual functions and obligations and is not related to the degree of administrative capacity and fitness which is a totally different thing, and is, for the present, fixed at twenty-one.[26]

The age of 21 thus appears to be determined by the 'degree of administrative capacity and fitness' of an individual.

2. **The rights, privileges and duties of individual Bahá'ís are as set forth in the Writings of Bahá'u'lláh, 'Abdu'l-Bahá and Shoghi Effendi and as laid down by the Universal House of Justice.**

There are far too many relevant passages in the Bahá'í writings on the 'rights, privileges and duties of individual Bahá'ís' to cite them all here. For a contemporary and comprehensive statement by the Universal House of Justice on the subject, see *Individual Rights and Freedoms*.

II. LOCAL SPIRITUAL ASSEMBLIES

Whenever in any locality the number of Bahá'ís resident therein who have attained the age of twenty-one exceeds nine these shall on the First Day of Riḍván convene and elect a local administrative body of nine members to be known as the Spiritual

Assembly of the Bahá'ís of that locality.

This paragraph of the By-Laws mirrors almost exactly the wording of Article VII of the By-Laws of the National Spiritual Assembly. In the Kitáb-i-Aqdas, Bahá'u'lláh reveals:

> The Lord hath ordained that in every city a House of Justice be established wherein shall gather counsellors to the number of Bahá, and should it exceed this number it doth not matter.[27]

Shoghi Effendi has explained that the Spiritual Assemblies of today are essentially the same entities that in the future will be called by 'their permanent and more descriptive title of "Houses of Justice", bestowed upon them by the Author of the Bahá'í Revelation'.[28] The election of each Local Spiritual Assembly by the Bahá'ís who reside in that locality thus expresses obedience to the above ordinance from the Most Holy Book.

Early in his ministry Shoghi Effendi instructed the Bahá'ís to raise up Local Spiritual Assemblies wherever possible:

> And, now that this all-important Work may suffer no neglect, but rather function vigorously and continuously in every part of the Bahá'í world; that the unity of the Cause of Bahá'u'lláh may remain secure and inviolate, it is of the utmost importance that in accordance with the explicit text of the Kitáb-i-Aqdas, the Most Holy Book, in every locality, be it city or hamlet, where the number of adult (21 years and above) declared believers exceeds nine, a local 'Spiritual Assembly' be forthwith established. To it all local matters pertaining to the Cause must be directly and immediately referred for full consultation and decision. The importance, nay the absolute necessity of these local Assemblies is manifest when we realize that in the days to come they will evolve into the local Houses of Justice, and at present provide the firm foundation on which the structure of the Master's Will is to be reared in future.[29]

These local Spiritual Assemblies will have to be elected directly by the friends, and every declared believer of 21 years and above, far from standing aloof and assuming an indifferent or independent attitude, should regard it his sacred duty to take part conscientiously and diligently, in the election, the consolidation and the efficient working of his own local Assembly.[30]

The Guardian summarized these requirements in *God Passes By*:

. . . instituted, without any exception, in every city, town and village where nine or more adult believers are resident; annually and directly elected, on the first day of the greatest Bahá'í Festival by all adult believers, men and women alike . . .[31]

The Festival of Riḍván, called by Bahá'u'lláh 'the King of Festivals', celebrates the Declaration of His mission to a small group of His family and companions in the Garden of Riḍván, outside Baghdad, in 1863. The Festival runs for 12 days from 21 April to 2 May. The annual election of Local Spiritual Assemblies was fixed on the first day of Riḍván by Shoghi Effendi (see below).

Every such Spiritual Assembly shall be elected annually thereafter upon each successive First Day of Riḍván.

The election of Local Spiritual Assemblies on the first day of Riḍván was a policy established by Shoghi Effendi, pending the establishment of the Universal House Justice:

With these Assemblies, local as well as national, harmoniously, vigorously, and efficiently functioning throughout the Bahá'í world, the only means for the establishment of the Supreme House of Justice will have been secured. And when this Supreme Body will have been properly established, it will have to consider afresh the whole situation, and lay down the principle which shall direct, so long as it deems advisable, the affairs of the Cause.

Pending its establishment, and to insure uniformity throughout the East and throughout the West, all local Assemblies will have to be re-elected once a year, during the first day of Riḍván, and the result of polling, if possible, be declared on that day.[32]

The Universal House of Justice has confirmed this policy by incorporating it into its By-Laws. From 1977, however, the House of Justice decided that in some cases it would be permissible for Local Assemblies to be elected on another day during the Riḍván Festival. This was because of circumstances at the time, when the Bahá'í Faith had expanded rapidly for two decades, especially in remote rural areas. From the start of the Five Year Plan (1974–9), the House of Justice also permitted Assemblies being formed for the first time to be elected at any point during the year.

At the start of the Four Year Plan (1996–2000), however, the Universal House of Justice reintroduced the formal requirement to elect all Local Spiritual Assemblies on the first day of Riḍván.[33] In making this decision, the Universal House of Justice explained that the previous temporary provisions had:

. . . enabled the believers in a large number of localities to receive assistance in electing their Local Spiritual Assemblies, and much experience has been gained in strengthening Local Assemblies under diverse conditions in a vast array of cultural settings. Nevertheless, in principle, the initiative and responsibility for electing a Local Spiritual Assembly belong primarily to the Bahá'ís in the locality, and assistance from outside is ultimately fruitful only if the friends become conscious of this sacred responsibility.[34]

This may be an example of the Universal House of Justice

abrogating its own earlier enactment – see the annotations to paragraph 12 of the Declaration of Trust.

The members shall hold office for the term of one year or until their successors are elected.

This rule is implied in the instruction from Shoghi Effendi, cited above, that Assemblies are to be re-elected once a year. If an Assembly member is removed or resigns from the Assembly for any reason, a by-election will usually be held to elect a replacement member. A member of an Assembly may serve less than a year if he is elected as a result of a by-election; he will then serve until the next Riḍván, when the whole Assembly is re-elected.

When, however, the number of Bahá'ís as aforesaid in any locality is exactly nine, these shall on the First Day of Riḍván constitute themselves the Local Spiritual Assembly by joint declaration.

The Universal House of Justice explained this procedure in a letter written on its behalf to the National Spiritual Assembly of Iceland in 1980:

There is nothing in the directives of the beloved Guardian or in the by-laws of Local Spiritual Assemblies to require that the joint declaration of a new Local Spiritual Assembly be signed. The way the declaration is made is within the discretion of the National Spiritual Assembly to determine, and it may or may not require signatures.

Wherever at Riḍván there are nine or more adult believers resident in an area properly qualified for the establishment of a Local Spiritual Assembly, the Assembly must be formed at Riḍván.

If the number of adult resident believers is exactly nine the Local Spiritual Assembly must be formed by joint declaration in a manner acceptable to the National Spiritual Assembly and the secretary of the National Spiritual Assembly will record the formation of the Local Assembly.

When the Spiritual Assembly is to be formed for the first time and one or more of the adult believers refuses to join in the declaration, the Spiritual Assembly cannot be formed.[35]

In a letter to the National Spiritual Assembly of New Zealand in 1969, the Universal House of Justice further emphasized that:

> . . . it is the duty of every Bahá'í in such a situation to take part in the joint declaration. If a Bahá'í, however, refuses to do so he should be helped to realize that he has committed a grave dereliction of his Bahá'í duty. In this stage of the development of the Cause a National Spiritual Assembly should not, generally, deprive a believer of his voting rights for such an offence, but should lovingly and patiently educate the friends in the importance of their responsibilities.[36]

1. The general powers and duties of a Local Spiritual Assembly are as set forth in the Writings of Bahá'u'lláh, 'Abdu'l-Bahá and Shoghi Effendi and as laid down by the Universal House of Justice.

This statement mirrors almost exactly the wording of Article VII, Section 2 of the By-Laws of the National Spiritual Assembly. Some of the 'most outstanding obligations of the members of every Spiritual Assembly'[37] were outlined by Shoghi Effendi early in his ministry, summarizing a number of statements scattered through the writings of Bahá'u'lláh and 'Abdu'l-Bahá:

> The matter of Teaching, its direction, its ways and means, its extension, its consolidation, essential as they are to the interests of the Cause, constitute by no means the only issue

141

which should receive the full attention of these Assemblies. A careful study of Bahá'u'lláh's and 'Abdu'l-Bahá's Tablets will reveal that other duties, no less vital to the interests of the Cause, devolve upon the elected representatives of the friends in every locality.

It is incumbent upon them to be vigilant and cautious, discreet and watchful, and protect at all times the Temple of the Cause from the dart of the mischief-maker and the onslaught of the enemy.

They must endeavour to promote amity and concord amongst the friends, efface every lingering trace of distrust, coolness and estrangement from every heart, and secure in its stead an active and whole-hearted cooperation for the service of the Cause.

They must do their utmost to extend at all times the helping hand to the poor, the sick, the disabled, the orphan, the widow, irrespective of colour, caste and creed.

They must promote by every means in their power the material as well as the spiritual enlightenment of youth, the means for the education of children, institute, whenever possible, Bahá'í educational institutions, organize and supervise their work and provide the best means for their progress and development.

They must make an effort to maintain official, regular, and frequent correspondence with the various Bahá'í centres throughout the world, report to them their activities, and share the glad-tidings they receive with all their fellow-workers in the Cause.

They must encourage and stimulate by every means at their command, through subscription, reports and articles, the development of the various Bahá'í magazines . . .

They must undertake the arrangement of the regular meetings of the friends, the feasts and the anniversaries, as well as the special gatherings designed to serve and promote the social, intellectual and spiritual interests of their fellow-men.

They must supervise in these days when the Cause is still in its infancy all Bahá'í publications and translations, and provide in general for a dignified and accurate presentation of all Bahá'í literature and its distribution to the general public.[38]

Shoghi Effendi summarized some of the powers and duties of these Assemblies in *God Passes By*:

. . . invested with an authority rendering them unanswerable for their acts and decisions to those who elect them; solemnly pledged to follow, under all conditions, the dictates of the 'Most Great Justice' that can alone usher in the reign of the 'Most Great Peace' which Bahá'u'lláh has proclaimed and must ultimately establish; charged with the responsibility of promoting at all times the best interests of the communities within their jurisdiction, of familiarizing them with their plans and activities and of inviting them to offer any recommendations they might wish to make; cognizant of their no less vital task of demonstrating, through association with all liberal and humanitarian movements, the universality and comprehensiveness of their Faith; dissociated entirely from all sectarian organizations, whether religious or secular; assisted by committees annually appointed by, and directly responsible to, them, to each of which a particular branch of Bahá'í activity is assigned for study and action; supported by local funds to which all believers voluntarily contribute . . .[39]

The Universal House of Justice has also called attention to these responsibilities in a number of its messages.[40]

2. A Local Spiritual Assembly shall exercise full jurisdiction over all Bahá'í activities and affairs within its locality, subject to the provisions of the Local Bahá'í Constitution [By-Laws of a Local Spiritual Assembly].

This statement of jurisdiction is put in different words in Article VII, Section 3 of the By-Laws of the National Spiritual Assembly and in Article III of the By-Laws of the Local Spiritual Assembly. Shoghi Effendi gave the following counsel in relation to each Local Spiritual Assembly:

> To it all local matters pertaining to the Cause must be directly and immediately referred for full consultation and decision.[41]

Article VII, Section 3 of the By-Laws of the National Spiritual Assembly states:

> Among its more specific duties a Local Spiritual Assembly shall have full jurisdiction of all Bahá'í activities and affairs within the local community, subject, however, to the exclusive and paramount authority of the National Spiritual Assembly as defined herein.[42]

3. The area of jurisdiction of a Local Spiritual Assembly shall be decided by the National Spiritual Assembly in accordance with the principle laid down for each country by the Universal House of Justice.

The delegation of this responsibility to National Assemblies was first directed by Shoghi Effendi:

> As to the principle according to which the area of the jurisdiction of a Local Assembly is to be determined, he feels this to be the function of the National Spiritual Assembly; whatever principle they uphold should be fairly applied to all localities without any distinction whatever.[43]

This was explained in more detail in a letter written on behalf of the Guardian to the National Spiritual Assembly of Australia and New Zealand in 1956:

The matter of the areas under the jurisdiction of a Local Spiritual Assembly is one which the National Assembly must study, and apply the principles laid down by the Guardian; namely, that within a municipal area, where the people resident in the area pay taxes and vote, the Assembly can be elected, and holds jurisdiction. Anyone living outside of that area is not a member of that Community, and cannot enjoy the administrative privileges of that Community. Although this will affect your Assembly roll, it will place the work of the Faith on a much sounder basis, and increase the number of Centres where Bahá'ís reside . . . It will challenge the friends to work harder to create new Assemblies and make up for those dissolved . . .[44]

In a letter to the National Spiritual Assembly of Zambia in 1978, the Universal House of Justice pointed out that the 'general principle' is that 'Local Spiritual Assemblies may be formed in the smallest civil administrative units of the country', as determined by the government.[45]

III. NATIONAL SPIRITUAL ASSEMBLIES

Whenever it is decided by the Universal House of Justice to form in any country or region a National Spiritual Assembly,

Whereas a Local Spiritual Assembly is formed by election or joint declaration once the number of adult Bahá'ís reaches a threshold number of nine, the Universal House of Justice, as head of the Bahá'í Faith, alone has the prerogative to determine when and how the election of each National Spiritual Assembly will take place. In a letter to a Bahá'í couple in 1988, the Universal House of Justice explained the criteria for the establishment of National Spiritual Assemblies:

The decisions about the formation in any country or region

of a National Spiritual Assembly, and the area of jurisdiction of the National Assembly, are assigned to the Universal House of Justice in Section III of the By-laws forming part of the Constitution of the Universal House of Justice. However, it should be noted that the existence of a group of believers sharing a distinct culture is not sufficient reason to form a National Spiritual Assembly. Rather, the Bahá'í Faith aims to demonstrate its power to create unified organic units in which cultural diversity is fostered, which are free from parochial attitudes and from ethnic or cultural prejudices, and in which all believers regard each other as true brothers and sisters. As the Faith progresses, the contrast is growing in many parts of the world, between the fragmented and mutually-antagonistic elements of society on the one hand, and the unified and harmonious Bahá'í community on the other hand.[46]

There were 56 National and Regional Spiritual Assemblies worldwide at the end of the Guardian's Ten Year Crusade in 1963, when the Universal House of Justice was first elected; at Riḍván 2003, 40 years later, there were 182. The first National Spiritual Assemblies were formed in the British Isles (1923), Germany (1923), India (1923), Egypt (1924), the United States of America (1925) (superseding the institution of the Bahá'í Temple Unity formed during 'Abdu'l-Bahá's ministry), Iraq (1931), Persia (1934) and Australia (1934).

In general, the Universal House of Justice has a policy of forming National Spiritual Assemblies in sovereign states, as stated in this letter in response to an individual's inquiry about the possibility of establishing a separate National Spiritual Assembly in French Canada, dated 17 April 1977:

The Universal House of Justice has received your letter . . . and instructs us to say that while it fully appreciates the reasons you have given for the establishment of a separate National Spiritual Assembly in French Canada, it does not wish to depart from its current policy of forming National

Spiritual Assemblies in sovereign independent States. The National Assemblies of Alaska and of Hawaii, which you cite, were formed because of the very great distances separating these large territories from the mainland of the United States.[47]

From the following cable sent by Shoghi Effendi to a European Teaching Conference it is evident that the Guardian clearly envisaged the formation of National Spiritual Assemblies in principalities, dependencies and islands, as well as in sovereign independent states:

HAIL THIS CROWNING EXPLOIT [FORMATION OF THE ITALO-SWISS NATIONAL SPIRITUAL ASSEMBLY] SECOND SEVEN YEAR PLAN AS FORERUNNER FORMATION RAPID SUCCESSION COURSE THIRD PHASE PLAN CONCEIVED CENTRE BAHA'U'LLAH'S COVENANT REGIONAL NATIONAL ASSEMBLIES SCANDINAVIA BENELUX COUNTRIES IBERIAN PENINSULA THEMSELVES PRELUDE ESTABLISHMENT PRESENT SUCCEEDING EPOCHS EVOLUTION DIVINE PLAN SEPARATE NATIONAL ASSEMBLIES EACH SOVEREIGN STATE PRINCIPALITY CHIEF DEPENDENCY EUROPEAN CONTINENT AS WELL AS NEIGHBOURING PRINCIPAL ISLANDS MEDITERRANEAN ATLANTIC OCEAN NORTH SEA.[48]

Thus the Universal House of Justice may choose to form a National Spiritual Assembly with jurisdiction over a region rather than a country. Some National Spiritual Assemblies have jurisdiction over a region which is less than a whole country: as noted above, there are separate National Assemblies for the United States of America (with jurisdiction over all the contiguous states), for Hawaii and for Alaska. Conversely, a National Spiritual Assembly may be formed temporarily to have jurisdiction over a region covering more than one country. Thus, for example, the National Spiritual Assembly of the Bahá'ís of Australia and New Zealand was formed in 1934, and a Regional Assembly of Central and East Africa was initially formed where there are now several National Spiritual Assemblies. Furthermore, one National Spiritual Assembly will sometimes be given temporary administrative responsibility for another country or region until the Bahá'ís there can form their own National Assembly.

> **the voting members of the Bahá'í community of that country or region shall, in a manner and at a time to be decided by the Universal House of Justice, elect their delegates to their National Convention. These delegates shall, in turn, elect in the manner provided in the National Bahá'í Constitution [Declaration of Trust and By-Laws of a National Spiritual Assembly] a body of nine members to be known as the National Spiritual Assembly of the Bahá'ís of that country or region.**

This method of electing the National Spiritual Assembly comes from 'Abdu'l-Bahá's instructions concerning the election of the Universal House of Justice, as Shoghi Effendi has explained:

Regarding the method to be adopted for the election of the National Spiritual Assemblies, it is clear that the text of the Beloved's Testament gives us no indication as to the manner in which these Assemblies are to be elected. In one of His earliest Tablets, however, addressed to a friend in Persia, the following is expressly recorded:–

'At whatever time all the beloved of God in each country appoint their delegates, and these in turn elect their representatives, and these representatives elect a body, that body shall be regarded as the Supreme Baytu'l-'Adl (Universal House of Justice).'

These words clearly indicate that a three-stage election has been provided by 'Abdu'l-Bahá for the formation of the International House of Justice, and as it is explicitly provided in His Will and Testament that the 'Secondary House of Justice (i.e., National Assemblies) must elect the members of the Universal One', it is obvious that the members of the National Spiritual Assemblies will have to be indirectly elected by the body of the believers in their respective provinces. In view of these complementary instructions the principle, set forth in my letter of March 12th, 1923, has been established requiring the believers (the beloved of God) in every country to elect a certain number of delegates who, in turn, will elect their national representatives (Secondary House of Justice or National Spiritual Assembly) whose sacred obligation and privilege will be to elect in time God's Universal House of Justice.[49]

The provisions for the election of the National Spiritual Assembly are set out in Article VIII of the By-Laws of the National Spiritual Assembly.

The members shall continue in office for a period of one year or until their successors shall be elected.

This statement mirrors the wording in Article III of the By-Laws of the National Spiritual Assembly. It was Shoghi Effendi who established the policy of re-electing National Spiritual Assemblies each year:

This National Spiritual Assembly, which, pending the establishment of the Universal House of Justice, will have to be re-elected once a year . . .[50]

It is possible that a member of a National Assembly may serve for a shorter term, as in the case of Local Spiritual Assemblies (see above).

1. The general powers and duties of a National Spiritual Assembly are as set forth in the Writings

of 'Abdu'l-Bahá and Shoghi Effendi and as laid down by the Universal House of Justice.

The institution of the National Spiritual Assembly – or rather, strictly speaking, the institution of the Secondary House of Justice – was created by 'Abdu'l-Bahá in His Will and Testament; its powers and duties were therefore never discussed by Bahá'u'lláh. Shoghi Effendi, who assumed the responsibility of bringing these bodies into being, described their functions on several occasions. The Guardian condensed and summarized the powers and duties of National Spiritual Assemblies in a passage in *God Passes By*:

> Designated by 'Abdu'l-Bahá in His Will as the 'Secondary Houses of Justice', they constitute the electoral bodies in the formation of the International House of Justice, and are empowered to direct, unify, coordinate and stimulate the activities of individuals as well as local Assemblies within their jurisdiction. Resting on the broad base of organized local communities, themselves pillars sustaining the institution which must be regarded as the apex of the Bahá'í Administrative Order, these Assemblies are elected, according to the principle of proportional representation, by delegates representative of Bahá'í local communities assembled at Convention during the period of the Riḍván Festival; are possessed of the necessary authority to enable them to insure the harmonious and efficient development of Bahá'í activity within their respective spheres; are freed from all direct responsibility for their policies and decisions to their electorates; are charged with the sacred duty of consulting the views, of inviting the recommendations and of securing the confidence and cooperation of the delegates and of acquainting them with their plans, problems and actions; and are supported by the resources of national funds to which all ranks of the faithful are urged to contribute.[51]

2. The National Spiritual Assembly shall have exclusive jurisdiction and authority over all the activities and affairs of the Bahá'í Faith throughout its area.

This statement reflects the wording of Article I of the By-Laws of the National Spiritual Assembly. The principle enunciated here was emphasized by Shoghi Effendi on several occasions. This is from a letter he wrote to the Bahá'ís of the world in 1923:

> This National Spiritual Assembly, which, pending the establishment of the Universal House of Justice, will have to be re-elected once a year, obviously assumes grave responsibilities, for it has to exercise full authority over all the local Assemblies in its province, and will have to direct the activities of the friends, guard vigilantly the Cause of God, and control and supervise the affairs of the Movement in general.
>
> Vital issues, affecting the interests of the Cause in that country such as the matter of translation and publication, the Mashriqu'l-Adhkár, the Teaching Work, and other similar matters that stand distinct from strictly local affairs, must be under the full jurisdiction of the National Assembly.[52]

The Guardian explained that the National Spiritual Assembly has the right to decide whether a certain matter is local or national in scope:

> With it, too, rests the decision whether a certain point at issue is strictly local in its nature, and should be reserved for the consideration and decision of the local Assembly, or whether it should fall under its own province and be regarded as a matter which ought to receive its special attention. The National Spiritual Assembly will also decide upon such matters which in its opinion should be referred to the Holy Land for consultation and decision.[53]

A few more of Shoghi Effendi's statements are cited here to show the importance of the principle expressed in this part of the By-Laws:

> I wish to reaffirm in clear and categorical language, the principle already enunciated upholding the supreme authority of the National Assembly in all matters that affect the interests of the Faith in that land. There can be no conflict of authority, no duality under any form or circumstances in any sphere of Bahá'í jurisdiction whether local, national or international.[54]

> Just as the National Assembly has full jurisdiction over all its local Assemblies, the Guardian has full jurisdiction over all National Assemblies . . .[55]

> . . . the Guardian wishes me to again affirm his view that the authority of the National Spiritual Assembly is undivided and unchallengeable in all matters pertaining to the administration of the Faith . . . and that, therefore, the obedience of individual Bahá'ís, delegates, groups, and assemblies to that authority is imperative, and should be whole-hearted and unqualified. He is convinced that the unreserved acceptance and complete application of this vital provision of the Administration is essential to the maintenance of the highest degree of unity among the believers, and is indispensable to the effective working of the administrative machinery of the Faith in every country.[56]

It shall endeavour to stimulate, unify and coordinate the manifold activities of the Local Spiritual Assemblies and of individual Bahá'ís in its area

The wording of this term of reference comes from Shoghi Effendi:

Its immediate purpose is to **stimulate, unify and coordinate** by frequent personal consultations, **the manifold activities** of the friends as well as the local Assemblies; and by keeping in close and constant touch with the Holy Land, initiate measures, and direct in general the affairs of the Cause in that country.[57]

Almost identical wording appears in *God Passes By*, written more than 20 years later:

Designated by 'Abdu'l-Bahá in His Will as the 'Secondary Houses of Justice', they constitute the electoral bodies in the formation of the International House of Justice, and are empowered to direct, **unify, coordinate and stimulate the activities of individuals as well as local Assemblies** within their jurisdiction.[58]

Shoghi Effendi explained the relationship between the National Spiritual Assembly and the Local Spiritual Assemblies in its area in this letter written on his behalf to an individual in 1933:

. . . the best way to insure and consolidate the organic unity of the Faith is to strengthen the authority of the Local Assemblies and to bring them within the full orbit of the National Assembly's jurisdiction. The National Assembly is the head, and the Local Assemblies are the various organs of the body of the Cause. To insure full cooperation between these various parts is to safeguard the best interests of the Faith by enabling it to counteract those forces which threaten to create a breach within the ranks of the faithful. This is the delicate and highly significant mission with which the Guardian wishes to entrust you. Not only to teach the outsiders, through public lecturing, but in addition to that, and in view of making your efforts more varied and successful, to acquaint the friends with the essentials of the Administration, upon the full understanding of which the future progress of the Cause greatly depends.[59]

and by all possible means assist them to promote the oneness of mankind.

This duty is also stated in Article I of the By-Laws of the National Spiritual Assembly. In His Tablets of the Divine Plan, 'Abdu'l-Bahá places an obligation on the Bahá'ís of every locality to promote this principle:

Consequently, those souls who are in a condition of the utmost severance, purified from the defects of the world of nature, sanctified from attachment to this earth, vivified with the breaths of eternal life – with luminous hearts, with heavenly spirit, with attraction of consciousness, with celestial magnanimity, with eloquent tongues and with clear explanations – such souls must hasten and travel through all parts of the Central States. In every city and village they must occupy themselves with the diffusion of the divine exhortations and advices, guide the souls and **promote the oneness** of the world of humanity. They must play the melody of international conciliation with such power that every deaf one may attain hearing, every extinct person may be set aglow, every dead one may obtain new life and every indifferent soul may find ecstasy. It is certain that such will be the consummation.[60]

The By-Laws of the Universal House of Justice thus make it a duty of National Spiritual Assemblies to assist local Bahá'ís and Assemblies in the execution of this task.

It shall furthermore represent its national Bahá'í community in relation to other national Bahá'í communities and to the Universal House of Justice.

This statement reflects the wording of Article I of the By-Laws of the National Spiritual Assembly. Shoghi Effendi sometimes referred to a National Spiritual Assembly as representing its national community.[61]

3. The area of jurisdiction of a National Spiritual Assembly shall be as defined by the Universal House of Justice.

See the annotations to Article II, above, for a discussion of the relevant principles. Each National Spiritual Assembly's area of jurisdiction is set out clearly in its Declaration of Trust.

4. The principal business of the National Convention shall be consultation on Bahá'í activities, plans and policies and the election of the members of the National Spiritual Assembly, as set forth in the National Bahá'í Constitution.

This statement mirrors almost exactly wording in Article VIII, Section 8 of the By-Laws of the National Spiritual Assembly. Shoghi Effendi has described the business of the National Convention in some depth, such as in the following broad summary from the early years of his ministry:

Hitherto the National Convention has been primarily called together for the consideration of the various circumstances attending the election of the National Spiritual Assembly. I feel, however, that in view of the expansion and the growing importance of the administrative sphere of the Cause, the general sentiments and tendencies prevailing among the friends, and the signs of increasing interdependence among the National Spiritual Assemblies throughout the world, the assembled accredited representatives of the American believers should exercise not only the vital and responsible right of electing the National Assembly, but should also fulfil the functions of an enlightened, consultative and cooperative body that will enrich the experience, enhance the prestige, support the authority, and assist the deliberations of the National Spiritual Assembly. It is my firm conviction that it is the bounden duty, in the interest of the Cause we

145

all love and serve, of the members of the incoming National Assembly, once elected by the delegates at Convention time, to seek and have the utmost regard, individually as well as collectively, for the advice, the considered opinion and the true sentiments of the assembled delegates. Banishing every vestige of secrecy, of undue reticence, of dictatorial aloofness, from their midst, they should radiantly and abundantly unfold to the eyes of the delegates, by whom they are elected, their plans, their hopes, and their cares. They should familiarize the delegates with the various matters that will have to be considered in the current year, and calmly and conscientiously study and weigh the opinions and judgements of the delegates. The newly elected National Assembly, during the few days when the Convention is in session and after the dispersal of the delegates, should seek ways and means to cultivate understanding, facilitate and maintain the exchange of views, deepen confidence, and vindicate by every tangible evidence their one desire to serve and advance the common weal. Not infrequently, nay oftentimes, the most lowly, untutored and inexperienced among the friends will, by the sheer inspiring force of selfless and ardent devotion, contribute a distinct and memorable share to a highly involved discussion in any given Assembly. Great must be the regard paid by those whom the delegates call upon to serve in high position to this all-important though inconspicuous manifestation of the revealing power of sincere and earnest devotion.

. . . The seating of delegates to the Convention, i.e., the right to decide upon the validity of the credentials of the delegates at a given Convention, is vested in the outgoing National Assembly, and the right to decide who has the voting privilege is also ultimately placed in the hands of the National Spiritual Assembly, either when a local Spiritual Assembly is for the first time being formed in a given locality, or when differences arise between a new applicant and an already established local Assembly. While the Convention is in session and the accredited delegates have already elected from among the believers throughout the country the members of the National Spiritual Assembly for the current year, it is of infinite value and a supreme necessity that as far as possible all matters requiring immediate decision should be fully and publicly considered, and an endeavour be made to obtain after mature deliberation, unanimity in vital decisions. Indeed, it has ever been the cherished desire of our Master, 'Abdu'l-Bahá, that the friends in their councils, local as well as national, should by their candour, their honesty of purpose, their singleness of mind, and the thoroughness of their discussions, achieve unanimity in all things. Should this in certain cases prove impracticable the verdict of the majority should prevail, to which decision the minority must under all circumstances, gladly, spontaneously and continually, submit.[62]

A compilation of extracts from the Bahá'í writings on the subject of the National Convention was prepared by the Research Department of the Universal House of Justice in December 1992.[63]

a) If in any year the National Spiritual Assembly shall consider that it is impracticable or unwise to hold the National Convention, the said Assembly shall provide ways and means by which the annual election and the other essential business of the Convention may be conducted.

This statement mirrors almost exactly wording in Article VIII, Section 6 of the By-Laws of the National Spiritual Assembly. In the passage from *Bahá'í Administration* cited above,[64] Shoghi Effendi established the principle that the outgoing National Spiritual Assembly has decision-making authority in terms of the arrangements of the National Convention – its seating arrangements, who has voting rights and so on. Here, the Universal House of Justice clarifies that this authority extends to the decision whether to hold the Convention at all. In her biography of

Shoghi Effendi, for example, Amatu'l-Bahá Rúḥíyyih Khánum records that, because of the distances separating the two countries and the expense of travelling between them, the Australian and New Zealand Bahá'ís held only three Conventions in a decade: one in 1934, one in 1937 and one in 1944.[65]

Shoghi Effendi made certain administrative details relating to the election of Assemblies contingent upon the approval of the Universal House of Justice (see annotations above on the legislative powers of the House). It is the prerogative of the House of Justice to delegate certain details such as these relating to National Conventions to the National Spiritual Assemblies.

b) Vacancies in the membership of the National Spiritual Assembly shall be filled by a vote of the delegates composing the Convention which elected the Assembly, the ballot to be taken by correspondence or in any other manner decided by the National Spiritual Assembly.

This statement mirrors almost exactly wording in Article VIII, Section 12 of the By-Laws of the National Spiritual Assembly. It states that the same delegates to a National Convention who elected a National Spiritual Assembly are also responsible for voting in by-elections during the course of the Bahá'í year until the following Riḍván, when new delegates elect the new National Assembly. It is unnecessary, therefore, to re-elect delegates every time there is a vacancy in the membership of the National Spiritual Assembly. According to this provision, by-elections to fill vacancies on a National Spiritual Assembly may be taken by calling for postal ballots or in any other way decided by the National Spiritual Assembly.

IV. OBLIGATIONS OF MEMBERS OF SPIRITUAL ASSEMBLIES

Among the most outstanding and sacred duties incumbent upon those who have been called upon to

148

initiate, direct and coordinate the affairs of the Cause of God as members of its Spiritual Assemblies are: to win by every means in their power the confidence and affection of those whom it is their privilege to serve; to investigate and acquaint themselves with the considered views, the prevailing sentiments and the personal convictions of those whose welfare it is their solemn obligation to promote; to purge their deliberations and the general conduct of their affairs of self-contained aloofness, the suspicion of secrecy, the stifling atmosphere of dictatorial assertiveness and of every word and deed that may savour of partiality, self-centredness and prejudice; and while retaining the sacred right of final decision in their hands, to invite discussion, ventilate grievances, welcome advice and foster the sense of interdependence and co-partnership, of understanding and mutual confidence between themselves and all other Bahá'ís.

These are the words of Shoghi Effendi, from a letter written to the members of the National Spiritual Assembly of the Bahá'ís of the United States and Canada, in 1927:

Let it be made clear to every inquiring reader that among the most outstanding and sacred duties incumbent upon those who have been called upon to initiate, direct and coordinate the affairs of the Cause, are those that require them to win by every means in their power the confidence and affection of those whom it is their privilege to serve. Theirs is the duty to investigate and acquaint themselves with the considered views, the prevailing sentiments, the personal convictions of those whose welfare it is their solemn obligation to promote. Theirs is the duty to purge once for all their deliberations and the general conduct of their affairs from that air of self-contained aloofness, from the suspicion of secrecy, the stifling atmosphere of dictatorial assertiveness, in short, from every word and deed that might savour of partiality, self-centeredness and prejudice. Theirs is the duty, while retaining the sacred and exclusive right of final decision in their hands, to invite discussion, provide information, ventilate grievances, welcome advice from even the most humble and insignificant members of the Bahá'í family, expose their motives, set forth their plans, justify their actions, revise if necessary their verdict, foster the sense of interdependence and co-partnership, of understanding and mutual confidence between them on one hand and all local Assemblies and individual believers on the other.[66]

This language is also mirrored in Article XI of the By-Laws of the National Spiritual Assembly.

V. THE UNIVERSAL HOUSE OF JUSTICE

The Universal House of Justice shall consist of nine men who have been elected from the Bahá'í community in the manner hereinafter provided.

Bahá'u'lláh designated the members of the Universal House of Justice as 'the Men of the House of Justice'.[67] In several places 'Abdu'l-Bahá has interpreted this designation as confining the membership of the House of Justice to men:

Know thou, O handmaid, that in the sight of Bahá, women are accounted the same as men, and God hath created all humankind in His own image, and after His own likeness. That is, men and women alike are the revealers of His names and attributes, and from the spiritual viewpoint there is no difference between them. Whosoever draweth nearer to God, that one is the most favoured, whether man or woman. How many a handmaid, ardent and devoted, hath, within the sheltering shade of Bahá, proved superior to the men, and surpassed the famous of the earth.

The House of Justice, however, according to the explicit text of the Law of God, is confined to men; this for a wisdom of the Lord God's, which will ere long be made manifest as clearly as the sun at high noon.[68]

Another Tablet by 'Abdu'l-Bahá restates the same principle, referring more specifically to the Universal House of Justice:

According to the ordinances of the Faith of God, women are the equals of men in all rights save only that of membership on the Universal House of Justice, for, as hath been stated in the text of the Book, both the head and the members of the House of Justice are men. However, in all other bodies, such as the Temple Construction Committee, the Teaching Committee, the Spiritual Assembly, and in charitable and scientific associations, women share equally in all rights with men.[69]

In yet another Tablet in Persian to an individual, 'Abdu'l-Bahá writes:

As regards the constitution of the House of Justice, Bahá'u'lláh addresses the men. He says: 'O ye men of the House of Justice!'

But when its members are to be elected, the right which belongs to women, so far as their voting and their voice is concerned, is indisputable. When the women attain to the ultimate degree of progress, then, according to the exigency of the time and place and their great capacity, they shall obtain extraordinary privileges. Be ye confident on these accounts. His Holiness Bahá'u'lláh has greatly strengthened the cause of women, and the rights and privileges of women is one of the greatest principles of 'Abdu'l-Bahá. Rest ye assured! Ere long the days shall come when the men addressing the women, shall say: 'Blessed are ye! Blessed are ye! Verily ye are worthy of every gift. Verily ye deserve to adorn your heads with the crown of everlasting glory, because in sciences and arts, in virtues and perfections ye shall become equal to man, and as regards tenderness of heart and the abundance of mercy and sympathy ye are superior.'[70]

Shoghi Effendi several times affirmed that 'Abdu'l-Bahá's interpretation of the words of Bahá'u'lláh were binding in this respect:

As regards the membership of the International House of Justice, 'Abdu'l-Bahá states in a Tablet that it is confined to men, and that the wisdom of it will be revealed as manifest as the sun in the future. In any case the believers should know that, as 'Abdu'l-Bahá Himself has explicitly stated, that sexes are equal except in some cases, the exclusion of women from the International House of Justice should not be surprising. From the fact that there is no equality of functions between the sexes one should not, however, infer that either sex is inherently superior or inferior to the other, or that they are unequal in their rights.[71]

As regards your question concerning the membership of the Universal House of Justice, there is a Tablet from 'Abdu'l-Bahá in which He definitely states that the membership of the Universal House is confined to men and that the wisdom of it will be fully revealed in the future. In the local, as well as the National Houses of Justice, however, women have the full right of membership. It is, therefore, only to the International House that they cannot be elected. The Bahá'ís should accept this statement of the Master in a spirit of deep faith, confident that there is a divine guidance and wisdom behind it, which will be gradually unfolded to the eyes of the world.[72]

Regarding your question, the Master said the wisdom of having no women on the International House of Justice, would become manifest in the future. We have no other indication than this.

At present there are women on the International Council, and this will continue as long as it exists, but when the International House of Justice is elected, there will only be men on it, as this is the law of the Aqdas.[73]

The Universal House of Justice has emphasized that the confining of its membership to men is a stipulation of the holy text and as such the House of Justice itself has no authority to legislate to permit the election of women:

Further, in response to a number of questions about eligibility for membership and procedures for election of the Universal House of Justice, the Guardian's secretary writing on his behalf distinguished between those questions which could be answered by reference to the 'explicitly revealed' Text and those which could not. Membership to the Universal House of Justice fits into the former category. The letter stated:

The membership of the Universal House of Justice is confined to men. Fixing the number of the members, the procedures for election and the term of membership will be known later, as these are not explicitly revealed in the Holy Text. (27 May 1940)

Hence, 'Abdu'l Bahá and the Guardian progressively have revealed, in accordance with divine inspiration, the meaning and implications of Bahá'u'lláh's seminal teachings. Their interpretations are fundamental statements of truth which cannot be varied through legislation by the Universal House of Justice.[74]

The Universal House of Justice continues:

As mentioned earlier, the law regarding the membership of the Universal House of Justice is embedded in the Text and has been merely restated by the divinely appointed interpret-

153

ers. It is therefore neither amenable to change nor subject to speculation about some possible future condition.

With regard to the status of women, the important point for Bahá'ís to remember is that in face of the categorical pronouncements in Bahá'í Scripture establishing the equality of men and women, the ineligibility of women for membership of the Universal House of Justice does not constitute evidence of the superiority of men over women. It must also be borne in mind that women are not excluded from any other international institution of the Faith. They are found among the ranks of the Hands of the Cause. They serve as members of the International Teaching Centre and as Continental Counsellors. And, there is nothing in the Text to preclude the participation of women in such future international bodies as the Supreme Tribunal.

Though at the present time, it may be difficult for the believers to appreciate the reason for the circumscription of membership on the Universal House of Justice to men, we call upon the friends to remain assured by the Master's promise that clarity of understanding will be achieved in due course. The friends, both women and men, must accept this with faith that the Covenant of Bahá'u'lláh will aid them and the institutions of His World Order to see the realization of every principle ordained by His unerring Pen, including the equality of men and women, as expounded in the Writings of the Cause.[75]

1. Election

The members of the Universal House of Justice shall be elected by secret ballot by the members of all National Spiritual Assemblies at a meeting to be known as the International Bahá'í Convention.

The method of electing the Universal House of Justice is described by 'Abdu'l-Bahá in His Will and Testament and other Tablets. The following quotation is from Part One of the Will and Testament, stipulating that the members of the Universal House of Justice are to be elected by the members of the 'secondary Houses of Justice' (currently called National Spiritual Assemblies):

> And now, concerning the House of Justice which God hath ordained as the source of all good and freed from all error, it must be elected by universal suffrage, that is, by the believers. Its members must be manifestations of the fear of God and daysprings of knowledge and understanding, must be steadfast in God's faith and the well-wishers of all mankind. By this House is meant the Universal House of Justice, that is, in all countries a secondary House of Justice must be instituted, and these secondary Houses of Justice must elect the members of the Universal one.[76]

This is from Part Two of that same document:

> By this House is meant that Universal House of Justice which is to be elected from all countries, that is from those parts in the East and West where the loved ones are to be found, after the manner of the customary elections in Western countries such as those of England.[77]

This is from a Tablet of 'Abdu'l-Bahá, again indicating that the manner of the election must be like that of western countries:

> The Supreme House of Justice should be elected according to the system followed in the election of the parliaments of Europe. And when the countries would be guided, the Houses of Justice of the various countries would elect the Supreme House of Justice.
>
> At whatever time all the beloved of God in each country appoint their delegates, and these in turn elect their representatives, and these representatives elect a body, that body

shall be regarded as the Supreme House of Justice. The establishment of that House is not dependent upon the conversion of all the nations of the world. For example, if conditions were favourable and no disturbances would be caused, the friends in Persia would elect their representatives, and likewise the friends in America, in India, and other areas would also elect their representatives, and these would elect a House of Justice. That House of Justice would be the Supreme House of Justice. That is all.[78]

The Guardian specified that all Bahá'í elections should be conducted by secret ballot.[79] This method is necessary to maintain the spiritual nature of Bahá'í elections (see Article VI of the By-Laws of the Universal House of Justice and annotations below).

Just as National Spiritual Assemblies are elected at National Conventions, the Universal House of Justice is elected at an International Convention. There is no reference in the Bahá'í writings to an International Convention. The usefulness of holding such an international gathering may be inferred from Shoghi Effendi's direction to Bahá'í communities to hold conventions at the local (unit) and national levels but the decision to do so was entirely at the discretion of the Universal House of Justice. This part of the By-Laws, therefore, is to a large extent an application at the international level of principles already set out for the conduct of National Conventions.

The first election of the Universal House of Justice was held at an international convention called by the Hands of the Cause in 1963 (see paragraph 17 of the Declaration of Trust and annotations above).

a) An election of the Universal House of Justice shall be held once every five years unless otherwise decided by the Universal House of Justice, and those elected shall continue in office until such time as their successors shall be elected and the first meeting of these successors is duly held.

There is nothing in the writings of Bahá'u'lláh, 'Abdu'l-Bahá or Shoghi Effendi that stipulates how often the Universal House of Justice should be elected, although 'Abdu'l-Bahá has in one Tablet recommended that a Spiritual Assembly be elected once every five years.[80] The House of Justice was therefore free to legislate on this point. This paragraph of the By-Laws makes it clear that the Universal House of Justice may hold its elections as frequently as it wishes but that the normal period between elections is five years.

The By-Laws do not specify what time of the year the International Convention and election should be held. However, all International Conventions so far have been held during the Riḍván period and it is interesting to note this statement in a letter written on behalf of Shoghi Effendi: 'The convention – all Bahá'í Conventions – must be held within the Riḍván period . . .'[81]

After the first election of the Universal House of Justice in 1963, further elections were held in 1968, 1973, 1978, 1983, 1988, 1993, 1998 and 2003.

The first meeting of the Universal House of Justice after each election is to be called, in the normal course, by the individual who receives the highest number of votes (see Article V, Section 4 of the By-Laws of the Universal House of Justice and annotations below). The newly elected members of the Universal House of Justice take office at the first meeting after each election.

b) Upon receiving the call to Convention each National Spiritual Assembly shall submit to the Universal House of Justice a list of the names of its members. The recognition and seating of the delegates to the International Convention shall be vested in the Universal House of Justice.

Prior to each International Convention the Universal House of Justice issues a call to all National Spiritual Assemblies. At that time, every National Assembly must send to the Universal

House of Justice a list of its members. The Universal House of Justice reserves the right not to recognize any delegate to the International Convention (i.e. a member of a National Spiritual Assembly) and to refuse to allow him to take part in the Convention. Presumably, this provision is included in the By-Laws to clarify that the House of Justice may exclude from the International Convention individuals who are known by it to be in violation of Bahá'í law or practice and whose presence at the Convention would be detrimental to its proceedings.

The second sentence of this paragraph (b) mirrors Article VIII, Section 4 of the By-Laws of the National Spiritual Assembly, which derives from the following directive from Shoghi Effendi:

> The seating of delegates to the Convention, i.e., the right to decide upon the validity of the credentials of the delegates at a given Convention, is vested in the outgoing National Assembly, and the right to decide who has the voting privilege is also ultimately placed in the hands of the National Spiritual Assembly, either when a local Spiritual Assembly is for the first time being formed in a given locality, or when differences arise between a new applicant and an already established local Assembly.[82]

c) The principal business of the International Convention shall be to elect the members of the Universal House of Justice, to deliberate on the affairs of the Bahá'í Cause throughout the world, and to make recommendations and suggestions for the consideration of the Universal House of Justice.

The 'principal business' of the International Convention mirrors that of the National Convention (see Article III, Section 4 of the By-Laws of the Universal House of Justice and annotations above). Of the delegates to the National Convention, Shoghi Effendi wrote that they had the 'vital and responsible right of electing the National Assembly' and 'should also fulfil the functions of an enlightened, consultative and cooperative body'.[83] More specifically, he wrote that they had the 'twofold function . . . to **elect** their national representatives [i.e. the members of the National Spiritual Assembly] and to submit to them any **recommendations** they may feel inclined to make'.[84] Elsewhere, he wrote that the 'Annual Bahá'í Convention' had a 'twofold function of electing the body of the National Spiritual Assembly, and of offering any constructive **suggestions** in regard to the general administration of the Cause'.[85]

The purposes of the National Convention are stated at Article VIII, Section 8 of the By-Laws of the National Spiritual Assembly.

d) The sessions of the International Convention shall be conducted in such manner as the Universal House of Justice shall from time to time decide.

There is nothing in the writings of Bahá'u'lláh, 'Abdu'l-Bahá or Shoghi Effendi about how the International Convention is to be conducted. The Universal House of Justice therefore has the authority to decide how it will be structured, the manner in which the election and consultation are to take place and so on.

The conduct of sessions at the National Convention is similarly to be determined by the National Spiritual Assembly, according to Article VIII, Section 9 of the By-Laws of the National Spiritual Assembly.

e) The Universal House of Justice shall provide a procedure whereby those delegates who are unable to be present in person at the International Convention shall cast their ballots for the election of the members of the Universal House of Justice.

The ability of National Spiritual Assembly members to attend an International Convention may be restricted by any number of factors including, for example, local conditions at the time and the costs of travel. Those who are unable to attend the Convention nevertheless have the right and duty to participate in the election of the Universal House of Justice. The House of Justice will ensure that this is possible by providing a procedure whereby they may cast their ballots. Paragraph (h) below suggests that ballots may be sent by mail. There is a parallel provision concerning the National Convention in Article VIII, Section 5 of the By-Laws of the National Spiritual Assembly.

f) If at the time of an election the Universal House of Justice shall consider that it is impracticable or unwise to hold the International Convention it shall determine how the election shall take place.

The reasons why an International Convention may not be held are that it is either 'impracticable' or 'unwise'. Among other possibilities, this may be due to disturbances in the Holy Land or more generally in the world. Although the International Convention may be unable to deliberate 'on the affairs of the Bahá'í Cause throughout the world' or make 'recommendations and suggestions for the consideration of the Universal House of Justice' (see paragraph (c) above), it can nevertheless carry out its essential elective function.

This provision of the By-Laws has been invoked only once. On 4 April 2003, the Universal House of Justice wrote to all National Spiritual Assemblies:

> We have been following closely developments in the world as they affect the Middle East, in the hope that the passage of events would make it possible for the International Bahá'í Convention to be held as planned. However, for the sake of all concerned we can wait no longer. To our regret, current conditions are such that we feel compelled to cancel the holding of the International Convention, and we write to so inform you.

This is the first time we have had to implement the provision of the Constitution of the Universal House of Justice that states: 'If at the time of an election the Universal House of Justice shall consider that it is impracticable or unwise to hold the International Convention it shall determine how the election shall take place.' The ballots of the members of all National Spiritual Assemblies are arriving daily, and we are arranging for the nineteen delegates chosen to be tellers to come to the Holy Land to count the votes on the Ninth Day of Riḍván. Should circumstances make it impossible for these friends to come, we shall adopt another means for the discharge of this task.[86]

The Universal House of Justice later commented on the war in the Middle East that had broken out earlier that year:

The disruptions caused by this and other situations in the world . . . have dashed the preparations for the Ninth International Convention at the World Centre of our Faith. But, however disappointing, this calls for no dismay. When the Major Plan of God interferes with His Minor Plan, there should be no doubt that in due course a way will providentially be opened to an opportunity of stellar possibilities for advancing the interests of His glorious Cause.[87]

Compare this provision of the By-Laws with the power of a National Spiritual Assembly to decide not to hold a National Convention in any year (see Article III, Section 4 (a) of the By-Laws of the Universal House of Justice and annotations above. Article VIII, Section 6 of the By-Laws of the National Spiritual Assembly provides for similar contingencies.). Note that the By-Laws of the Universal House of Justice only specify that the House shall determine how the election shall take place if an International Convention is not held. The By-Laws of the National Spiritual Assembly, on the other hand, make it incumbent upon the National Assembly to provide means by which both the election 'and the other essential business' of the National Convention may be conducted 'by mail'.[88]

g) On the day of the election the ballots of all voters shall be scrutinized and counted and the result certified by tellers appointed in accordance with the instructions of the Universal House of Justice.

Tellers are to be appointed for each International Convention 'in accordance with the instructions of the Universal House of Justice'. These tellers have the duties of inspecting the ballots of all voters at the International Convention and of certifying the results of the election.

h) If a member of a National Spiritual Assembly who has voted by mail ceases to be a member of that National Spiritual Assembly between the time of casting his ballot and the date of the counting of the ballots, his ballot shall nevertheless remain valid unless in the interval his successor shall have been elected and the ballot of such successor shall have been received by the tellers.

This provision applies only to ballots sent by mail. A member of a National Spiritual Assembly who sends his postal ballot for the election of the Universal House of Justice may cease to be a member of the National Assembly before the ballots are actually counted. If so, his ballot will still be valid and his vote counted. The exception is where he has sent his postal ballot and another individual has been subsequently elected to the National Spiritual Assembly and the new member has been able to cast his vote (whether by mail or in person).

i) In case by reason of a tie vote or votes the full membership of the Universal House of Justice is not determined on the first ballot, then one or more

additional ballots shall be held on the persons tied until all members are elected. The electors in the case of additional ballots shall be the members of National Spiritual Assemblies in office at the time each subsequent vote is taken.

This provision does not restrict the participants in additional ballots to delegates who are present at the International Convention. Presumably, then, some means will be found to receive the ballots of those members of National Spiritual Assemblies who are unable to attend the Convention.

Article VIII, Section 10 of the By-Laws of the National Spiritual Assembly contains a parallel provision for holding additional ballots.

2. Vacancies in membership

A vacancy in the membership of the Universal House of Justice will occur upon the death of a member or in the following cases:

a) Should any member of the Universal House of Justice commit a sin injurious to the common weal, he may be dismissed from membership by the Universal House of Justice.

The wording of this clause comes from Part One of the Will and Testament of 'Abdu'l-Bahá:

> Should any of the members commit **a sin, injurious to the common weal**, the guardian of the Cause of God hath at his own discretion the right to expel him, whereupon the people must elect another one in his stead.[89]

It should be noted that this quotation does not say that *only* the Guardian may expel a member from membership of the Universal House of Justice. It does say, however, that the Guardian may do so 'at his own discretion' – i.e. without a decision of the Universal House of Justice. Early on in its ministry the Universal House of Justice confirmed that, in the absence of a living Guardian, the House of Justice would bear this responsibility alone. This letter was written in 1965 to the National Spiritual Assembly of the Netherlands:

> The third group of queries raised by the friends concerns details of functioning of the Universal House of Justice in the absence of the Guardian, particularly the matter of expulsion of members of the House of Justice. Such questions will be clarified in the Constitution of the House of Justice, the formulation of which is a goal of the Nine Year Plan. Meanwhile the friends are informed that any member committing a 'sin injurious to the common weal', may be expelled from membership of the House of Justice by a majority vote of the House itself. Should any member, God forbid, be guilty of breaking the Covenant, the matter would be investigated by the Hands of the Cause of God, and the Covenant-breaker would be expelled by decision of the Hands of the Cause of God residing in the Holy Land, subject to the approval of the House of Justice, as in the case of any other believer. The decision of the Hands in such a case would be announced to the Bahá'í world by the Universal House of Justice.[90]

One year later the Universal House of Justice wrote the following to an individual Bahá'í:

> As the Universal House of Justice has already announced, it cannot legislate to make possible the appointment of a successor to Shoghi Effendi, nor can it legislate to make possible the appointment of any more Hands of the Cause, but it must do everything within its power to ensure the performance of all those functions which it shares with these two mighty

institutions . . . it must make provision in its Constitution for
the removal of any of its members who commits a sin 'injurious to the common weal'.[91]

**b) The Universal House of Justice may at its discretion
declare a vacancy with respect to any member who
in its judgement is unable to fulfil the functions of
membership.**

This provision differs from the preceding one: it is concerned
with the inability of a member to fulfil his functions, not his
commission of a sin. It states that a vacancy will declared, not
that the member concerned will be expelled from membership
of the Universal House of Justice.

**c) A member may relinquish his membership on the
Universal House of Justice only with the approval of
the Universal House of Justice.**

The situation provided for in this paragraph arose in 1967
when a member of the House of Justice, Dr Luṭfu'lláh Ḥakím,
resigned from the Universal House of Justice owing to ill health.
The Universal House of Justice wrote that it had 'regretfully
accepted Dr Ḥakím's resignation'.[92]

3. By-election

**If a vacancy in the membership of the Universal
House of Justice occurs, the Universal House of
Justice shall call a by-election at the earliest possible
date unless such date, in the judgement of the
Universal House of Justice, falls too close to the date
of a regular election of the entire membership, in
which case the Universal House of Justice may, at
its discretion, defer the filling of the vacancy to the
time of the regular election. If a by-election is held,**

the voters shall be the members of the National Spiritual Assemblies in office at the time of the by-election.

Just as in the case of Local and National Spiritual Assemblies, vacancies on the Universal House of Justice are filled by way of by-elections. If the vacancy arises very near the date of a regular election, the House of Justice may decide not to hold a by-election.

A by-election of the Universal House of Justice has been held three times: in 1983, when Glenford Mitchell was elected to the Universal House of Justice to fill a vacancy caused by the passing of Amoz Gibson;[93] in 1987, when Peter Khan was elected to fill a vacancy caused by the passing of Charles Wolcott; and in 2000 when Kiser Barnes was elected after the passing of Adib Taherzadeh.

4. Meetings

a) After the election of the Universal House of Justice the first meeting shall be called by the member elected by the highest number of votes or, in his absence or other incapacity, by the member elected by the next highest number of votes or, in case two or more members have received the same highest number of votes, then by the member selected by lot from among those members. Subsequent meetings shall be called in the manner decided by the Universal House of Justice.

This paragraph provides a method for calling the first meeting of a newly elected Universal House of Justice. If the House of Justice had been elected during the ministry of the Guardian, no doubt he as its 'permanent head' would have called its meetings. In the absence of a living Guardian, some other method had to be devised. The member of the House of Justice who has received the highest number of votes calls the first meeting after the election. If two or more members receive the same highest number of votes, then those members shall select one of them by lot to call the first meeting. The Universal House of Justice itself shall then decide how to call subsequent meetings. These provisions are similar to those set out for Local Assemblies in Article VIII of the By-Laws of the Local Spiritual Assembly, except that subsequent meetings of a Local Assembly are to be called by its responsible officers, whereas the Universal House of Justice has no officers.

b) The Universal House of Justice has no officers.

The only officer of the Universal House of Justice mentioned in the Bahá'í writings is the Guardian. In Part One of His Will and Testament, 'Abdu'l-Bahá wrote that 'the guardian of the Cause of God is its sacred head and the distinguished member for life of that body'.[94] Referring to this appointment in the Will and Testament, Shoghi Effendi confirmed that 'the Guardian of the Faith has been made the permanent head of so august a body'.[95] The House of Justice has confirmed that only the Guardian can fulfil this function:

> While the specific responsibility of the Guardian is the interpretation of the Word, he is also invested with all the powers and prerogatives necessary to discharge his function as Guardian of the Cause, its Head and supreme protector. He is, furthermore, made the irremovable head and member for life of the supreme legislative body of the Faith. It is as the head of the Universal House of Justice, and as a member of that body, that the Guardian takes part in the process of legislation. If the following passage, which gave rise to your query, is considered as referring to this last relationship, you will see that there is no contradiction between it and the other texts: 'Though the Guardian of the Faith has been made the permanent head of so august a body he can

167

never, even temporarily, assume the right of exclusive legislation. He cannot override the decision of the majority of his fellow members, but is bound to insist upon a reconsideration by them of any enactment he conscientiously believes to conflict with the meaning and to depart from the spirit of Bahá'u'lláh's revealed utterances.[96]

There is thus no scriptural warrant for any officers on the Universal House of Justice other than the Guardian, who would have been its permanent head. The House of Justice has decided that no one of its members should have that function and the chairing of meetings of the Universal House of Justice is therefore rotated among its members.

It shall provide for the conduct of its meetings and shall organize its activities in such manner as it shall from time to time decide.

In the course of describing its own relationship with the Guardianship, the Universal House of Justice has provided this revealing description of its decision-making process:

It may help the friends to understand this relationship if they are aware of some of the processes that the Universal House of Justice follows when legislating. First, of course, it observes the greatest care in studying the Sacred Texts and the interpretations of the Guardian as well as considering the views of all the members. After long consultation the process of drafting a pronouncement is put into effect. During this process the whole matter may well be reconsidered. As a result of such reconsideration the final judgement may be significantly different from the conclusion earlier favoured, or possibly it may be decided not to legislate at all on that subject at that time. One can understand how great would be the attention paid to the views of the Guardian during the above process were he alive.[97]

c) **The business of the Universal House of Justice shall be conducted by the full membership in consultation, except that the Universal House of Justice may from time to time provide for quorums of less than the full membership for specified classes of business.**

All nine members of the Universal House of Justice serve on that body in a full-time capacity. This paragraph provides that, in general, the business of the House of Justice is conducted when all nine are present at a meeting. However, there are certain categories of business that do not require the attention of the full membership and these may be handled by a quorum of less than nine.

5. Signature

The signature of the Universal House of Justice shall be the words 'The Universal House of Justice' or in Persian 'Baytu'l-'Adl-i-A'ẓam' written by hand by any one of its members upon authority of the Universal House of Justice, to which shall be affixed in each case the Seal of the Universal House of Justice.

In English, the Universal House of Justice is also called by Shoghi Effendi the 'International House of Justice'. However, this clause affirms that the official name of that body is the more commonly known title. The seal of the Universal House of Justice is at the foot of page 7 of the Declaration of Trust.

6. Records

The Universal House of Justice shall provide for the recording and verification of its decisions in such manner as it shall, from time to time, judge necessary.

The Universal House of Justice addressed this issue in a letter of 4 August 1974 written on its behalf to an individual:

As mentioned in the By-laws of the Constitution of the Universal House of Justice, there is no hard and fast rule for the verification of its decisions and this applies to letters. Various procedures are followed which are reviewed from time to time.[98]

VI. BAHÁ'Í ELECTIONS

In order to preserve the spiritual character and purpose of Bahá'í elections the practices of nomination or electioneering, or any other procedure or activity detrimental to that character and purpose shall be eschewed. A silent and prayerful atmosphere shall prevail during the election so that each elector may vote for none but those whom prayer and reflection inspire him to uphold.

Shoghi Effendi left the manner of carrying out Bahá'í elections to the ultimate discretion of the Universal House of Justice:

In connection with the best and most practical methods of procedure to be adopted for the election of Bahá'í Spiritual Assemblies, I feel that in view of the fact that definite and detailed regulations defining the manner and character of Bahá'í elections have neither been expressly revealed by Bahá'u'lláh nor laid down in the Will and Testament of 'Abdu'l-Bahá, it devolves upon the members of the Universal House of Justice to formulate and apply such system of laws as would be in conformity with the essentials and requisites expressly provided by the Author and Interpreter of the Faith for the conduct of Bahá'í administration.[99]

Shoghi Effendi did, however, establish certain policies as to the conduct of Bahá'í elections, which have been ratified by the House of Justice and continue to the present day. The following passage explains the reasoning behind these policies:

> . . . the practice of nomination so detrimental to the atmosphere of a silent and prayerful election, is viewed with mistrust inasmuch as it gives the right to the majority of a body that, in itself under the present circumstances, often constitutes a minority of all the elected delegates, to deny that God-given right of every elector to vote only in favour of those who he is conscientiously convinced are the most worthy candidates. Should this simple system be provisionally adopted, it would safeguard the spiritual principle of the unfettered freedom of the voter, who will thus preserve intact the sanctity of the choice he first made. It would avoid the inconvenience of securing advance nominations from absent delegates, and the impracticality of associating them with the assembled electors in the subsequent ballots that are often required to meet the exigencies of majority vote.[100]

This passage also addresses the absence of nominations in Bahá'í elections:

> As to the practice of nomination in Bahá'í elections, this the Guardian firmly believes to be in fundamental disaccord with the spirit which should animate and direct all elections held by the Bahá'ís, be they of a local or national character and importance. It is, indeed, the absence of such a practice that constitutes the distinguishing feature and the marked superiority of the Bahá'í electoral methods over those commonly associated with political parties and factions. The practice of nomination being thus contrary to the spirit of Bahá'í Administration should be totally discarded by all the friends. For otherwise the freedom of the Bahá'í elector in choosing the members of any Bahá'í assembly will be seriously endangered, leaving the way open for the domination

of personalities. Not only that; but the mere act of nomination leads eventually to the formation of parties – a thing which is totally alien to the spirit of the Cause. In addition to these serious dangers, the practice of nomination has the great disadvantage of killing in the believer the spirit of initiative, and of self-development. Bahá'í electoral procedures and methods have, indeed, for one of their essential purposes the development in every believer of the spirit of responsibility. By emphasizing the necessity of maintaining his full freedom in the elections, they make it incumbent upon him to become an active and well-informed member of the Bahá'í community in which he lives. To be able to make a wise choice at the election time, it is necessary for him to be in close and continued contact with all of his fellow-believers, to keep in touch with all local activities, be they teaching, administrative or otherwise, and to fully and whole-heartedly participate in the affairs of the local as well as national committees and Assemblies in his country. It is only in this way that a believer can develop a true social consciousness and acquire a true sense of responsibility in matters affecting the interests of the Cause. Bahá'í community life thus makes it a duty for every loyal and faithful believer to become an intelligent, well-informed and responsible elector, and also gives him the opportunity of raising himself to such a station. And since the practice of nomination hinders the development of such qualities in the believer, and in addition leads to corruption and partisanship, it has to be entirely discarded in all Bahá'í elections.[101]

The principle of electing by secret ballot was also emphasized by Shoghi Effendi, as he wrote in this letter to the Bahá'ís in Persia:

Let them exercise the utmost vigilance so that the elections are carried out freely, universally and by secret ballot. Any form of intrigue, deception, collusion and compulsion must be stopped and is forbidden.[102]

172

Shoghi Effendi has written that at the time of elections, the Bahá'ís 'should be in the mood of prayer, disinterestedness and detachment from worldly motives',[103] should 'turn completely to God, and with a purity of motive, a freedom of spirit and a sanctity of heart, participate in the elections'.[104]

In 1971 the Universal House of Justice wrote a letter to all National Spiritual Assemblies on the subject of the 'Spiritual Character of Bahá'í Elections';[105] a compilation of the same name was put out at the same time and revised in 1989.[106]

1. All Bahá'í elections, except elections of officers of Local and National Spiritual Assemblies and committees, shall be by plurality vote taken by secret ballot.

Early in his ministry Shoghi Effendi explained the principle behind plurality votes:

The general practice prevailing throughout the East is the one based upon the principle of plurality rather than absolute majority, whereby those candidates that have obtained the highest number of votes, irrespective of the fact whether they command an absolute majority of the votes cast or not, are automatically and definitely elected. It has been felt, with no little justification, that this method, admittedly disadvantageous in its disregard of the principle that requires that each elected member must secure a majority of the votes cast, does away on the other hand with the more serious disadvantage of restricting the freedom of the elector who, unhampered and unconstrained by electoral necessities, is called upon to vote for none but those whom prayer and reflection have inspired him to uphold.[107]

This subject is also addressed by the Guardian in other letters, such as this:

In connection with this, the Guardian wishes to draw your Assembly's attention to the necessity of adopting the system of plurality voting rather than that of absolute majority voting. For the latter, by making the repetition of elections a necessity, causes, though indirectly, much pressure to bear upon the person of the elector. The Bahá'í elector, as already emphasized, should be given full freedom in his choice. Anything, therefore, which can in the least interfere with such a freedom should be considered as disastrous and hence should be completely wiped out. In all elections, it is always difficult, that more than a few individuals of high position should obtain a majority of the votes of the electorate. Most of those elected have a plurality of votes. To enforce the principle of majority voting, therefore, it requires that the election be repeated again and again and until all the members to be elected have obtained more than half of the votes cast – a thing which becomes the more difficult when it is a matter of electing an assembly of nine persons. So, repetition in elections becomes inevitable. And such a repetition is in itself a restriction imposed upon the freedom of the electorate. The only course, therefore, is for every elector to write down the name of nine who he thinks are most worthy. These nine who obtain the highest number of votes, irrespective of the majority of the votes cast, will constitute the members of the Assembly.[108]

The principle of plurality voting for the members of Bahá'í Assemblies is also enshrined in Article XI, Section 2 of the By-Laws of the Local Spiritual Assembly and in Articles VII and VIII of the By-Laws of the National Spiritual Assembly. Not all Bahá'í elections are determined by a plurality vote: see Article VI, Section 2 below. However, all Bahá'í elections must be held by secret ballot, as explained above.

2. Election of the officers of a Spiritual Assembly or committee shall be by majority vote of the Assembly or committee taken by secret ballot.

The requirement of majority vote for election of officers is established in the By-Laws of the National Spiritual Assembly and By-Laws of the Local Spiritual Assembly, as the Universal House of Justice points out:

> While it is certainly true that the permanent officers of an Assembly should be elected immediately following the election of that Assembly, it is equally important, as stated in Article IV of the By-laws of the National Assembly, that 'The officers shall be elected by a majority vote of the *entire* membership of the Assembly taken by secret ballot.' That is all members of the Assembly must be properly notified and given an opportunity to vote, and in cases of unavoidable absence it does not contravene the spirit of the By-laws if the absent member should cast his ballot by mail or even by telephone.
>
> Temporary officers may be elected until all nine are properly notified of the election.[109]

The corresponding provisions in the By-Laws of the Local Spiritual Assembly are in Article VII.

3. In case by reason of a tie vote or votes the full membership of an elected body is not determined on the first ballot, then one or more additional ballots shall be taken on the persons tied until all members are elected.

The Universal House of Justice explained this principle in a letter written on its behalf to the National Spiritual Assembly of the Bahamas in 1982:

> Following the voting in an election of an Assembly, Local or National, results of the balloting should be announced, including the names of those tied for ninth place. A new ballot must then be cast to decide between those who have

received the same number of votes for ninth place. Only those who are tied are to be voted for on the ballot, and the tie may be broken by the delegates present at the convention.[110]

4. The duties and rights of a Bahá'í elector may not be assigned nor may they be exercised by proxy.

In many political systems an individual may assign his right to vote in an election to another individual or may tell that other individual how to vote on his behalf. In the Bahá'í system, the right to vote in an election is a sacred duty that cannot be performed on one's behalf by another person. The principle requiring secret ballots makes voting by proxy an impossibility in Bahá'í elections. Article VIII, Section 3 of the By-Laws of the National Spiritual Assembly parallels this provision in relation to the National Convention.

VII. THE RIGHT OF REVIEW

The Universal House of Justice has the right to review any decision or action of any Spiritual Assembly, National or Local, and to approve, modify or reverse such decision or action. The Universal House of Justice also has the right to intervene in any matter in which a Spiritual Assembly is failing to take action or to reach a decision and, at its discretion, to require that action be taken, or itself to take action directly in the matter.

The right of review derives from the 'powers and duties' of the Universal House of Justice, as stated in its Declaration of Trust including, among others, 'to deliberate and decide upon all problems which have caused difference' and 'to safeguard the personal rights, freedom and initiative of individuals'.[111]

Thus if the Universal House of Justice decides that any decision or action of a Local or National Assembly is unjust

176

or harmful to the Faith or to the rights of any individual or institution, it may intervene and modify or reverse that decision or action. Similarly, any harmful or unjust inaction can be remedied by direct intervention of the Universal House of Justice itself. Article IX of the By-Laws of the National Spiritual Assembly affirms the overall power of the Universal House of Justice to review any decision of the National Spiritual Assembly (which itself has the power to review the decisions of Local Spiritual Assemblies).

VIII. APPEALS

The right of appeal exists in the circumstances, and shall be exercised according to the procedures, outlined below:

1. a) Any member of a local Bahá'í community may appeal from a decision of his Local Spiritual Assembly to the National Spiritual Assembly which shall determine whether it shall take jurisdiction of the matter or refer it back to the Local Spiritual Assembly for reconsideration. If such an appeal concerns the membership of a person in the Bahá'í community, the National Spiritual Assembly is obliged to take jurisdiction of and decide the case.

The right to appeal a decision of a Local Spiritual Assembly to the National Spiritual Assembly was established by Shoghi Effendi in a letter written on his behalf to an individual:

. . . whenever there is any infringement of Bahá'í rights, or lapse in the proper procedure. the friends should take the matter up with the Assembly concerned, and if not satisfied, then with the National Spiritual Assembly. This is both their privilege and their duty.[112]

The appeal to the higher authority must be combined with loyalty to and support for the Assembly involved, as another letter, written on behalf of the Guardian to an individual, describes:

> When the Local Assembly has given its decision in the matter, you then have the right to appeal, if you wish, to the National Spiritual Assembly for further consideration of your case. But before taking such an action it is your duty as a loyal and steadfast believer to whole-heartedly and unreservedly accept the National Spiritual Assembly's request to enter into joint conference with your Local Assembly. You should have confidence that in obeying the orders of your National Assembly you will not only succeed in solving your own personal problems with the friends, but will in addition set a noble example before them.[113]

The Universal House of Justice has more recently restated this right in general terms:

> The individual has the responsibility to establish and maintain the Assembly through election, the offering of advice, moral support and material assistance; and he has the right to be heard by it, to receive its guidance and assistance, and to appeal from any Assembly decision which he conscientiously feels is unjust or detrimental to the interests of the community.[114]

The method of appeal to the National Spiritual Assembly is set out in Article X, Section 1 of the By-Laws of the Local Spiritual Assembly and in Article VII, Section 9 of the By-Laws of the National Spiritual Assembly. Also see Article II, Section 2 of the By-Laws of the Universal House of Justice and annotations, above, on the 'full jurisdiction' of a Local Spiritual Assembly over Bahá'í activities within its locality.

Membership in the Bahá'í community is a matter of fundamental import to any individual Bahá'í (see Article I of the By-Laws and annotations above). Therefore, decisions on such cases come under the jurisdiction of National Spiritual Assemblies, or the Universal House of Justice on appeal.

b) Any Bahá'í may appeal from a decision of his National Spiritual Assembly to the Universal House of Justice which shall determine whether it shall take jurisdiction of the matter or leave it within the final jurisdiction of the National Spiritual Assembly.

During his ministry the Guardian was the final arbiter of appeals, as this letter establishes, written on his behalf to the National Spiritual Assembly of Germany and Austria in 1949:

> Appeal can be made from the Local Assembly's decision to the National Assembly, and from the National Assembly's decision to the Guardian [now to the Universal House of Justice]. But the principle of authority invested in our elected bodies must be upheld. This is not something which can be learned without trial and test.[115]

This was written in 1925 on behalf of Shoghi Effendi to an individual:

> . . . we must do all we can to strengthen and support the Local and National Assemblies by exercising great care in the elections, so as to secure the return of the wisest and most suitable members, then by loyal co-operation and obedience. If we disapprove of their decisions we must be careful to avoid discussing such matters with other believers who have no authority to put them right. We must put our views frankly before the Assembly itself and only in the case of not getting a satisfactory reply appeal to the National Assembly, if it is a question of the conduct of the Local Assembly, and to Shoghi Effendi if the National Assembly is concerned.[116]

In yet another letter the Guardian emphasizes the ultimate right to appeal to the head of the Faith:

Anything whatsoever affecting the interests of the Cause and in which the National Assembly as a body is involved should, if regarded as unsatisfactory by Local Assemblies and individual believers, be immediately referred to the National Assembly itself. Neither the general body of the believers, nor any Local Assembly, nor even the delegates to the annual Convention, should be regarded as having any authority to entertain appeals against the decision of the National Assembly. Should the matter be referred to the Guardian it will be his duty to consider it with the utmost care and to decide whether the issues involved justify him to consider it in person, or to leave it entirely to the discretion of the National Assembly.[117]

Bahá'ís may now appeal to the Universal House of Justice, as head of the Bahá'í Faith. This function can be regarded as deriving from a number of the 'powers and duties' of the Universal House of Justice, as stated in its Declaration of Trust, for example:

- to deliberate and decide upon all problems which have caused difference
- to adjudicate disputes falling within its purview
- to safeguard the personal rights, freedom and initiative of individuals
- to be responsible for ensuring that no body or institution within the Cause abuse its privileges or decline in the exercise of its rights and prerogatives

The By-Laws of the National Spiritual Assembly state that a National Assembly has the right to make 'final decisions' on certain matters (see, for example, Articles I and VII of those By-Laws). It may seem that there is a contradiction between this and the right of appeal to the Universal House of Justice. In a letter written on its behalf to the National Spiritual Assembly of Spain in 1982, the Universal House of Justice addressed this apparent contradiction:

The House of Justice instructs us to explain that wherever 'final' jurisdiction is given to the Local or National Spiritual Assembly in its constitution there is a balancing provision. For example:

Article IV of the Local Assembly By-Laws states: 'while retaining the sacred right of final decision in all matters pertaining to the Bahá'í community, the Spiritual Assembly shall ever seek the advice and consultation of all members of the community, keep the community informed of all its affairs, and invite full and free discussion on the part of the community in all matters affecting the Faith.' Yet, Article III of those same Local By-Laws states: 'The Spiritual Assembly, however, shall recognize the authority and right of the National Spiritual Assembly to declare at any time what activities and affairs of the Bahá'í community of . . . are national in scope and hence subject to the jurisdiction of the National Assembly.' And in Article II is stated: '. . . the Spiritual Assembly shall act in conformity with the functions of a Local Spiritual Assembly as defined in the By-Laws adopted by the National Spiritual Assembly . . .'

With respect to those articles that accord final jurisdiction to the National Spiritual Assembly, there is the over-riding provision of Article IX of the National By-Laws: 'Where the National Spiritual Assembly has been given in these By-Laws exclusive and final jurisdiction, and paramount executive authority, in all matters pertaining to the activities and affairs of the Bahá'í Cause in . . . it is understood that any decision made or action taken upon such matters shall be subject in every instance to ultimate review and approval by the Universal House of Justice.'

It is clear, therefore, that the word 'final' is not used in an absolute sense. It is, rather, an indication of the principle enunciated by 'Abdu'l-Bahá that the believers should whole-heartedly and loyally support their Assemblies and abide by their decisions, even if they see them to be in error. At the same time, the Assemblies have the duty to lovingly and frankly consult with those who are under their jurisdiction and, if a believer (or Local Assembly) feels that a serious injustice is being committed or the interests of the Faith are being adversely affected, he has the right of appeal. When an appeal is made, the Assembly whose decision is being questioned should lovingly collaborate in the process and join with the appellant in submitting all relevant information to the higher body for decision.

The whole matter of appeals is clearly summarized in Articles VII and VIII of the By-Laws of the Universal House of Justice.[118]

c) If any differences arise between two or more Local Spiritual Assemblies and if these Assemblies are unable to resolve them, any one such Assembly may bring the matter to the National Spiritual Assembly which shall thereupon take jurisdiction of the case. If the decision of the National Spiritual Assembly thereon is unsatisfactory to any of the Assemblies concerned, or if a Local Spiritual Assembly at any time has reason to believe that actions of its National Spiritual Assembly are affecting adversely the welfare and unity of that Local Assembly's community, it shall, in either case, after seeking to compose its difference of opinion with the National Spiritual Assembly, have the right to appeal to the Universal House of Justice, which shall determine whether it shall take jurisdiction of the matter or leave it within the final jurisdiction of the National Spiritual Assembly.

This paragraph, mirroring very closely the language in Article X, Sections 2 and 3 of the By-Laws of the Local Spiritual Assembly (also see Article VII, Section 11 of the By-Laws of the National Spiritual Assembly), establishes that Local Assemblies also have a right of appeal, in the first instance to their National Spiritual Assembly and afterwards to the Universal House of Justice. An appeal to the latter may be made on the basis that either a) the decision of the National Spiritual Assembly thereon is unsatisfactory or b) the Local Spiritual Assembly has reason to believe that the actions of the National Spiritual Assembly 'are affecting adversely the welfare and unity of that Local Assembly's community'. The Local Spiritual Assemblies concerned should first try to resolve their differences together, and then with the National Spiritual Assembly, before taking the next step in the appeal process.

The National Spiritual Assembly's jurisdiction in these circumstances derives from its 'exclusive jurisdiction and authority over all the activities and affairs of the Bahá'í Cause' throughout its area, stated in Article I of the By-Laws. The jurisdiction of the Universal House of Justice to settle differences between Assemblies derives from its 'powers and duties' to 'deliberate and decide upon all problems which have caused difference' and to 'adjudicate disputes falling within its purview'.[119]

2. **An appellant, whether institution or individual, shall in the first instance make appeal to the Assembly whose decision is questioned, either for reconsideration of the case by that Assembly or for submission to a higher body. In the latter case the Assembly is in duty bound to submit the appeal together with full particulars of the matter. If an Assembly refuses to submit the appeal, or fails to do so within a reasonable time, the appellant may take the case directly to the higher authority.**

This paragraph requires appellants, whether institutions or individuals, to submit their appeals to the Assembly whose decision they are appealing. The appellant may request the Assembly concerned either to reconsider the case or, alternatively, to submit the appeal to a higher body. Where the decision of a Local Spiritual Assembly is appealed, the 'higher body' is the appropriate National Spiritual Assembly; in the case of a decision of a National Spiritual Assembly, the 'higher body' is the Universal House of Justice itself.

The duty of an Assembly to submit an appeal to a higher body is stated in Article X, Section 1 of the By-Laws of the Local Spiritual Assembly and is reaffirmed by the Universal House of Justice:

> . . . if an appeal is turned down by the National Spiritual Assembly, the appellant's request for referral to the Universal House of Justice cannot be refused, nor should the referral be unduly delayed.[120]

Where the Assembly submits an appeal to the higher body, it must also provide full details of the case so that that body is fully informed before considering the matter. The Universal House of Justice has commented on the concept of due process in Bahá'í appeals and in doing so has elucidated this issue of obtaining full information:

> The Administrative Order has not adopted a formal set of procedures to be applied universally in the Bahá'í community for dealing with infringements of Bahá'í law. Rather, the National Spiritual Assembly in its operation is guided and constrained by the Teachings and committed to protect and preserve the rights of both the individual and the community. Hence, while there is no fixed procedure for the discovery of facts necessary for the adjudication of a case, it is a matter of principle that Assemblies must, before passing judgement, acquaint themselves, through means they them-

selves devise, with the facts of any case. The principal motive
is not to condemn and punish the individual but to assist him,
if necessary, to bring his behaviour into conformity with the
Teachings and also to protect the community.[121]

This paragraph in the By-Laws safeguards the rights of the
appellant individual or institution in cases where an Assembly
refuses to submit the appeal to the higher body. This was
emphasized in a letter of the Universal House of Justice to a
National Spiritual Assembly:

> It would seem that your National Assembly has misunder-
> stood the procedure for submitting appeals. Mr. and Mrs. . . .
> were quite correct in sending the appeal to your Assembly
> and you should have then forwarded it to the Universal
> House of Justice together with your comments on the case.
> It is true, as you state in your letter of 26th May 1975,
> that every Bahá'í may write direct to the Universal House of
> Justice but this does not apply in the case of appeals which
> should be submitted through the National Spiritual Assembly.
> Only if the Assembly fails to forward the appeal within a rea-
> sonable time should the appellant take the case directly to the
> Universal House of Justice. This process is explained in Article
> VIII of the Constitution of the Universal House of Justice.[122]

IX. THE BOARDS OF COUNSELLORS

**The institution of the Boards of Counsellors was
brought into being by the Universal House of Justice
to extend into the future the specific functions of
protection and propagation conferred upon the
Hands of the Cause of God. The members of these
boards are appointed by the Universal House of
Justice.**

In a note to paragraph 173 of the Kitáb-i-Aqdas we find the

following helpful explanation of the institution of the Hands of the Cause of God:

> The Hands of the Cause of God were individuals appointed by Bahá'u'lláh and charged with various duties, especially those of protecting and propagating His Faith. In *Memorials of the Faithful* 'Abdu'l-Bahá referred to other outstanding believers as Hands of the Cause, and in His Will and Testament He included a provision calling upon the Guardian of the Faith to appoint Hands of the Cause at his discretion. Shoghi Effendi first raised posthumously a number of the believers to the rank of Hands of the Cause, and during the latter years of his life appointed a total of 32 believers from all continents to this position. In the period between the passing of Shoghi Effendi in 1957 and the election of the Universal House of Justice in 1963, the Hands of the Cause directed the affairs of the Faith in their capacity as Chief Stewards of Bahá'u'lláh's embryonic World Commonwealth . . . In November 1964, the Universal House of Justice determined that it could not legislate to make it possible to appoint Hands of the Cause. Instead, by a decision of the House of Justice in 1968, the functions of the Hands of the Cause in relation to protecting and propagating the Faith were extended into the future by the creation of the Continental Boards of Counsellors, and in 1973 through the establishment of the International Teaching Centre, which has its seat in the Holy Land.[123]

The functions of propagation and protection of the Faith were given to the Hands of the Cause by 'Abdu'l-Bahá in the first Part of His Will and Testament. These passages enjoin upon the Hands the function of protecting the Bahá'í Faith:

> My object is to show that the Hands of the Cause of God must be ever watchful and so soon as they find anyone beginning to oppose and protest against the guardian of the Cause of God, cast him out from the congregation of the people of

186

Bahá and in no wise accept any excuse from him. How often hath grievous error been disguised in the garb of truth, that it might sow the seeds of doubt in the hearts of men! . . .

O friends! The Hands of the Cause of God must be nominated and appointed by the guardian of the Cause of God. All must be under his shadow and obey his command. Should any, within or without the company of the Hands of the Cause of God disobey and seek division, the wrath of God and His vengeance will be upon him, for he will have caused a breach in the true Faith of God.[124]

These passages from the Will and Testament create an obligation on the Hands of the Cause to propagate the Bahá'í Faith:

The obligations of the Hands of the Cause of God are to diffuse the Divine Fragrances, to edify the souls of men, to promote learning, to improve the character of all men and to be, at all times and under all conditions, sanctified and detached from earthly things. They must manifest the fear of God by their conduct, their manners, their deeds and their words.

This body of the Hands of the Cause of God is under the direction of the guardian of the Cause of God. He must continually urge them to strive and endeavour to the utmost of their ability to diffuse the sweet savours of God, and to guide all the peoples of the world, for it is the light of Divine Guidance that causeth all the universe to be illumined.[125]

The above quotation stipulates that the Hands of the Cause were to be appointed by, and responsible to, the Guardian. The passing of Shoghi Effendi without a successor therefore raised several questions in relation to the continuing functioning of the institution of the Hands. The Universal House of Justice referred to these issues early in its ministry, announcing that while it could not 'legislate to make possible the appointment of any more Hands of the Cause', it nevertheless had to 'make provision for the proper discharge in future of the functions of protection and propagation'.[126]

In paragraph 8 of its Declaration of Trust the Universal House of Justice is said to have a duty of 'ensuring the continuing discharge of the functions of protection and propagation vested' in the Hands of the Cause of God. In paragraph 13 of the Declaration of Trust, the House of Justice has the power and duty 'to found institutions'. On 21 June 1968 the Universal House of Justice sent a cable to National Spiritual Assemblies announcing the establishment of Continental Boards of Counsellors.[127] Three days later, on 24 June 1968, the Universal House of Justice elaborated on this decision in a letter to the Bahá'ís of the world:

Following the passing of the Guardian of the Cause of God, it fell to the House of Justice to devise a way, within the Administrative Order, of developing 'the Institution of the Hands of Cause with a view to extension into the future of its appointed functions of protection and propagation', and this was made a goal of the Nine Year Plan. Much thought and study has been give to the question over the past four years, and the texts have been collected and reviewed. During the last two months, this goal, as announced in our cable to the National Conventions, has been the object of prolonged and prayerful consultation between the Universal House of Justice and the Hands of the Cause of God. All this has made evident the framework within which this goal was to be achieve, namely:

The Universal House of Justice sees no way in which additional Hands of the Cause of God can be appointed.

The absence of the Guardian of the Faith brought about an entirely new relationship between the Universal House of Justice and the Hands of the Cause and called for the progressive unfoldment by the Universal House of Justice of the manner in which the Hands of the Cause would carry out their divinely conferred functions of protection and propagation.

Whatever new development or institution is initiated should come into operation as soon as possible in order to reinforce and supplement the work of the Hands of the Cause while at the same time taking full advantage of the opportunity of having the Hands themselves assist in launching and guiding the new procedures.

Any such institution must grow and operate in harmony with the principles governing the functioning of the Institution of the Hands of the Cause of God.

In the light of these considerations the Universal House of Justice decided . . . to establish Continental Boards of Counsellors for the protection and propagation of the Faith. Their duties will include directing the Auxiliary Boards in their respective areas, consulting and collaborating with National Spiritual Assemblies, and keeping the Hands of the Cause and the Universal House of Justice informed concerning the conditions of the Cause in their areas.[128]

The first appointments to the Continental Boards of Counsellors were in 1968[129] and the Universal House of Justice issued an important elucidation of their functions in 1972.[130] A document issued by the Universal House of Justice in 2001, called *The Institution of the Counsellors*, summarizes the guidance of the House of Justice regarding the role played by the members of this institution and its relationship with the other bodies in the Administrative Order of the Bahá'í Faith. This document should be studied for more details of the functioning of the Counsellors.

1. The term of office of a Counsellor, the number of Counsellors on each Board, and the boundaries of the zone in which each Board of Counsellors shall operate, shall be decided by the Universal House of Justice.

The details of the functioning of the Counsellors have varied over time, in accordance with the authority of the Universal House of Justice to abrogate its own enactments (see paragraph 12 of the Declaration of Trust, and annotations). In 1968 the Universal House of Justice established 11 Boards, with 36 Counsellors altogether; the term of office of these initial appointments was not specified.[131] In 1969 the number of Counsellors was raised to 38[132] and in 1973 the House of Justice expanded this institution to 54 Counsellors, operating in 12 zones.[133] In 1979 the House announced that the term of office of the Counsellors would be five years, starting from the Day of the Covenant on 26 November 1980.[134]

In 1980, in a further step in the maturation of the institution of the Counsellors, the Universal House of Justice reduced the number of zones to five (Africa, the Americas, Asia, Australasia and Europe) and increased the number of Counsellors to 63.[135] In 1985 the number of Counsellors was increased from 63 to 72 and adjustments were made in their geographical distribution.[136] In 1986 Turkey was transferred from the area of responsibility of the Continental Board of Counsellors in Asia to that of the Continental Board of Counsellors in Europe.[137] The geographical distribution of Counsellors in the various zones was further adjusted in 1990, though the total number remained 72.[138] The zones of the Continental Boards of Counsellors are unchanged today but there are now 81 Continental Counsellors worldwide.

2. A Counsellor functions as such only within his zone and should he move his residence out of the zone for which he is appointed he automatically relinquishes his appointment.

As well as only being appointed for a specific term, Counsellors differ from Hands of the Cause of God in that the former only operate as such within the continental zones in which they have been appointed to serve. In contrast, the Hands of the Cause operate worldwide. Compare this with Article X, Section 1 of the By-Laws, below, dealing with the residence of Auxiliary Board members.

3. The rank and specific duties of a Counsellor render him ineligible for service on local or national administrative bodies. If elected to the Universal House of Justice he ceases to be a Counsellor.

When the institution of the Continental Boards of Counsellors was first established the Universal House of Justice made it clear that, while serving in that capacity, the members of the Boards would 'not be eligible for membership on national or local administrative bodies'.[139] There is one exception to this rule:

> Should the membership of a community drop to nine, a Counsellor may serve temporarily on the Local Spiritual Assembly, and as an officer if so elected, until a replacement is available.[140]

In contrast, a Counsellor may be elected to the Universal House of Justice but then ceases to be a Counsellor. Compare this with Article X, Section 3 of the By-Laws of the Universal House of Justice, below, dealing with the eligibility of Auxiliary Board members for elective offices.

In 1978 the House of Justice explained the implications of the statement that 'the Boards of Counsellors outrank the National Institutions of the Faith':

> A Board of Counsellors has the particular responsibility of caring for the protection and propagation of the Faith throughout a continental zone which contains a number of national Bahá'í communities. In performing these tasks it neither directs nor instructs the Spiritual Assemblies or individual believers, but it has the necessary rank to enable

it to ensure that it is kept properly informed and that the Spiritual Assemblies give due consideration to its advice and recommendations. However, the essence of the relationships between Bahá'í institutions is loving consultation and a common desire to serve the Cause of God rather than a matter of rank or station.[141]

X. THE AUXILIARY BOARDS

In each zone there shall be two Auxiliary Boards, one for the protection and one for the propagation of the Faith, the numbers of whose members shall be set by the Universal House of Justice. The members of these Auxiliary Boards shall serve under the direction of the Continental Boards of Counsellors and shall act as their deputies, assistants and advisers.

In 1952 Shoghi Effendi directed the Hands of the Cause to appoint, at Riḍván 1954, five Auxiliary Boards – one in each continent, with nine members each. These Auxiliary Boards were to act as their 'adjuncts, or deputies' and would assist the Hands of the Cause of God in 'the efficient, prompt execution' of the Ten Year Crusade.[142] In early 1954 Shoghi Effendi wrote:

The hour is ripe for the fifteen Hands residing outside the Holy Land to proceed during Riḍván with the appointment, in each continent separately, from among the resident Bahá'ís of that Continent, of Auxiliary Boards, whose members, acting as **deputies, assistants and advisers** of the Hands, must increasingly lend their assistance for the promotion of the interests of the Ten Year Crusade.[143]

In April 1954 the Guardian predicted that the duties of these Auxiliary Boards would in the future assist the Hands of the Cause 'in the discharge of their dual and sacred task of safeguarding the Faith and of promoting its teaching activities'.[144] In October 1957 Shoghi Effendi called for the Hands of the Cause to appoint:

> . . . an additional Auxiliary Board, equal in membership to the existing one, and charged with the specific duty of watching over the security of the Faith, thereby complementing the function of the original Board, whose duty will henceforth be exclusively concerned with assisting the prosecution of the Ten-Year Plan.[145]

When the Continental Boards of Counsellors were created in 1968 they were given the responsibility of directing the Auxiliary Boards for Protection and Propagation in close collaboration with the Hands of the Cause.[146] The Auxiliary Boards were thenceforth to report to the Continental Boards of Counsellors, who would also appoint their members.[147]

In 1973, the year following the publication of its Constitution, the Universal House of Justice raised the number of Auxiliary Board members worldwide to 270; 81 of this number were for Protection and 189 for Propagation.[148] Also in 1973 the Universal House of Justice decided to give to each Continental Board of Counsellors the discretion to authorize individual Auxiliary Board members to appoint assistants:

> The exact nature of the duties and the duration of the appointment of the assistants is also left to each Continental Board to decide for itself. Their aims should be to activate and encourage Local Spiritual Assemblies, to call the attention of Local Spiritual Assembly members to the importance of holding regular meetings, to encourage local communities to meet for the Nineteen Day Feasts and Holy Days, to help deepen their fellow-believers' understanding of the Teachings, and generally to assist the Auxiliary Board members in the discharge of their duties.[149]

Since 1973 the Universal House of Justice has raised incrementally the worldwide number of Auxiliary Board members. Since 1997 the number of Auxiliary Board members worldwide has been 990: 495 for Protection and 495 for Propagation.

Extracts from other important messages about the functions of the Auxiliary Board members and their assistants can be found in the compilation *Lights of Guidance*.[150] *The Institution of the Counsellors* likewise summarizes the guidance received from the Universal House of Justice regarding the duties and activities of the Auxiliary Board members and their assistants.

1. The members of the Auxiliary Boards shall be appointed from among the believers of that zone by the Continental Board of Counsellors.

As with the Continental Counsellors, Auxiliary Board members must reside within the continental zone that they serve: compare this with Article IX, Section 2 of the By-Laws above dealing with the residence of Counsellors. It is not strictly necessary that Auxiliary Board members reside within the specific area they are allotted (see Section 2 below). This is likely to be an important consideration, however, as the Universal House of Justice wrote in a letter to the International Teaching Centre on 4 February 1976:

> As you know, the beloved Guardian repeatedly emphasized the importance of Auxiliary Board members' visiting Assemblies and groups in the respective areas served by them. While details concerning the appointment and functioning of the members of Auxiliary Boards are left to the Counsellors, in light of the Guardian's instructions cited above, they should take into consideration, in making a new appointment, the advisability of that appointee residing in the area which he serves.[151]

The guidance regarding the appointment of Auxiliary Board members is summarized here:

The members of the Auxiliary Boards are appointed from among the believers of each continent by the Continental Board of Counsellors for five-year periods beginning on the Day of the Covenant of the year following the appointment of the Counsellors themselves. They should be twenty-one years of age or older. The full membership of the Continental Board makes the appointments in consultation, which, if necessary, can be carried out by mail.

The members of an Auxiliary Board are responsible individually to the Board of Counsellors which appoints them.[152]

2. Each Auxiliary Board member shall be allotted a specific area in which to serve and, unless specifically deputized by the Counsellors, shall not function as a member of the Auxiliary Board outside that area.

The areas which Auxiliary Board members serve are allotted to them by the Continental Boards of Counsellors that appoint them. The Universal House of Justice has explained, in general terms, the duties of Auxiliary Board members within their allotted areas:

Each Auxiliary Board Member who is allotted a specific area in which to serve, should establish contact with the Local Spiritual Assemblies and other localities of his area, encourage and guide all such centres in the implementation of the goals of the Plan, become informed of the relative strength and weakness of each locality, and feel responsible before God in the discharge of his responsibilities. Should he lose contact with a particular Local Spiritual Assembly or locality, he should use his initiative in finding a satisfactory solution to the problem. He should also send his reports and recommendations to the Counsellors on a regular basis.[153]

It is interesting to note that an Auxiliary Board member's allotted area may straddle two or more countries:

Each Auxiliary Board member is assigned a specific territory, and although for practical purposes such a territory may coincide with a particular country or National Assembly area, there is no hard and fast rule that it must do so. Auxiliary Boards are continental institutions, and there need not be any correlation between the boundaries of the territories assigned to their members and national frontiers . . . For obvious reasons, it is preferable for Auxiliary Board members to reside in the area they serve; however, if an area has no suitable candidate for this post, the Counsellors may decide to make an alternative arrangement.[154]

3. An Auxiliary Board member is eligible for any elective office but if elected to an administrative post on a national or local level must decide whether to retain membership on the Board or accept the administrative post, since he may not serve in both capacities at the same time. If elected to the Universal House of Justice he ceases to be a member of the Auxiliary Board.

An Auxiliary Board member who has been elected to a Local or National Spiritual Assembly, or a member of an Assembly who has been appointed to serve on an Auxiliary Board, must choose which path of service he or she will take. As with the Continental Counsellors, an Auxiliary Board member who is elected to the Universal House of Justice ceases to be a Board member: see Article IX, Section 3 of the By-Laws of the Universal House of Justice, above, on the eligibility of Counsellors for elective positions.

As with the Continental Counsellors, there is one exceptional circumstance in which an Auxiliary Board member may serve on a Local Spiritual Assembly, as explained by the Universal House of Justice in a letter to the National Spiritual Assembly of the United States in 1966:

In all three areas of election, Auxiliary Board members are eligible to be elected. Therefore, a ballot should not be invalidated because it contains the name of a member of an Auxiliary Board. The basic principle involved is that the Board member himself must decide whether or not to accept his election. As you have stated in your letter, if the membership in a Bahá'í community drops to nine, including the Auxiliary Board member resident there, the Auxiliary Board member may serve temporarily as a member of the Assembly to preserve its Assembly status.[155]

XI. AMENDMENT

This Constitution may be amended by decision of the Universal House of Justice when the full membership is present.

The Universal House of Justice is free to amend its own Constitution. For it to do so, all nine members of the House of Justice must be present. However, Article XI does not require a unanimous decision: a majority of the Universal House of Justice will suffice to amend the Constitution. This is consistent with this promise of 'Abdu'l-Bahá in His Will and Testament that all of the decisions of the Universal House of Justice will be divinely guided, without any requirement of consensus among its members: 'That which this body, whether unanimously or by a majority doth carry, that is verily the Truth and the Purpose of God Himself.'[155]

6

Questions and Exercises on the By-Laws

Discussion Questions and Exercises

1. What are the 'elected councils, universal, secondary and local' referred to in the Preamble to the By-Laws?

2. What are the differences between 'legislative', 'executive' and 'judicial' powers?

3. Look again at the powers and duties of the Universal House of Justice as enumerated in the Declaration of Trust. Try to categorize each of these as either 'legislative', 'executive' or 'judicial' in nature.

4. Do the same exercise with the Local Spiritual Assembly By-Laws at appendix II and the National Spiritual Assembly Declaration of Trust and By-Laws at appendix III. Try to categorize the powers and duties of each of these institutions as either 'legislative', 'executive' or 'judicial' in nature.

5. What are the 'qualifications of Bahá'í faith and practice'?

6. How many stages are there in the election of the Universal

House of Justice? Explain what these stages are and why they are required by the Bahá'í writings.

7. Make a numbered list of 'the most outstanding and sacred duties' of the members of Spiritual Assemblies, as listed in the Article IV of the By-Laws. Try to find other passages in the Bahá'í writings that describe special duties of these institutions and their members.

8. Why is it not possible to vote by proxy or assign one's vote in a Bahá'í election?

9. What procedure should you follow if an Assembly takes a decision or action that you feel is incorrect, harmful or detrimental to the Faith?

10. Why was the institution of the Counsellors brought into being?

11. What are the duties of the Auxiliary Boards for Protection and Propagation? How do they differ?

12. What limitations are there, if any, on the ability of the Universal House of Justice to amend its own Constitution? What aspects of the Constitution can be changed? What aspects cannot be changed, even by the Universal House of Justice itself?

Self-Testing Quiz

1. What two qualities describe the believers who are appointed for the specific purposes of protecting and propagating the Faith under the guidance of the Universal House of Justice?

2. Complete this sentence: The Bahá'í 'Administrative Order is the _____ and _____ of the World Order adumbrated by Bahá'u'lláh.'

3. How old do you have to be to vote and be elected to a Spiritual Assembly in the Bahá'í community?

4. How many Bahá'ís must there be in a local community before the Local Spiritual Assembly can be formed?

5. Who decides when a National Spiritual Assembly should be formed and what area each National Spiritual Assembly should have jurisdiction over?

6. Complete this sentence: The National Spiritual Assembly 'shall endeavour to _____, _____ ____ and coordinate the manifold activities of the Local Spiritual Assemblies and of individual Bahá'ís in its area and by all possible means assist them to promote the ____ _____ of _____.'

7. What is the principal business of National Bahá'í Conventions?

8. Who elects National Spiritual Assemblies?

9. How often is the Universal House of Justice elected?

10. Who elects the Universal House of Justice?

11. In what four ways can a vacancy arise in the membership of the Universal House of Justice?

12. What is the signature of the Universal House of Justice in Persian?

13. Complete these sentences: In 'Bahá'í elections, the practices of _____ or electioneering . . . shall be eschewed. A _____ and _____ ___ atmosphere shall prevail so that each elector may vote for none but those whom _____ and _____ inspire him to uphold.'

14. Which were created first, the Counsellors or the Auxiliary Boards?

15. Who created the Auxiliary Boards?

16. How many Auxiliary Boards are there in any zone?

17. How can the Constitution of the Universal House of Justice be amended?

Appendix 1

The Constitution of the Universal House of Justice

Declaration of Trust

IN THE NAME OF GOD, THE ONE, THE INCOMPARABLE, THE
ALL-POWERFUL, THE ALL-KNOWING, THE ALL-WISE.

*The light that is shed from the heaven of bounty, and the benediction
that shineth from the dawning-place of the will of God, the Lord of
the Kingdom of Names, rest upon Him Who is the Supreme Mediator,
the Most Exalted Pen, Him Whom God hath made the dawning-place
of His most excellent names and the dayspring of His most exalted
attributes. Through Him the light of unity hath shone forth above the
horizon of the world, and the law of oneness hath been revealed amidst
the nations, who, with radiant faces, have turned towards the Supreme
Horizon, and acknowledged that which the Tongue of Utterance hath
spoken in the kingdom of His knowledge: 'Earth and heaven, glory and
dominion, are God's, the Omnipotent, the Almighty, the Lord of grace
abounding!'*

With joyous and thankful hearts we testify to the abundance of
God's Mercy, to the perfection of His Justice and to the fulfilment of His Ancient Promise.

Bahá'u'lláh, the Revealer of God's Word in this Day, the

Source of Authority, the Fountainhead of Justice, the Creator of a new World Order, the Establisher of the Most Great Peace, the Inspirer and Founder of a world civilization, the Judge, the Lawgiver, the Unifier and Redeemer of all mankind, has proclaimed the advent of God's Kingdom on earth, has formulated its laws and ordinances, enunciated its principles, and ordained its institutions. To direct and canalize the forces released by His Revelation He instituted His Covenant, whose power has preserved the integrity of His Faith, maintained its unity and stimulated it world-wide expansion throughout the successive ministries of 'Abdu'l-Bahá and Shoghi Effendi. It continues to fulfil its life-giving purpose through the agency of the Universal House of Justice whose fundamental object, as one of the twin successors of Bahá'u'lláh and 'Abdu'l-Bahá, is to ensure the continuity of that divinely-appointed authority which flows from the Source of Faith, to safeguard the unity of its followers and to maintain the integrity and flexibility of its teachings.

The fundamental purpose animating the Faith of God and His Religion, declares Bahá'u'lláh, *is to safeguard the interests and promote the unity of the human race, and to foster the spirit of love and fellowship amongst men. Suffer it not to become a source of dissension and discord, of hate and enmity. This is the straight Path, the fixed and immovable foundation. Whatsoever is raised on this foundation, the changes and chances of the world can never impair its strength, nor will the revolution of countless centuries undermine its structure.*

Unto the Most Holy Book, 'Abdu'l-Bahá declares in His Will and Testament, *every one must turn, and all that is not expressly recorded therein must be referred to the Universal House of Justice.*

The provenance, the authority, the duties, the sphere of action of the Universal House of Justice all derive from the revealed Word of Bahá'u'lláh which, together with the interpretations and expositions of the Centre of the Covenant and the Guardian of the Cause – who, after 'Abdu'l-Bahá, is the sole authority in the interpretation of Bahá'í Scripture – constitute the binding terms of reference of the Universal

House of Justice and are its bedrock foundation. The authority of these Texts is absolute and immutable until such time as Almighty God shall reveal His new Manifestation to Whom will belong all authority and power.

There being no successor to Shoghi Effendi as Guardian of the Cause of God, the Universal House of Justice is the Head of the Faith and its supreme institution, to which all must turn, and on it rests the ultimate responsibility for ensuring the unity and progress of the Cause of God. Further, there devolve upon it duties of directing and coordinating the work of the Hands of the Cause, of ensuring the continuing discharge of the functions of protection and propagation vested in the institution, and of providing for the receipt and disbursement of the Ḥuqúqu'lláh.

Among the powers and duties with which the Universal House of Justice has been invested are:

To ensure the preservation of the Sacred Texts and to safeguard their inviolability; to analyze, classify, and coordinate the Writings; and to defend and protect the Cause of God and emancipate it from the fetters of repression and persecution;

To advance the interests of the Faith of God; to proclaim, propagate and teach its Message; to expand and consolidate the institutions of its Administrative Order; to usher in the World Order of Bahá'u'lláh; to promote the attainment of those spiritual qualities which should characterize Bahá'í life individually and collectively; to do its utmost for the realization of greater cordiality and comity amongst the nations and for the attainment of universal peace; and to foster that which is conducive to the enlightenment and illumination of the souls of men and the advancement and betterment of the world;

To enact laws and ordinances not expressly recorded in the Sacred Texts; to abrogate, according to the changes and requirements of the time, its own enactments; to deliberate and decide upon all problems which have caused difference;

to elucidate questions that are obscure; to safeguard the personal rights, freedom and initiative of individuals; and to give attention to the preservation of human honour, to the development of countries and the stability of states;

To promulgate and apply the laws and principles of the Faith; to safeguard and enforce that rectitude of conduct which the Law of God enjoins; to preserve and develop the Spiritual and Administrative Centre of the Bahá'í Faith, permanently fixed in the twin cities of 'Akká and Haifa; to administer the affairs of the Bahá'í community throughout the world; to guide, organize, coordinate and unify its activities; to found institutions; to be responsible for ensuring that no body or institution within the Cause abuse its privileges or decline in the exercise of its rights and prerogatives; and to provide for the receipt, disposition, administration and safeguarding of the funds, endowments and other properties that are entrusted to its care;

To adjudicate disputes falling within its purview; to give judgement in cases of violation of the laws of the Faith and to pronounce sanctions for such violations; to provide for the enforcement of its decisions; to provide for the arbitration and settlement of disputes arising between peoples; and to be the exponent and guardian of that Divine Justice which can alone ensure the security of, and establish the reign of law and order in, the world.

The members of the Universal House of Justice, designated by Bahá'u'lláh 'the Men of Justice', 'the people of Bahá who have been mentioned in the Book of Names', 'the Trustees of God amongst His servants and the daysprings of authority in His countries', shall in the discharge of their responsibilities ever bear in mind the following standards set forth by Shoghi Effendi, the Guardian of the Cause of God:

'In the conduct of the administrative affairs of the Faith, in the enactment of the legislation necessary to supplement the laws of the Kitáb-i-Aqdas, the members of the Universal House of Justice, it should be borne in mind, are not, as Bahá'u'lláh's utterances clearly imply, responsible to those whom they represent, nor are they allowed to be governed by the feelings, the general opinion, and even the convictions of the mass of the faithful, or of those who directly elect them. They are to follow, in a prayerful attitude, the dictates and promptings of their conscience. They may, indeed they must, acquaint themselves with the conditions prevailing among the community, must weigh dispassionately in their minds the merits of any case presented for their consideration, but must reserve for themselves the right of an unfettered decision. *"God will verily inspire them with whatsoever He willeth"*, is Bahá'u'lláh's incontrovertible assurance. They, and not the body of those who either directly or indirectly elect them, have thus been made the recipients of the divine guidance which is at once the life-blood and ultimate safeguard of this Revelation.'

The Universal House of Justice was first elected on the first day of the Festival of Riḍván in the one hundred and twentieth year of the Bahá'í Era [21 April 1963 AD], when the members of the National Spiritual Assemblies, in accordance with the provisions of the Will and Testament of 'Abdu'l-Bahá, and in response to the summons of the Hands of the Cause of God, the Chief Stewards of Bahá'u'lláh's embryonic World Commonwealth, brought into being this 'crowning glory' of the administrative institutions of Bahá'u'lláh, the very 'nucleus and forerunner' of His World Order. Now, therefore, in obedience to the Command of God and with entire reliance upon Him, we, the members of the Universal House of Justice, set our hands and its seal to this Declaration of Trust which, together with the By-Laws hereto appended, form the Constitution of the Universal House of Justice.

[signed]

Hugh E. Chance
Hushmand Fatheazam
Amoz E. Gibson
David Hofman
H. Borrah Kavelin
Ali Nakhjavani
David S. Ruhe
Ian C. Semple
Charles Wolcott

Signed in the city of Haifa on the fourth day of the month of Qawl in the one hundred and twenty-ninth year of the Bahá'í Era, corresponding to the twenty-sixth day of the month of November in the year 1972 according to the Gregorian calendar.

[seal affixed]

By-Laws

Preamble

The Universal House of Justice is the supreme institution of an Administrative Order whose salient features, whose authority and whose principles of operation are clearly enunciated in the Sacred Writings of the Bahá'í Faith and their authorized interpretations. This Administrative Order consists, on the one hand, of a series of elected councils, universal, secondary and local, in which are vested legislative, executive and judicial powers over the Bahá'í community and, on the other, of eminent and devoted believers appointed for the specific purposes of protecting and propagating the Faith of Bahá'u'lláh under the guidance of the Head of that Faith.

This Administrative Order is the nucleus and pattern of the World Order adumbrated by Bahá'u'lláh. In the course of its divinely propelled organic growth its institutions will expand, putting forth auxiliary branches and developing subordinate agencies, multiplying their activities and diversifying their functions, in consonance with the principles and purposes revealed by Bahá'u'lláh for the progress of the human race.

I. Membership in the Bahá'í Community

The Bahá'í community shall consist of all persons recognized by the Universal House of Justice as possessing the qualifications of Bahá'í faith and practice.

1. In order to be eligible to vote and hold elective office, a Bahá'í must have attained the age of twenty-one years.

2. The rights, privileges and duties of individual Bahá'ís are as set forth in the Writings of Bahá'u'lláh, 'Abdu'l-Bahá and Shoghi Effendi and as laid down by the Universal House of Justice.

II. Local Spiritual Assemblies

Whenever in any locality the number of Bahá'ís resident therein who have attained the age of twenty-one exceeds nine, these shall on the First Day of Riḍván convene and elect a local administrative body of nine members to be known as the Spiritual Assembly of the Bahá'ís of that locality. Every such Spiritual Assembly shall be elected annually thereafter upon each successive First Day of Riḍván. The members shall hold office for the term of one year or until their successors are elected. When, however, the number of Bahá'ís as aforesaid in any locality is exactly nine, these shall on the First Day of Riḍván constitute themselves the Local Spiritual Assembly by joint declaration.

1. The general powers and duties of a Local Spiritual Assembly are as set forth in the Writings of Bahá'u'lláh, 'Abdu'l-Bahá and Shoghi Effendi and as laid down by the Universal House of Justice.

2. A Local Spiritual Assembly shall exercise full jurisdiction

over all Bahá'í activities and affairs within its locality, subject to the provisions of the Local Bahá'í Constitution [By-Laws of a Local Spiritual Assembly].

3. The area of jurisdiction of a Local Spiritual Assembly shall be decided by the National Spiritual Assembly in accordance with the principle laid down for each country by the Universal House of Justice.

III. National Spiritual Assemblies

Whenever it is decided by the Universal House of Justice to form in any country or region a National Spiritual Assembly, the voting members of the Bahá'í community of that country or region shall, in a manner and at a time to be decided by the Universal House of Justice, elect their delegates to their National Convention. These delegates shall, in turn, elect in the manner provided in the National Bahá'í Constitution [Declaration of Trust and By-Laws of a National Spiritual Assembly] a body of nine members to be known as the National Spiritual Assembly of the Bahá'ís of that country or region. The members shall continue in office for a period of one year or until their successors shall be elected.

1. The general powers and duties of a National Spiritual Assembly are as set forth in the Writings of 'Abdu'l-Bahá and Shoghi Effendi and as laid down by the Universal House of Justice.

2. The National Spiritual Assembly shall have exclusive jurisdiction and authority over all the activities and affairs of the Bahá'í Faith throughout its area. It shall endeavour to stimulate, unify and coordinate the manifold activities of the Local Spiritual Assemblies and of individual Bahá'ís in its area and by all possible means assist them to promote the oneness of mankind. It shall furthermore represent its national Bahá'í community in relation to

other national Bahá'í communities and to the Universal House of Justice.

3. The area of jurisdiction of a National Spiritual Assembly shall be as defined by the Universal House of Justice.

4. The principal business of the National Convention shall be consultation on Bahá'í activities, plans and policies and the election of the members of the National Spiritual Assembly, as set forth in the National Bahá'í Constitution.

    a) If in any year the National Spiritual Assembly shall consider that it is impracticable or unwise to hold the National Convention, the said Assembly shall provide ways and means by which the annual election and the other essential business of the Convention may be conducted.

    b) Vacancies in the membership of the National Spiritual Assembly shall be filled by a vote of the delegates composing the Convention which elected the Assembly, the ballot to be taken by correspondence or in any other manner decided by the National Spiritual Assembly.

IV. Obligations of Members of Spiritual Assemblies

Among the most outstanding and sacred duties incumbent upon those who have been called upon to initiate, direct and coordinate the affairs of the Cause of God as members of its Spiritual Assemblies are: to win by every means in their power the confidence and affection of those whom it is their privilege to serve; to investigate and acquaint themselves with the considered views, the prevailing sentiments and the personal convictions of those whose welfare it is their solemn obligation to promote; to purge their deliberations and the general conduct of their affairs of self-contained aloofness, the suspicion of secrecy, the stifling atmosphere of dictatorial assertiveness and of every word and deed that may savour of partiality, self-centredness and prejudice; and while retaining the sacred right of final decision in their hands, to invite discussion, ventilate grievances, welcome advice and foster the sense of interdependence and co-partnership, of understanding and mutual confidence between themselves and all other Bahá'ís.

V. The Universal House of Justice

The Universal House of Justice shall consist of nine men who have been elected from the Bahá'í community in the manner hereinafter provided.

1. *Election*

The members of the Universal House of Justice shall be elected by secret ballot by the members of all National Spiritual Assemblies at a meeting to be known as the International Bahá'í Convention.

a) An election of the Universal House of Justice shall be held once every five years unless otherwise decided by the Universal House of Justice, and those elected shall continue in office until such time as their successors shall be elected and the first meeting of these successors is duly held.

b) Upon receiving the call to Convention each National Spiritual Assembly shall submit to the Universal House of Justice a list of the names of its members. The recognition and seating of the delegates to the International Convention shall be vested in the Universal House of Justice.

c) The principal business of the International Convention shall be to elect the members of the Universal House of Justice, to deliberate on the affairs of the Bahá'í Cause throughout the world, and to make recommendations and suggestions for the consideration of the Universal House of Justice.

d) The sessions of the International Convention shall be conducted in such manner as the Universal House of Justice shall from time to time decide.

e) The Universal House of Justice shall provide a procedure whereby those delegates who are unable to be present in person at the International Convention shall cast their ballots for the election of the members of the Universal House of Justice.

f) If at the time of an election the Universal House of Justice shall consider that it is impracticable or unwise to hold the International Convention it shall determine how the election shall take place.

g) On the day of the election the ballots of all voters shall be scrutinized and counted and the result certified by tellers appointed in accordance with the instructions of the Universal House of Justice.

h) If a member of a National Spiritual Assembly who has voted by mail ceases to be a member of that National Spiritual Assembly between the time of casting his ballot and the date of the counting of the ballots, his ballot shall nevertheless remain valid unless in the interval his successor shall have been elected and the ballot of such successor shall have been received by the tellers.

i) In case by reason of a tie vote or votes the full membership of the Universal House of Justice is not determined on the first ballot, then one or more additional ballots shall be held on the persons tied until all members are elected.

The electors in the case of additional ballots shall be the members of National Spiritual Assemblies in office at the time each subsequent vote is taken.

2. *Vacancies in Membership*

A vacancy in the membership of the Universal House of Justice will occur upon the death of a member or in the following cases:

a) Should any member of the Universal House of Justice commit a sin injurious to the common weal, he may be dismissed from membership by the Universal House of Justice.

b) The Universal House of Justice may at its discretion declare a vacancy with respect to any member who in its judgement is unable to fulfil the functions of membership.

c) A member may relinquish his membership on the Universal House of Justice only with the approval of the Universal House of Justice

3. *By-Election*

If a vacancy in the membership of the Universal House of Justice occurs, the Universal House of Justice shall call a by-election at the earliest possible date unless such date, in the judgement of the Universal House of Justice, falls too close to the date of a regular election of the entire membership, in which case the Universal House of Justice may, at its discretion, defer the filling of the vacancy to the time of the regular election. If a by-election is held, the voters shall be the members of the National Spiritual Assemblies in office at the time of the by-election.

4. *Meetings*

a) After the election of the Universal House of Justice the

first meeting shall be called by the member elected by the highest number of votes or, in his absence or other incapacity, by the member elected by the next highest number of votes or, in case two or more members have received the same highest number of votes, then by the member selected by lot from among those members. Subsequent meetings shall be called in the manner decided by the Universal House of Justice.

b) The Universal House of Justice has no officers. It shall provide for the conduct of its meetings and shall organize its activities in such manner as it shall from time to time decide.

c) The business of the Universal House of Justice shall be conducted by the full membership in consultation, except that the Universal House of Justice may from time to time provide for quorums of less than the full membership for specified classes of business.

5. *Signature*

The signature of the Universal House of Justice shall be the words 'The Universal House of Justice' or in Persian 'Baytu'l-'Adl-i-A'ẓam' written by hand by any one of its members upon authority of the Universal House of Justice, to which shall be affixed in each case the Seal of the Universal House of Justice.

6. *Records*

The Universal House of Justice shall provide for the recording and verification of its decisions in such manner as shall, from time to time, judge necessary.

VI. Bahá'í Elections

In order to preserve the spiritual character and purpose of Bahá'í elections the practices of nomination or electioneering, or any other procedure or activity detrimental to that character and purpose shall be eschewed. A silent and prayerful atmosphere shall prevail during the election so that each elector may vote for none but those whom prayer and reflection inspire him to uphold.

1. All Bahá'í elections, except elections of officers of Local and National Spiritual Assemblies and committees, shall be by plurality vote taken by secret ballot.

2. Election of the officers of a Spiritual Assembly or committee shall be by a majority vote of the Assembly or committee taken by secret ballot.

3. In case by reason of a tie vote or votes the full membership of an elected body is not determined on the first ballot, then one or more additional ballots shall be taken on the persons tied until all members are elected.

4. The duties and rights of a Bahá'í elector may not be assigned nor may they be exercised by proxy.

VII. The Right of Review

The Universal House of Justice has the right to review any decision or action of any Spiritual Assembly, National or Local, and to approve, modify or reverse such decision or action. The Universal House of Justice also has the right to intervene in any matter in which a Spiritual Assembly is failing to take action or to reach a decision and, at its discretion, to require that action be taken, or itself to take action directly in the matter.

VIII. Appeals

The right of appeal exists in the circumstances, and shall be exercised according to the procedures, outlined below:

1. a) Any member of a local Bahá'í community may appeal

from a decision of his Local Spiritual Assembly to the National Spiritual Assembly which shall determine whether it shall take jurisdiction of the matter or refer it back to the Local Spiritual Assembly for reconsideration. If such an appeal concerns the membership of a person in the Bahá'í community, the National Spiritual Assembly is obliged to take jurisdiction of and decide the case.

b) Any Bahá'í may appeal from a decision of his National Spiritual Assembly to the Universal House of Justice which shall determine whether it shall take jurisdiction of the matter or leave it within the final jurisdiction of the National Spiritual Assembly.

c) If any differences arise between two or more Local Spiritual Assemblies and if these Assemblies are unable to resolve them, any one such Assembly may bring the matter to the National Spiritual Assembly which shall thereupon take jurisdiction of the case. If the decision of the National Spiritual Assembly thereon is unsatisfactory to any of the Assemblies concerned, or if a Local Spiritual Assembly at any time has reason to believe that actions of its National Spiritual Assembly are affecting adversely the welfare and unity of that Local Assembly's community, it shall, in either case, after seeking to compose its difference of opinion with the National Spiritual Assembly, have the right to appeal to the Universal House of Justice, which shall determine whether it shall take jurisdiction of the matter or leave it within the final jurisdiction of the National Spiritual Assembly.

2. An appellant, whether institution or individual, shall in the first instance make appeal to the Assembly whose decision is questioned, either for reconsideration of the case by that Assembly or for submission to a higher body.

In the latter case the Assembly is in duty bound to submit the appeal together with full particulars of the matter. If an Assembly refuses to submit the appeal, or fails to do so within a reasonable time, the appellant may take the case directly to the higher authority.

IX. The Boards of Counsellors

The institution of the Boards of Counsellors was brought into being by the Universal House of Justice to extend into the future the specific functions of protection and propagation conferred upon the Hands of the Cause of God. The members of these Boards are appointed by the Universal House of Justice.

1. The term of office of a Counsellor, the number of Counsellors on each Board, and the boundaries of the zone in which each Board of Counsellors shall operate, shall be decided by the Universal House of Justice.

2. A Counsellor functions as such only within his zone and should he move his residence out of the zone for which he is appointed he automatically relinquishes his appointment.

3. The rank and specific duties of a Counsellor render him ineligible for service on local and national administrative bodies. If elected to the Universal House of Justice he ceases to be a Counsellor.

X. The Auxiliary Boards

In each zone there shall be two Auxiliary Boards, one for the protection and one for the propagation of the Faith, the numbers of whose members shall be set by the Universal House of Justice. The members of these Auxiliary Boards shall serve under the direction of the Continental Boards of Counsellors and shall act as their deputies, assistants and advisers.

1. The members of the Auxiliary Boards shall be appointed

from among the believers of that zone by the Continental Board of Counsellors.

2. Each Auxiliary Board member shall be allotted a specific area in which to serve and, unless specifically deputized by the Counsellors, shall not function as a member of the Auxiliary Board outside that area.

3. An Auxiliary Board member is eligible for any elective office but if elected to an administrative post on a national or local level must decide whether to retain membership on the Board or accept the administrative post, since he may not serve in both capacities at the same time. If elected to the Universal House of Justice he ceases to be a member of the Auxiliary Board.

XI. Amendment

This Constitution may be amended by decision of the Universal House of Justice when the full membership is present.

Appendix II

By-Laws of a Local Spiritual Assembly[1]

WE, the undersigned members of the Spiritual Assembly of the Bahá'ís of . . . , desiring to incorporate this body do hereby adopt the following By-Laws:

ARTICLE I

The Trustees, i.e., the members of the Spiritual Assembly, recognize that this action has been taken in full unanimity and agreement. They acknowledge for themselves and on behalf of their successors the sacred meaning and universal purpose of the Bahá'í Faith, the teachings and principles of which fulfil the divine promise of all former revealed religions.

ARTICLE II

In administering the affairs of the Bahá'í religion under this Corporation for the benefit of the Bahá'ís of . . . in accordance with the religious teachings and administrative principles of this Faith, the Spiritual Assembly shall act in conformity with the functions of a Local Spiritual Assembly as defined in the By-Laws adopted by the National Spiritual Assembly and published by that body for the information and guidance of Bahá'ís throughout . . . [Name of country or region].

ARTICLE III

The Spiritual Assembly, in the fulfilment of its obligations and responsibilities under this Corporation, shall have exclusive jurisdiction and authority over all the local activities and affairs of the Bahá'í community of . . . , including paramount authority in the administration of this Corporation. It shall be responsible for maintaining the integrity and accuracy of all Bahá'í teaching, whether written or oral, undertaken throughout the local community. It shall make available the published literature of the Faith. It shall represent the community in relationship to the National Spiritual Assembly, the Universal House of Justice, other local Bahá'í communities and the general public in . . . It shall be charged with the recognition of all applicants requesting membership in the local Bahá'í community. It shall pass upon the right of any and all members of the community whose membership is in question to retain their status as voting members of the community. It shall call the meetings of the community, including the Bahá'í Anniversaries and Feasts, the Meetings of consultation, and the Annual Meeting at which the members of the Assembly are elected. It shall appoint and supervise all committees of the Bahá'í community. It shall collect and disburse all funds intended for the maintenance of this Corporation. It shall have full and complete custody of the headquarters or meeting place of the Bahá'í community. It shall have exclusive authority to conduct Bahá'í marriage ceremonies and issue Bahá'í marriage certificates within the area of its jurisdiction. It shall report to the National Spiritual Assembly annually, or when requested, the membership roll of the Bahá'í community, for the information and approval of the National Assembly. The Spiritual Assembly, however, shall recognize the authority and right of the National Spiritual Assembly to declare at any time what activities and affairs of the Bahá'í community of . . . are national in scope and hence subject to the jurisdiction of the National Assembly. It shall likewise recognize the right of any member of the community to appeal to the National Assembly for review and decision of any matter in which the previous decision of the Local Spiritual Assembly is felt by the member to be contrary to the explicit teachings of the Bahá'í Faith or opposed to its best interests. It shall, on the other hand, have the authority and right to appeal from the decision of the National Assembly to the Universal House of Justice for review and final decision of any matter related to the Faith in . . . .

ARTICLE IV

The Spiritual Assembly, in administering this Corporation, shall ever bear in mind the ideals upheld in the sacred Writings of the Bahá'í Faith respecting relationships of a Spiritual Assembly to its Bahá'í community, respecting the relations of Bahá'ís to one another in the community, and relationships of Bahá'ís to all non-Bahá'ís, without prejudice of race, creed or nationality. The Assembly shall therefore above all recognize its sacred duty to maintain full and complete unity throughout the Bahá'í community, to relieve and comfort the sick and distressed, to assist the poor and destitute, to protect the orphans, the crippled and the aged, to educate the children of Bahá'ís according to the highest religious and intellectual standards, to compose differences and disagreements among members of the community, to promulgate the principles of Divine Civilization revealed by Bahá'u'lláh, and to promote in every way possible the Bahá'í aim of the oneness of mankind. It shall faithfully and devotedly uphold the general Bahá'í activities and affairs initiated and sustained by the National Spiritual Assembly. It shall co-operate wholeheartedly with other Local Spiritual Assemblies throughout . . . [name of country or region] in all matters declared by the National Spiritual Assembly to be of general Bahá'í importance and concern. It shall rigorously abstain from any action or influence, direct or indirect, that savours of intervention on the part of the Bahá'í body in matters of public politics and civil jurisdiction. It shall encourage intercourse between the Bahá'í community of . . . and other recognized Bahá'í communities, issuing letters of introduction to Bahá'ís travelling from . . . and passing upon letters of introduction issued by other Bahá'í Assemblies. It shall regard its authority as a means of rendering service to Bahá'ís and non-Bahá'ís and not as a source of arbitrary power. While retaining the sacred right of final decision in all matters pertaining to the Bahá'í community, the Spiritual Assembly shall ever seek the advice and consultation of all members of the community, keep the community informed of all its affairs, and invite full and free discussion on the part of the community of all matters affecting the Faith.

ARTICLE V

The Bahá'ís of . . . for whose benefit this Corporation has been established shall consist of all persons of age of 15 years or over resident in . . . who are accepted by the National Spiritual Assembly as possessing the qualifications of Bahá'í faith and practice required under the following standard set forth by the Guardian of the Faith:

Full recognition of the station of the Báb, the Forerunner; of Bahá'u'lláh, the Author; and of 'Abdu'l-Bahá, the True Exemplar of the Bahá'í religion; unreserved acceptance of, and submission to, whatsoever has been revealed by their Pen; loyal and steadfast adherence to every clause of 'Abdu'l-Bahá's sacred Will; and close association with the spirit as well as the form of Bahá'í Administration throughout the world.

Upon attaining the age of 21 years, a Bahá'í is eligible to vote and to hold elective office.

ARTICLE VI

The Spiritual Assembly shall consist of nine Trustees chosen from among the Bahá'ís of . . . , who shall be elected by these Bahá'ís in a manner hereinafter provided and who shall continue in office for the period of one year, or until their successors shall be elected.

ARTICLE VII

The officers of the Spiritual Assembly shall consist of a Chairman, Vice-Chairman, Secretary and Treasurer, and such other officers as may be found necessary for the proper conduct of its affairs. The officers shall be elected by a majority vote of the entire membership of the Assembly taken by secret ballot.

ARTICLE VIII

The first meeting of a newly-elected Assembly shall be called by the member elected to membership by the highest number of votes, or, in case two or more members have received the same said highest number of votes, then by the member selected by lot from among those members; and this member shall preside until the permanent Chairman shall be chosen. All subsequent meetings shall be called by the Secretary of the Assembly at the request of the Chairman or, in his absence or incapacity, of the Vice-Chairman, or of any three members of the Assembly; provided, however, that the Annual Meeting of the Assembly shall be held on April 21, in accordance with the administrative principles recognized by all Bahá'í Assemblies.

SECTION 1. Five members of the Assembly present at a meeting shall constitute a quorum, and a majority vote of those present and constituting a quorum shall be sufficient for the conduct of business, except as otherwise provided in these By-Laws, and with due regard to the principle of unity and cordial fellowship involved in the institution of a Spiritual Assembly. The transactions and decisions of the Assembly shall be recorded at each meeting by the Secretary, who shall have the minutes adopted and approved by the Assembly, and preserve them in the official records of the Assembly.

SECTION 2. Vacancies in the membership of the Spiritual Assembly shall be filled by election at a special meeting of the local Bahá'í community duly called for that purpose by the

Assembly. In the event that the number of vacancies exceeds four, making a quorum of the Spiritual Assembly impossible, the election shall be under the supervision of the National Spiritual Assembly.

ARTICLE IX

The sphere of jurisdiction of the Spiritual Assembly, with respect to residential qualification of membership, and voting rights of a believer in the Bahá'í community, shall be the locality included within the civil limits of . . .

ARTICLE X

SECTION 1. In the event that any decision of the Assembly is unacceptable to any member or members of the community, the Assembly shall, after endeavouring to compose the difference of opinion, invite the said member or members to make appeal to the National Spiritual Assembly and notify that body of the condition of the matter and the readiness of the Assembly to become party to the appeal.

SECTION 2. In the same manner, if any difference arises between the Assembly and another Local Assembly, or Assemblies, in . . . [name of country or region], the Assembly shall report the matter to the National Assembly and inform that body of its readiness to make joint appeal together with the other Assembly or Assemblies.

SECTION 3. If, however, the result of such appeal is unsatisfactory to the Spiritual Assembly, or the Assembly at any time has reason to believe that actions of the National Spiritual Assembly are affecting adversely the welfare and unity of the Bahá'í community of . . . , it shall, after seeking to compose its difference of opinion with the National Assembly in direct consultation, have the right to make appeal to the Universal House of Justice.

SECTION 4. The Assembly shall likewise have the right to make complaint to the National Spiritual Assembly in the event that matters of local Bahá'í concern and influence are referred to the national body by a member or members of the local community without previous opportunity for action by the Local Assembly.

ARTICLE XI

The Annual Meeting of the Corporation at which its Trustees shall be elected shall be held on April 21, at an hour and place to be fixed by the Assembly, which shall give not less than fifteen days' notice of the meeting to all members of the local Bahá'í community.

SECTION 1. The Assembly shall accept those votes transmitted to the Assembly before the election by members who by reason of sickness or other unavoidable reason are unable to be present at the election in person.

SECTION 2. The election of members to the Spiritual Assembly shall be by plurality vote.

SECTION 3. All voting members of the local Bahá'í community are eligible for election as members of the Spiritual Assembly.

SECTION 4. The Assembly shall prepare an agenda for the Annual Meeting in which shall be included reports of the activities of the Assembly since its election, a financial statement showing all income and expenditure of its fund, reports of its committees and presentation of any other matters pertaining to the affairs of the Bahá'í community. The Assembly, both preceding and following the annual election, shall invite discussion and welcome suggestions from the community, in order that its plans may reflect the community mind and heart.

SECTION 5. The result of the election shall be reported by the Spiritual Assembly to the National Assembly.

ARTICLE XII

In addition to the Annual Meeting, the Assembly shall arrange for regular meetings of the Bahá'í community throughout the year at intervals of nineteen days, in accordance with the calendar incorporated in the teachings of the Bahá'í Faith.

ARTICLE XIII

The seal of the Corporation shall be circular in form, bearing the following inscription: The Spiritual Assembly of the Bahá'ís of . . .

ARTICLE XIV

Alternative 'A'

These By-Laws may be amended by majority vote of the Spiritual Assembly at any of its regular or special meetings, provided that at least fourteen days prior to the date fixed for the said meeting a copy of the proposed amendment or amendments is mailed to each member of the Assembly by the Secretary.

Alternative 'B'

These By-Laws may be amended only by majority action of the National Spiritual Assembly, which, in making amendments, does so for the By-Laws of all Local Spiritual Assemblies throughout . . . [name of country or region].

226

Appendix III

A Model Declaration of Trust and By-Laws for a National Spiritual Assembly[1]

Declaration of Trust
by the National Spiritual Assembly of the Bahá'ís of
. . .

WE,

duly chosen by the representatives of the Bahá'ís of . . . at the Annual Meeting held at . . ., on . . ., to be the National Spiritual Assembly of the Bahá'ís of . . ., with full power to establish a Trust as hereinafter set forth, hereby declare that from this date the powers, responsibilities, rights, privileges and obligations reposed in said National Spiritual Assembly of the Bahá'ís of . . . by Bahá'u'lláh, Founder of the Bahá'í Faith, by 'Abdu'l-Bahá, its Interpreter and Exemplar, by Shoghi Effendi, its Guardian, and by the Universal House of Justice, ordained by Bahá'u'lláh in His sacred Writings as the supreme body of the Bahá'í religion, shall be exercised, administered and carried on by the above-named National Spiritual Assembly and their duly qualified successors under this Declaration of Trust.

The National Spiritual Assembly in adopting this form of association, union and fellowship, and in selecting for itself the designation of Trustees of the Bahá'ís of . . ., does so as the administrative body of a religious community which has had

227

continuous existence and responsibility for . . . In consequence of these activities the National Spiritual Assembly is called upon to administer such ever-increasing diversity and volume of affairs and properties for the Bahá'ís of . . ., that we, its members, now feel it both desirable and necessary to give our collective functions more definite legal form. This action is taken in complete unanimity and with full recognition of the sacred relationship thereby created. We acknowledge in behalf of ourselves and our successors in this Trust the exalted religious standard established by Bahá'u'lláh for Bahá'í administrative bodies in the utterance: *Be ye Trustees of the Merciful One among men*; and seek the help of God and His guidance in order to fulfil that exhortation.

Date   *(Signatures of the nine members)*

ARTICLE I

The name of said Trust shall be 'the National Spiritual Assembly of the Bahá'ís of . . .'

ARTICLE II

Sharing the ideals and assisting the efforts of our fellow Bahá'ís to establish, uphold and promote the spiritual, educational and humanitarian teachings of human brotherhood, radiant faith, exalted character and selfless love revealed in the lives and utterances of all the Prophets and Messengers of God, Founders of the world's revealed religions – and given renewed creative energy and universal application to the conditions of this age in the life and utterances of Bahá'u'lláh – we declare the purpose and objects of this Trust to be to administer the affairs of the Cause of Bahá'u'lláh for the benefit of the Bahá'ís of . . . according to the principles of Bahá'í affiliation and administration created and established by Bahá'u'lláh, defined and explained by 'Abdu'l-Bahá, interpreted and amplified by Shoghi Effendi, and supplemented and applied by the Universal House of Justice.

228

These purposes are to be realized by means of devotional meetings; by public meetings and conferences of an educational, humanitarian and spiritual character; by the publication of books, magazines and newspapers; by the construction of temples of universal worship and of other institutions and edifices for humanitarian service; by supervising, unifying, promoting and generally administering the activities of the Bahá'ís of . . . in the fulfilment of their religious offices, duties and ideals; and by any other means appropriate to these ends, or any of them.

Other purposes and objects of this Trust are:

a. The right to enter into, make, perform and carry out contracts of every sort and kind for the furtherance of the objects of this Trust with any person, firm, association, corporation, private, public or municipal or body politic, or any state, territory or colony thereof, or any foreign government; and in this connection, and in all transactions under the terms of this Trust, to do any and all things which a copartnership or natural person could do or exercise, and which now or hereafter may be authorized by law.

b. To hold and be named as beneficiary under any trust established by law or otherwise or under any will or other testamentary instrument in connection with any gift, devise, or bequest in which a trust or trusts is or are established in any part of the world as well as in . . .; to receive gifts, devises or bequests of money or other property.

c. All and whatsoever the several purposes and objects set forth in the written utterances of Bahá'u'lláh, 'Abdu'l-Bahá and Shoghi Effendi, and enactments of the Universal House of Justice, under which certain jurisdiction, powers and rights are granted to National Spiritual Assemblies.

d. Generally to do all things and acts which in the judgement of said Trustees, i.e., the National Spiritual Assembly of the Bahá'ís of . . ., are necessary, proper and advantageous to promote the complete and successful administration of this Trust.

ARTICLE III

SECTION 1. All persons, firms, corporations and associations extending credit to, contracting with or having any claim against the Trustees, i.e., the National Spiritual Assembly, and the members thereof, of any character whatsoever whether legal or equitable and whether arising out of contract or tort, shall look solely to the funds of the Trust and to the property of the Trust estate for payment or indemnity, or for payment of any debt, damage, judgement or decree or any money that may otherwise become due or payable from the Trustees, so that neither the Trustees nor any of them, nor any of their officers or agents appointed by them hereunder, nor any beneficiary or beneficiaries herein named shall be personally liable therefor.

SECTION 2. Every note, bond, proposal, obligation or contract in writing or other agreement or instrument made or given under this Trust shall be explicitly executed by the National Spiritual Assembly, as Trustees, by their duly authorized officers or agents.

ARTICLE IV

The Trustees, i.e., the National Spiritual Assembly, shall adopt for the conduct of the affairs entrusted to them under this Declaration of Trust, such by-laws, rules of procedure or regulations as are required to define and carry on its own administrative functions and those of the several local and other elements composing the body of the Bahá'ís of . . ., not inconsistent with the terms of this instrument and all in accordance with the instructions and enactments of the Universal House of Justice.

ARTICLE V

The central office of the corporation shall be located in . . .

ARTICLE VI

The seal of this Trust shall be circular in form, bearing the following inscription: National Spiritual Assembly of the Bahá'ís of . . .

ARTICLE VII

This Declaration of Trust may be amended by majority vote of the National Spiritual Assembly of the Bahá'ís of . . . at any special meeting duly called for that purpose, provided that at least thirty (30) days prior to the date fixed for said meeting a copy of the proposed amendment or amendments is mailed to each member of the Assembly by the Secretary.

By-Laws of the National Spiritual Assembly

ARTICLE I

The National Spiritual Assembly, in the fulfilment of the sacred duties under this Trust, shall have exclusive jurisdiction and authority over all the activities and affairs of the Bahá'í Faith throughout . . ., including paramount authority in the administration of this Trust. It shall endeavour to stimulate, unify and coordinate the manifold activities of the Local Spiritual Assemblies (hereinafter defined) and of individual Bahá'ís in . . . and by all possible means assist them to promote the oneness of mankind. It shall be charged with the recognition of such Local Assemblies, the scrutiny of all membership rolls, the calling of the Annual Meeting or special meetings and the seating of delegates to the Annual Meeting and their apportionment among the various electoral districts. It shall appoint all national Bahá'í committees and shall supervise the publication and distribution of Bahá'í literature, the reviewing of all writings pertaining to the Bahá'í Cause, the construction and administration of the Mashriqu'l-Adhkár and its accessory activities, and the collection and disbursement of all funds for the carrying on of this Trust. It shall decide whether any matter lies within its own jurisdiction or within the jurisdiction of any Local Spiritual Assembly. It shall, in such cases as it considers suitable and necessary, entertain appeals from the decisions of Local Spiritual Assemblies and shall have the right of final decision in all cases where the qualification of an individual or group for continued voting rights and membership in the Bahá'í body is in question. It shall furthermore represent the Bahá'ís of . . . in all their co-operative and spiritual activities with the Bahá'ís of other lands and shall constitute the sole electoral body of . . . in the election of the Universal House of Justice provided for in the sacred Writings of the Bahá'í Cause. Above all, the National Spiritual Assembly shall ever seek to attain that station of unity in devotion to the Revelation of Bahá'u'lláh which will attract the confirmations of the Holy Spirit and enable the Assembly to serve the founding of the Most Great Peace. In all its deliberation and action the National Spiritual Assembly shall have constantly before it as Divine guide and standard the utterance of Bahá'u'lláh:

> *It behoveth them* (i.e., members of Spiritual Assemblies) *to be the trusted ones of the Merciful among men and to regard themselves as the guardians appointed of God for all that dwell on earth. It is incumbent upon them to take counsel together and to have regard for the interests of the servants of God, for His sake, even as they regard their own interests, and to choose that which is meet and seemly.*

ARTICLE II

The Bahá'ís of . . . for whose benefit this Trust is established shall consist of all persons of the age of 15 years or over resident in . . . who are accepted by the National Spiritual Assembly as possessing the qualifications of Bahá'í faith and practice required under the following standard set forth by the Guardian of the Faith:

Full recognition of the station of the Báb, the Forerunner; of Bahá'u'lláh, the Author; and of 'Abdu'l-Bahá, the True Exemplar of the Bahá'í religion, unreserved acceptance of, and submission to, whatsoever has been revealed by their Pen; loyal and steadfast adherence to every clause of 'Abdu'l-Bahá's sacred Will; and close association with the spirit as well as the form of Bahá'í Administration throughout the world.

Those residing in the area of jurisdiction of any Local Spiritual Assembly recognized by the National Spiritual Assembly may declare their faith to, and be enrolled by, the Local Spiritual Assembly; those living outside any such area of local Bahá'í jurisdiction shall be enrolled in such manner as shall be prescribed by the National Assembly.

Upon attaining the age of 21 years, a Bahá'í is eligible to vote and to hold elective office.

ARTICLE III

The National Spiritual Assembly shall consist of nine members chosen from among the Bahá'ís of . . ., who shall be elected by the said Bahá'ís in manner hereinafter provided, and who shall continue for the period of one year, or until their successors shall be elected.

ARTICLE IV

The officers of the National Spiritual Assembly shall consist of a Chairman, Vice-Chairman, Secretary and Treasurer, and such other officers as may be found necessary for the proper conduct of its affairs. The officers shall be elected by a majority vote of the entire membership of the Assembly taken by secret ballot.

ARTICLE V

The first meeting of a newly-elected National Assembly shall be called by the member elected to membership by the highest number of votes or, in case two or more members have received the same said highest number of votes, then by the member selected by lot from among those members; and this member shall preside until the permanent Chairman shall be chosen. All subsequent meetings shall be called by the Secretary of the Assembly at the request of the Chairman or, in his absence or incapacity, of the Vice-Chairman, or of any three members of the Assembly; provided, however, that the Annual Meeting of the Assembly shall be held at a time and place to be fixed by a majority vote of the Assembly, as hereinafter provided.

Article VI

Five members of the National Spiritual Assembly present at a meeting shall constitute a quorum, and a majority vote of those present and constituting a quorum shall be sufficient for the conduct of business, except as otherwise provided in these By-Laws, and with due regard to the principle of unity and cordial fellowship involved in the institution of a Spiritual Assembly. The transactions and decisions of the National Assembly shall be recorded at each meeting by the Secretary, who shall supply copies of the minutes to the Assembly members after each meeting, and preserve the minutes in the official records of the Assembly.

Article VII

Whenever, in any locality of . . . , the number of Bahá'ís resident therein recognized by the National Spiritual Assembly exceeds nine, these shall on April 21st of any year convene and elect by plurality vote a local administrative body of nine members, to be known as the Spiritual Assembly of the Bahá'ís of that community. Every such Spiritual Assembly shall be elected annually thereafter upon each successive 21st day of April. The members shall hold office for the term of one year or until their successors are elected and qualified.

When, however, the number of Bahá'ís in any authorized civil area is exactly nine, these shall on April 21st of any year, or in successive years, constitute themselves the Local Spiritual Assembly by joint declaration. Upon the recording of such declaration by the Secretary of the National Spiritual Assembly, said body of nine shall become established with the rights, privileges and duties of a Local Spiritual Assembly as set forth in this instrument.

SECTION 1. Each newly-elected Local Spiritual Assembly shall at once proceed in the manner indicated in Articles IV and V of these By-Laws to the election of its officers, who shall consist of a Chairman, Vice-Chairman, Secretary and Treasurer, and such other officers as the Assembly finds necessary for the conduct of its business and the fulfilment of its spiritual duties. Immediately thereafter the Secretary chosen shall transmit to the Secretary of the National Assembly the names of the members of the newly-elected Assembly and a list of its officers.

SECTION 2. The general powers and duties of a Local Spiritual Assembly shall be as set forth in the writings of Bahá'u'lláh, 'Abdu'l-Bahá and Shoghi Effendi, and as laid down by the Universal House of Justice.

SECTION 3. Among its more specific duties, a Local Spiritual Assembly shall have full jurisdiction of all Bahá'í activities and affairs within the local community, subject, however, to the exclusive and paramount authority of the National Spiritual Assembly as defined herein.

SECTION 4. Vacancies in the membership of a Local Spiritual Assembly shall be filled by election at a special meeting of the local Bahá'í community duly called for that purpose by the Assembly. In the event that the number of vacancies exceeds four, making a quorum of the Local Assembly impossible, the election shall be held under the supervision of the National Spiritual Assembly.

SECTION 5. The business of the Local Assembly shall be conducted in like manner as provided for the deliberations of the National Assembly in Article VI above.

SECTION 6. The Local Assembly shall pass upon and approve the qualifications of each member of the Bahá'í community before such members shall be admitted to voting membership; but where an individual is dissatisfied with the ruling of the Local Spiritual Assembly upon his Bahá'í qualifications, such individual may appeal from the ruling to the National Assembly, which shall thereupon take jurisdiction of and finally decide the case.

SECTION 7. On or before the 1st day of November of each year the Secretary of each Local Assembly shall send to the Secretary of the National Assembly a duly certified list of the voting members of the local Bahá'í community for the information and approval of the National Assembly.

SECTION 8. All matters arising within a local Bahá'í community which are of purely local interest and do not affect the national interests of the Cause shall be under the primary jurisdiction of the Spiritual Assembly of that locality; but decision whether a particular matter involves the interest and welfare of the national Bahá'í body shall rest with the National Spiritual Assembly.

SECTION 9. Any member of a local Bahá'í community may appeal from a decision of his Spiritual Assembly to the National Assembly, which shall determine whether it shall take jurisdiction of the matter or leave it to the Local Spiritual Assembly for reconsideration. In the event that the National Assembly assumes jurisdiction of the matter, its findings shall be final.

SECTION 10. Where any dissension exists within a local Bahá'í community of such character that it cannot be remedied by the efforts of the Local Spiritual Assembly, this condition shall be referred by the Spiritual Assembly for consideration to the National Spiritual Assembly, whose action in the matter shall be final.

SECTION 11. All questions arising between two or more Local Spiritual Assemblies, or between members of different Bahá'í communities, shall be submitted in the first instance to the National Assembly, which shall have original and final jurisdiction in all such matters.

SECTION 12. The sphere of jurisdiction of a Local Spiritual Assembly, with respect to residential qualification of membership, and voting rights of a believer in any Bahá'í community, shall be the locality included within the recognized civil limits.

All differences of opinion concerning the sphere of jurisdiction of any Local Spiritual Assembly or concerning the affiliation of any Bahá'í or group of Bahá'ís in . . . shall be referred to the National Spiritual Assembly, whose decision in the matter shall be final.

ARTICLE VIII

The members of the National Spiritual Assembly shall be elected at an annual meeting to be known as the National Convention of the Bahá'ís of . . . This Convention shall be held at a time and place to be fixed by the National Assembly. The National Convention shall be composed jointly of representatives chosen by the Bahá'ís of each . . . under the principle of proportionate representation and the members of the National Spiritual Assembly.

Notice of the annual meeting shall be given by the National Spiritual Assembly sixty days in advance in the Convention Call which sets forth the number of delegates assigned to the various electoral units in proportion to the number of Bahá'ís resident in each such unit, to a total of . . . delegates for the Bahá'ís of . . . .

SECTION 1. All delegates to the Convention shall be elected by plurality vote. Bahá'ís who for illness or other unavoidable reasons are unable to be present at the election in person shall have the right to transmit their ballots to the meeting by mail. The meeting held in each . . . for the election of delegates shall be called by the National Spiritual Assembly and conducted by the Bahá'ís present under whatever procedure may be uniformly laid down by said body. Immediately after the meeting a certified report of the election containing the name and address of each delegate shall be transmitted to the National Spiritual Assembly.

SECTION 2. All delegates to be seated at the Convention must be recognized Bahá'ís and residents of the . . . represented by them.

SECTION 3. The rights and privileges of a delegate may not be assigned nor may they be exercised by proxy.

SECTION 4. The recognition and seating of delegates to the National Convention shall be vested in the National Spiritual Assembly.

SECTION 5. Delegates unable to be present in person at the Convention shall have the right to transmit their ballots for election of the members of the National Assembly under whatever procedure is adopted by the National Assembly.

SECTION 6. If in any year the National Spiritual Assembly shall consider that it is impracticable or unwise to assemble together the delegates to the National Convention, the said Assembly shall provide ways and means by which the annual election and the other essential business of the Convention may be conducted by mail.

SECTION 7. The presiding officer of the National Spiritual Assembly present at the Convention shall call together the delegates, who after roll call shall proceed to the permanent organization of the meeting, electing by ballot a Chairman, a Secretary and such other officers as are necessary for the proper conduct of the business of the Convention.

SECTION 8. The principal business of the annual meeting shall be consultation on Bahá'í activities, plans and policies, and the election of the nine members of the National Spiritual Assembly. Members of the National Spiritual Assembly, whether or not elected delegates, may take a full part in the consultation and discussion but only delegates may participate in the election of Convention officers or in the annual election of the members of the National Assembly. All action by the delegates, other than the organization of the Convention, the transmission of messages to the World Centre of the Bahá'í Faith, and the election of the National Assembly, shall constitute advice and recommendation for consideration by the said Assembly, final decision in all matters concerning the affairs of the Bahá'í Faith in . . . being vested solely in that body.

SECTION 9. The general order of business to be taken up at the Annual Convention shall be prepared by the National Spiritual Assembly in the form of an agenda, but any matter pertaining to the Bahá'í Faith introduced by any of the delegates may upon motion and vote be taken up as part of the Convention deliberations.

SECTION 10. The election of the members of the National Spiritual Assembly shall be by plurality vote of the delegates recognized by the outgoing National Spiritual Assembly, i.e., the members elected shall be the nine persons receiving the greatest number of votes on the first ballot cast by delegates present at the Convention and delegates whose ballot has been transmitted to the Secretary of the National Spiritual Assembly by mail. In case, by reason of a tie vote or votes, the full membership is not determined on the first ballot, then one or more additional ballots shall be taken on the persons tied until all nine members are elected.

SECTION 11. All official business transacted at the National Convention shall be recorded and preserved in the records of the National Assembly.

SECTION 12. Vacancies in the membership of the National Spiritual Assembly shall be filled by a plurality vote of the delegates composing the Convention which elected the Assembly, the ballot to be taken by correspondence or in any other manner decided upon by the National Assembly.

ARTICLE IX

Where the National Spiritual Assembly has been given in these By-Laws exclusive and final jurisdiction, and paramount executive authority, in all matters pertaining to the activities and affairs of the Bahá'í Cause in . . . , it is understood that any decision made or action taken upon such matters shall be subject in every instance to ultimate review and approval by the Universal House of Justice.

ARTICLE X

Whatever functions and powers are not specifically attributable to Local Spiritual Assemblies in these By-Laws shall be considered vested in the National Spiritual Assembly, which body is authorized to delegate such discretionary functions and powers as it deems necessary and advisable to the Local Spiritual Assemblies within its jurisdiction.

ARTICLE XI

In order to preserve the spiritual character and purpose of Bahá'í elections, the practice of nominations or any other electoral method detrimental to a silent and prayerful election shall not prevail, so that each elector may vote for none but those whom prayer and reflection have inspired him to uphold.

Among the most outstanding and sacred duties incumbent upon those who have been called upon to initiate, direct and co-ordinate the affairs of the Cause as members of Local or National Assemblies are:

To win by every means in their power the confidence and affection of those whom it is their privilege to serve, to investigate and acquaint themselves with the considered views, the prevailing sentiments and the personal convictions of those whose welfare it is their solemn obligation to promote, to purge their deliberations and the general conduct of their affairs of self-contained aloofness, the suspicion of secrecy, the stifling atmosphere of dictatorial assertiveness and of every word and deed that may savour of partiality, self-centredness and prejudice; and while retaining the sacred right of final decision in their hands, to invite discussion, ventilate grievances, welcome advice and foster the sense of inter-dependence and co-partnership, of understanding and mutual confidence between themselves and all other Bahá'ís.

ARTICLE XII

These By-Laws may be amended by majority vote of the National Spiritual Assembly at any of its regular or special meetings, provided that at least fourteen days prior to the date fixed for the said meeting a copy of the proposed amendment or amendments is mailed to each member of the Assembly by the Secretary.

Bibliography

'Abdu'l-Bahá. *Selections from the Writings of 'Abdu'l-Bahá*. Haifa: Bahá'í World Centre, 1978.

— *Some Answered Questions*. Wilmette, IL: Bahá'í Publishing Trust, 1981.

— *Tablets of Abdul-Baha Abbas*. New York: Bahá'í Publishing Committee; vol. 1, 1930.

— *Tablets of the Divine Plan*. Wilmette, IL: Bahá'í Publishing Trust, 1977.

— *The Will and Testament of 'Abdu'l-Bahá*. Wilmette, IL: Bahá'í Publishing Trust, 1991.

The Báb. *Selections from the Writings of the Báb*. Haifa: Bahá'í World Centre, 1976.

The Bahá'í World. vol. 4. 1930–1932, rpt. Wilmette, IL: Bahá'í Publishing Trust, 1980.

The Bahá'í World. vol. 12, 1950–1954. rpt. Wilmette, IL: Bahá'í Publishing Trust, 1980.

The Bahá'í World. vol. 20, 1986–1992. Haifa: Bahá'í World Centre, 1998.

Bahá'u'lláh. *Epistle to the Son of the Wolf*. Wilmette, IL: Bahá'í Publishing Trust, 1988.

— *Gleanings from the Writings of Bahá'u'lláh*. Wilmette, IL: Bahá'í Publishing Trust, 1994.

— *The Kitáb-i-Aqdas*. Haifa: Bahá'í World Centre, 1992.

— *Kitáb-i-Íqán*. Wilmette, IL: Bahá'í Publishing Trust, 1989.

— *Prayers and Meditations*. Wilmette, IL: Bahá'í Publishing Trust, 1987.

— *Tablets of Bahá'u'lláh*. Wilmette, IL: Bahá'í Publishing Trust, 1988.

The Compilation of Compilations. Prepared by the Universal House of Justice 1963–1990. 2 vols. [Sydney]: Bahá'í Publications Australia, 1991.

The Compilation of Compilations. Prepared by the Research Department of the Universal House of Justice, vol. 3. Ingleside: Bahá'í Publications Australia, 2000.

Directives from the Guardian. Compiled by Gertrude Garrida. New Delhi: Bahá'í Publishing Trust, 1973.

Lights of Guidance: A Bahá'í Reference File. Compiled by Helen Hornby. New Delhi: Bahá'í Publishing Trust, 2nd edn. 1988.

The Ministry of the Custodians, 1957–1963: An Account of the Stewardship of the Hands of the Cause. Haifa: Bahá'í World Centre, 1992.

National Convention: A Compilation. Mona Vale, Australia: Bahá'í Publications Australia, 1993.

Rabbaní, Rúḥíyyih. *The Priceless Pearl.* London: Bahá'í Publishing Trust, 1969.

Shoghi Effendi. *The Advent of Divine Justice.* Wilmette, IL: Bahá'í Publishing Trust, 1990.

— *Bahá'í Administration.* Wilmette, IL: Bahá'í Publishing Trust, 1995.

— *Citadel of Faith: Messages to America 1947–1957.* Wilmette, IL: Bahá'í Publishing Trust, 1995.

— *Dawn of a New Day: Messages to India 1923–1957.* New Delhi: Bahá'í Publishing Trust, 1970.

— *God Passes By.* Wilmette, IL: Bahá'í Publishing Trust, rev. edn. 1995.

— *The Light of Divine Guidance: The Messages from the Guardian of the Bahá'í Faith to the Bahá'ís of Germany and Austria.* 2 vols. Hofheim-Langenhain: Bahá'í-Verlag, 1982.

— *Messages to America.* Wilmette, IL: Bahá'í Publishing Committee, 1947.

— *Messages to the Antipodes: Communications from Shoghi Effendi to the Bahá'í Communities of Australasia.* Mona Vale NSW: Bahá'í Publications Australia, 1997.

— *Messages to the Bahá'í World.* Wilmette, IL: Bahá'í Publishing Trust, 1971.

— *Messages to Canada.* [Toronto]: National Spiritual Assembly of the Bahá'ís of Canada, 1965.

— *Messages of Shoghi Effendi to the Indian Subcontinent, 1923–1957.* New Delhi: Bahá'í Publishing Trust, 1995.

— *The Promised Day is Come.* Wilmette, IL: Bahá'í Publishing Trust, rev. edn. 1980.

— *The World Order of Bahá'u'lláh.* Wilmette, IL: Bahá'í Publishing Trust, 1991.

The Universal House of Justice. *The Guardianship and the Universal House of Justice – Selected Messages by or on Behalf of the Universal*

House of Justice. Riviera Beach: Palabra Publications, 1996.

— *Individual Rights and Freedoms in the World Order of Bahá'u'lláh*. Wilmette IL: Bahá'í Publishing Trust, 1989.

— *The Institution of the Counsellors*. Haifa: Bahá'í World Centre, 2001.

— 'Issues Related to the Study of the Bahá'í Faith'. Published as a supplement to the *Bahá'í Canada*, May 1998.

— *Messages from the Universal House of Justice 1963–1986: The Third Epoch of the Formative Age*. Wilmette, IL: Bahá'í Publishing Trust, 1996.

— *Rights and Responsibilities: The Complementary Roles of the Individual and Institutions*. Thornhill, ON: Bahá'í Canada Publications, 1997.

Notes and References

1. Introduction

1. Shoghi Effendi, *God Passes By*, pp. 213–14.
2. Bahá'u'lláh, *Kitáb-i-Aqdas*, para. 30.
3. ibid. 'Questions and Answers', no. 50, p. 122.
4. ibid. 'Questions and Answers', no. 49, p. 121.
5. Bahá'u'lláh, *Tablets*, pp. 26–7.
6. ibid. p. 68.
7. From the Naw-Rúz 111 (1954) letter of Shoghi Effendi to the Bahá'ís of the East, in *Compilation*, vol. 1, pp. 341–2, no. 760.
8. 'Abdu'l-Bahá, *Some Answered Questions*, p. 172.
9. Shoghi Effendi, *God Passes By*, p. 328.
10. Shoghi Effendi, *World Order*, pp. 3–4.
11. Shoghi Effendi, *God Passes By*, p. 328.
12. Shoghi Effendi, *World Order*, p. 148.
13. From a letter of Shoghi Effendi to the Bahá'ís of Persia, 17 November 1929, in *Compilation*, vol. 1, pp. 333–4, nos. 745–6.
14. From a letter of Shoghi Effendi to the Bahá'ís of the East, 19 December 1922, in ibid. p. 328, no. 738.
15. From a letter of Shoghi Effendi to the Bahá'ís of the East, 1924, in ibid. p. 329, no. 741.
16. From a letter of Shoghi Effendi to the Spiritual Assembly of Tihrán, 30 October 1924, in ibid. p. 329, no. 742.
17. From a letter of the Universal House of Justice to an individual, 7 December 1969, in ibid. p. 365, no. 765.
18. From a letter written on behalf of the Universal House of Justice to an individual, 3 June 1997, cited in *Issues Related to the Study of the Bahá'í Faith*, p. 14.

19. See *Messages from the Universal House of Justice 1963–1986*, pp. 50–8, no. 23.
20. See ibid. pp. 83–90, no. 35.
21. See ibid. pp. 156–61, no. 75.
22. See also the Universal House of Justice, *Guardianship and the Universal House of Justice*.
23. Shoghi Effendi, *World Order*, p. 148.
24. The Universal House of Justice, *Constitution*, p. 4, para. 7.
25. Shoghi Effendi, *World Order*, p. 6.
26. Shoghi Effendi, *Citadel of Faith*, p. 5.
27. ibid. p. 7.
28. See *Ministry of the Custodians*, pp. 1–22.
29. Shoghi Effendi, *Messages to the Bahá'í World*, pp. 7–8.
30. ibid.
31. ibid. p. 8.
32. *Ministry of the Custodians*, pp. 45, 282.
33. The Universal House of Justice, *Messages from the Universal House of Justice 1963–1986*, p. 32, no. 14.5.
34. ibid. p. 101, no. 42.8.
35. ibid. p. 158, no. 75.10.
36. ibid. p. 229, no. 123.2.
37. ibid. p. 238, no. 128.6.
38. Shoghi Effendi, *World Order*, p. 150.
39. Translated from the Persian by the Research Department of the Universal House of Justice, in an email written on behalf of the Universal House of Justice to the author, 25 February 2002, together with an attached memorandum by the Research Department of the Universal House of Justice.
40. *Bahá'í World*, vol. 4, pp. 159–65.
41. Rabbaní, *Priceless Pearl*, p. 303.
42. From a letter written on behalf of Shoghi Effendi to the National Spiritual Assembly of the United States, 5 July 1950, in *Lights of Guidance*, p. 64, no. 224.
43. Shoghi Effendi, *Messages to the Antipodes*, p. 269.
44. ibid. p. 262.
45. *Bahá'í World*, vol. 12, pp. 393–400; *Bahá'í World*, vol. 18, pp. 538–45; see also Shoghi Effendi, *Bahá'í Administration*, pp. 134–5, 142–4.
46. Shoghi Effendi, *Light of Divine Guidance*, vol. 1, p. 66.
47. Shoghi Effendi, *Bahá'í Administration*, p. 143.
48. Shoghi Effendi, *Unfolding Destiny*, p. 101.

49. Shoghi Effendi, *Light of Divine Guidance,* vol. 1, p. 66.
50. Shoghi Effendi, *God Passes By,* p. 335.
51. Translated from the Persian by the Research Department of the Universal House of Justice, in an email written on behalf of the Universal House of Justice to the author, 25 February 2002, together with an attached memorandum by the Research Department of the Universal House of Justice.
52. Cited in an email written on behalf of the Universal House of Justice to the author, 25 February 2002, together with an attached memorandum by the Research Department of the Universal House of Justice.
53. ibid.
54. The Universal House of Justice, *Messages from the Universal House of Justice 1963–1986,* p. 246, no. 132.1.
55. Shoghi Effendi, *World Order,* p. 6.

2. The Station of the Universal House of Justice

1. Bahá'u'lláh, *Tablets,* pp. 26–7.
2. ibid. p. 68.
3. 'Abdu'l-Bahá, *Will and Testament,* para. 17.
4. ibid. para. 56.
5. 'Abdu'l-Bahá, *Selections,* p. 68.
6. 'Abdu'l-Bahá, *Some Answered Questions,* pp. 172–3.
7. 'Abdu'l-Bahá, in *Compilation,* vol. 1, p. 322, no. 727.
8. 'Abdu'l-Bahá, in ibid. p. 323, no. 728.
9. Shoghi Effendi, *World Order,* p. 7.
10. From a letter of Shoghi Effendi to the Bahá'ís of the East, 19 December 1922, in *Compilation,* vol. 1, p. 328, no. 738.
11. From a letter of Shoghi Effendi to the Bahá'ís of the East, 1924, in ibid. p. 329, no. 741.
12. From a letter of Shoghi Effendi to the Spiritual Assembly of Tihrán 30 October 1924, in ibid. no. 742.
13. From a letter of Shoghi Effendi to the Bahá'ís of Persia, 27 November 1929, in ibid. p. 333, no. 745.
14. From a letter of Shoghi Effendi to the Bahá'ís of Persia, 27 November 1929, in ibid. pp. 333–4, no. 746.
15. From the Naw-Rúz letter of Shoghi Effendi to the Bahá'ís of the East, Naw-Rúz 111 (1954), in ibid. p. 341, no. 760.

3. Annotations to the Declaration of Trust

1. Shoghi Effendi, *God Passes By*, p. 219.
2. Bahá'u'lláh, *Epistle to the Son of the Wolf*, p. 1.
3. From a letter written on behalf of Shoghi Effendi to an individual, 29 April 1933, in *Messages to the Antipodes*, pp. 84–5.
4. Matthew 6:10; Luke 11:2
5. Bahá'u'lláh, *Kitáb-i-Íqán*, para. 62. Emphasis added.
6. Bahá'u'lláh, *Kitáb-i-Aqdas*, note 24, p. 176.
7. Bahá'u'lláh, *Kitáb-i-Aqdas*, Question and Answers, no. 39, p. 119. Emphasis added.
8. ibid. no. 43, p. 120. Emphasis added.
9. ibid. no. 100, p. 137. Emphasis added.
10. The Báb, *Selections*, p. 47. Emphasis added.
11. Bahá'u'lláh, *Prayers and Meditations*, p. 87. Emphasis added.
12. Shoghi Effendi, *God Passes By*, pp. 93–4. Emphasis added.
13. ibid. p. 170. Emphasis added
14. ibid. p. 214. Emphasis added
15. ibid. p. 221. Emphasis added
16. ibid. p. 237. Emphasis added
17. ibid. pp. 205–6. Emphasis added.
18. Shoghi Effendi, *World Order*, p. 21.
19. Shoghi Effendi, *God Passes By*, pp. 213–14. Emphasis added.
20. ibid. p. 216. Emphasis added
21. ibid. p. 237.
22. ibid. pp. 237–8. Emphasis added.
23. ibid. p. 323. Emphasis added
24. ibid. pp. 244–5. Emphasis added.
25. ibid. pp. 213–14. Emphasis added.
26. ibid. p. 295. Emphasis added
27. From a letter of Shoghi Effendi, 17 June 1954, in Shoghi Effendi, *Unfolding Destiny*, p. 337. Emphasis added.
28. Shoghi Effendi, *Bahá'í Administration*, p. 114. Emphasis added.
29. From a letter of Shoghi Effendi to an individual, 27 January 1945, in Shoghi Effendi, *Unfolding Destiny*, p. 442. Emphasis added.
30. Shoghi Effendi, *World Order*, pp. 19–20. Emphasis added.
31. See, for example, Shoghi Effendi, *Messages to America*, p. 32; Shoghi Effendi, *Messages to the Bahá'í World*, pp. 19, 75–6; Shoghi Effendi, *World Order*, pp. 18, 21–2, 147–8 and 156–7.
32. Shoghi Effendi, *World Order*, p. 147.

33. ibid. p. 148. Emphasis added.
34. From a letter of the Universal House of Justice, 27 May 1966, in *Messages from the Universal House of Justice 1963–1986*, p. 86, para. 35.7d.
35. Bahá'u'lláh, *Gleanings*, p. 215; Bahá'u'lláh, *Tablets*, p. 168.
36. 'Abdu'l-Bahá, *Will and Testament*, para. 37.
37. Shoghi Effendi, *World Order*, pp. 21–2.
38. ibid. p. 5.
39. ibid. p. 147.
40. Shoghi Effendi, *God Passes By*, p. 325.
41. Shoghi Effendi, *World Order*, p. 134.
42. 'Abdu'l-Bahá, *Will and Testament*, para. 16. Emphasis added.
43. Shoghi Effendi, *World Order*, pp. 149–50.
44. ibid. p. 151.
45. Shoghi Effendi, *God Passes By*, p. 326.
46. From a letter of Shoghi Effendi to an individual, 6 April 1928, in Shoghi Effendi, *Unfolding Destiny*, p. 423.
47. Shoghi Effendi, *Directives from the Guardian*, pp. 33–4.
48. From a letter written on behalf of Shoghi Effendi to an individual, 20 August 1956, in *Lights of Guidance*, p. 313, no. 1055.
49. Shoghi Effendi, *World Order*, p. 148.
50. From a letter of the Universal House of Justice to an individual, 7 December 1969, in *Messages from the Universal House of Justice 1963–1986*, p. 160, para. 75.16.
51. From a letter of the Universal House of Justice to all National Spiritual Assemblies, December 1967, in ibid. p. 123, para. 54.2.
52. Shoghi Effendi, *World Order*, p. 23. Emphasis added.
53. Bahá'u'lláh, *Kitáb-i-Íqán*, para. 103. Emphasis added.
54. Shoghi Effendi, *Promised Day is Come*, p. 99. Emphasis added.
55. Shoghi Effendi, *World Order*, p. 123. Emphasis added.
56. Bahá'u'lláh, *Kitáb-i-Aqdas*, para. 37; Bahá'u'lláh, *Gleanings*, p. 346.
57. Bahá'u'lláh, *Kitáb-i-Aqdas*, note 62, pp. 195–6.
58. 'Abdu'l-Bahá, *Selections*, p. 67.
59. 'Abdu'l-Bahá, quoted in *Compilation*, vol. 1, p. 322, no. 727.
60. Shoghi Effendi, *Directives from the Guardian*, pp. 61–2.
61. From a letter of a Universal House of Justice to all National Spiritual Assemblies, in *Messages of the Universal House of Justice 1963–1986*, p. 145, para. 5.1.

62. From a letter of the Universal House of Justice to a National Spiritual Assembly, 9 March 1965, in ibid. pp. 50–1, para. 23.3.

63. From a letter of the Universal House of Justice to an individual, 17 May 1966, in ibid. pp. 83–4, paras. 35.2–3.

64. Shoghi Effendi, *Directives from the Guardian*, p. 82. Emphasis added.

65. Shoghi Effendi, *Messages to America*, p. 94. Emphasis added.

66. Shoghi Effendi, *Messages to the Bahá'í World*, p. 7. Emphasis added.

67. Shoghi Effendi, *Bahá'í Administration*, p. 41.

68. 'Abdu'l-Bahá, *Will and Testament*, para. 56. Emphasis added.

69. ibid. para. 25.

70. Bahá'u'lláh, *Tablets*, p. 27.

71. From a letter of the Universal House of Justice to an individual, 7 December 1969, in *Messages of the Universal House of Justice 1963–1986*, p. 160, para. 75.15.

72. From a letter of the Universal House of Justice to an individual, 17 May 1966, in ibid. p. 89, para. 35.17. Emphasis added.

73. From a letter of the Universal House of Justice to the Continental Board of Counsellors and National Spiritual Assemblies, 24 April 1972, in ibid. pp. 216–17, para. 111.12.

74. Bahá'u'lláh, *Kitáb-i-Aqdas*, note 125, p. 218.

75. 'Abdu'l-Bahá, *Will and Testament*, para. 27.

76. ibid. paras. 16 and 20.

77. From a letter of the Universal House of Justice to an individual, 27 May 1966, in *Messages of the Universal House of Justice 1963–1986*, pp. 89–90, para. 35.18. Emphasis added.

78. Regarding the discharge of the functions of the Hands of the Cause, see the section on the Continental Boards of Counsellors in the By-Laws of the Universal House of Justice, Article IX and annotations, below.

79. Shoghi Effendi, *World Order*, p. 7.

80. From a letter of Universal House of Justice to all National Spiritual Assemblies, December 1967, in *Messages of the Universal House of Justice 1963–1986*, p. 123, paras. 54.2–3.

81. Letter of the Universal House of Justice to all National Spiritual Assemblies, 26 August 1984, in ibid. pp. 642–3.

82. From a letter of the Universal House of Justice to all National Spiritual Assemblies, 7 March 1967, in ibid. p. 97, para. 40.4.

83. From a letter of the Universal House of Justice to the Bahá'ís of the World, April 1964, in ibid. p. 32, para. 14.5. Emphasis added.

84. From a letter of the Universal House of Justice to the Bahá'ís of the World, Naw-Rúz 1974, in ibid. p. 262, para. 141.5.

85. From a letter of the Universal House of Justice to the Bahá'ís of the World, Naw-Rúz 1979, in ibid. p. 404, para. 221.11d. Emphasis added.

86. Email letter written on behalf of the Universal House of Justice to an individual, 4 July 2002.

87. Shoghi Effendi, *World Order*, p. 148. Emphasis added.

88. Shoghi Effendi, *Messages to the Bahá'í World*, p. 155. Emphasis added. See also Shoghi Effendi, *Advent of Divine Justice*, p. 15 and Shoghi Effendi, *God Passes By*, pp. xvii, 364 and 410–11.

89. From a letter of the Universal House of Justice to the Bahá'ís of the World, April 1964, in *Messages of the Universal House of Justice 1963–1986*, p. 32, para. 14.5.

90. Shoghi Effendi, *World Order*, p. 18. Emphasis added.

91. Shoghi Effendi, *Bahá'í Administration*, p. 173.

92. Shoghi Effendi, *Australia and New Zealand*, p. 62.

93. From a cable of Shoghi Effendi to a National Spiritual Assembly, 16 January 1951, in Shoghi Effendi, *Unfolding Destiny*, p. 257; and Shoghi Effendi, *Citadel of Faith*, p. 90.

94. From a letter of Shoghi Effendi, 25 February 1951, in Shoghi Effendi, *Unfolding Destiny*, p. 261.

95. From a letter of the Universal House of Justice to an individual, 27 May 1966, in *Messages of the Universal House of Justice 1963–1986*, p. 90, para. 35.18. Emphasis added.

96. From a letter of the Universal House of Justice to all National Spiritual Assemblies, 2 July 1967, in ibid. p. 111, para. 45.3.

97. Letter of the Universal House of Justice to the Peoples of the World, October 1985, in ibid. pp. 681–96.

98. Shoghi Effendi, *Messages to the Bahá'í World*, pp. 84–5.

99. From a letter of Shoghi Effendi, 26 February 1947, in Shoghi Effendi, *Unfolding Destiny*, p. 196. Emphasis added.

100. Shoghi Effendi, *Messages to the Bahá'í World*, p. 84.

101. Shoghi Effendi, *Messages to America*, pp. 8–9. Emphasis added.

102. Bahá'u'lláh, *Tablets*, pp. 129–30.

103. 'Abdu'l-Bahá, *Selections*, p. 132.

104. Bahá'u'lláh, *Tablets*, p. 89. Emphasis added.

105. ibid. p. 125. Emphasis added.
106. ibid. p. 127.
107. From a letter written on behalf of Shoghi Effendi to a National Spiritual Assembly, 14 March 1939, in *Compilation*, p. 194, no. 1625.
108. Letter of the Universal House of Justice to all National Spiritual Assemblies, 23 January 1985, in *Messages of the Universal House of Justice 1963–1986*, pp. 652–4.
109. Letter of the Universal House of Justice to the Peoples of the World, October 1985, in ibid. pp. 681–96; letter of the Universal House of Justice to all National Spiritual Assemblies, 25 November 1985, in ibid. p. 700; letter of the Universal House of Justice to a National Spiritual Assembly, 12 December 1985, in ibid. p. 701.
110. Bahá'u'lláh, *Tablets*, p. 128.
111. 'Abdu'l-Bahá, *Selections*, pp. 127–8.
112. Bahá'u'lláh, *Tablets*, p. 68.
113. Bahá'u'lláh, *Kitáb-i-Aqdas*, note 49, p. 121.
114. ibid. note 50, p. 122.
115. Bahá'u'lláh, *Tablets*, pp. 132–4.
116. Bahá'u'lláh, *Kitáb-i-Aqdas*, note 86, p. 204.
117. ibid. para. 146.
118. ibid. note 161, p. 235.
119. ibid. note 95, p. 209.
120. 'Abdu'l-Bahá, *Will and Testament*, para. 25.
121. ibid. para. 37.
122. ibid. para. 38
123. 'Abdu'l-Bahá, *Some Answered Questions*, p. 172.
124. 'Abdu'l-Bahá, quoted in *Compilation*, vol. 1, p. 322, no. 727.
125. Quoted in a letter of the Universal House of Justice to an individual, 27 May 1966, in *Messages of the Universal House of Justice 1963–1986*, pp. 85–6, paras. 35.7a–d. Emphasis added.
126. From a letter of Shoghi Effendi, Naw-Rúz 1954, in *Compilation*, vol. 1, p. 341, no. 760. Emphasis added.
127. Shoghi Effendi, *God Passes By*, p. 326. Emphasis added.
128. Shoghi Effendi, *Bahá'í Administration*, p. 78.
129. Shoghi Effendi, *World Order*, p. 153. Emphasis added.
130. Shoghi Effendi, *God Passes By*, pp. 218–19. Emphasis added.
131. Shoghi Effendi, *Directives from the Guardian*, pp. 3–4.
132. Shoghi Effendi, *Bahá'í Administration*, pp. 82–3.
133. ibid. p. 135.

134. ibid. pp. 135–6.
135. ibid. p. 40.
136. ibid. p. 41.
137. From a letter written on behalf of Shoghi Effendi in Persian to an individual, 27 May 1940, cited in a letter from the Universal House of Justice to a National Spiritual Assembly, 31 May 1988.
138. Shoghi Effendi, *Lights of Divine Guidance*, vol. 2, p. 82.
139. From a letter written on behalf of Shoghi Effendi, 27 December 1933, in *Dawn of a New Day*, pp. 196–7.
140. From a letter written on behalf of Shoghi Effendi to an individual, 27 June 1933, in *Light of Divine Guidance*, vol. 1, pp. 49–50.
141. Shoghi Effendi, *Directives from the Guardian*, p. 30.
142. From a letter written on behalf of Shoghi Effendi, 10 November 1955, in *Messages to Canada*, pp. 230–1.
143. From a letter written on behalf of Shoghi Effendi to a National Spiritual Assembly, 29 November 1955, in *Messages to the Antipodes*, p. 397.
144. From a letter written on behalf of Shoghi Effendi to a National Spiritual Assembly, 13 June 1956, in ibid. p. 411.
145. ibid. p. 412.
146. From a letter written on behalf of Shoghi Effendi to an individual, 25 August 1939, in *Messages to Canada*, p. 66.
147. From a letter written on behalf of Shoghi Effendi, 17 June 1954, in Shoghi Effendi, *Unfolding Destiny*, p. 334.
148. The Universal House of Justice made this law binding on all Bahá'ís in 1999.
149. From a letter written on behalf of Shoghi Effendi to an individual, 10 October 1936, cited in a letter written on behalf of the Universal House of Justice to the author, 13 August 2002, together with an enclosed memorandum by the Research Department of the Universal House of Justice.
150. From a letter written on behalf of Shoghi Effendi to an individual, 13 November 1940, cited in ibid.
151. From a letter written on behalf of Shoghi Effendi to an individual, 20 October 1953, cited in ibid.
152. From a letter written on behalf of Shoghi Effendi to an individual, 25 August 1939, in *Messages to Canada*, p. 66.
153. ibid. p. 67.
154. Shoghi Effendi, *Directives from the Guardian*, pp. 82–3.

155. From a letter of the Universal House of Justice, 17 May 1974, in *Lights of Guidance*, pp. 290–2, paras. 982 and 985.

156. From a letter written on behalf of the Universal House of Justice to a National Spiritual Assembly, 16 March 1983, in ibid. p. 344, no. 1154.

157. From a letter of the Universal House of Justice to an individual, 7 April 1974, in ibid. p. 350, no. 1174.

158. From a letter written on behalf of the Universal House of Justice to an individual, 5 June 1988, cited in a letter written on behalf of the Universal House of Justice to the author, 13 August 2002, together with an enclosed memorandum by the Research Department of the Universal House of Justice.

159. 'Abdu'l-Bahá, *Will and Testament*, para. 38.

160. Shoghi Effendi, *World Order*, p. 23. Emphasis added.

161. ibid. p. 149. Emphasis added

162. Shoghi Effendi, *Light of Divine Guidance*, p. 82.

163. See Article IX, Section 1 of the By-Laws of the Universal House of Justice, and annotations below.

164. See Article II of the By-Laws of the Universal House of Justice, and annotations, below.

165. 'Abdu'l-Bahá, *Will and Testament*, para. 25. Emphasis added.

166. ibid. para. 38. Emphasis added.

167. 'Abdu'l-Bahá, *Selections*, p. 215. Emphasis added.

168. Shoghi Effendi, *Bahá'í Administration*, pp. 62–3.

169. ibid. p. 46. Emphasis added.

170. From a letter of the Universal House of Justice to a National Spiritual Assembly, 9 March 1965, in *Messages of the Universal House of Justice 1963–1986*, p. 56, para. 23.20.

171. ibid. p. 57, paras. 23.22c–23.23.

172. From a letter of the Universal House of Justice to an individual, 25 October 1984, in ibid. p. 646, para. 412.4.

173. From a letter written on behalf of the Universal House of Justice to the author, 13 August 2002, together with an enclosed memorandum by the Research Department of the Universal House of Justice.

174. From a letter written on behalf of the Universal House of Justice to an individual, 16 August 1987, cited in a letter written on behalf of the Universal House of Justice to the author, 13 August 2002, together with an enclosed memorandum by the Research Department of the Universal House of Justice.

175. From a letter of the Universal House of Justice to a National

Spiritual Assembly, 9 March 1965, in *Messages of the Universal House of Justice 1963–1986*, p. 50, para. 23.3. Emphasis added.

176. Both letters cited in a letter written on behalf of the Universal House of Justice to the author, 13 August 2002, together with an enclosed memorandum by the Research Department of the Universal House of Justice.

177. From a letter of the Universal House of Justice to a National Spiritual Assembly, 19 July 1982, in *Messages of the Universal House of Justice 1963–1986*, pp. 549–50, para. 333.4 Emphasis added.

178. From a letter of the Universal House of Justice to the Continental Boards of Counsellors and National Spiritual Assemblies, 24 April 1972, in ibid. p. 214, para. 111.1. Emphasis added.

179. From a letter of the Universal House of Justice to an individual, 7 December 1969, in ibid. p. 161, para. 75.18. Emphasis added.

180. From a letter of the Universal House of Justice to all National Spiritual Assemblies, Naw-Rúz 1974, in ibid. p. 266, para. 142.1.

181. From a letter written on behalf of the Universal House of Justice to an individual, 27 April 1995. Emphasis added.

182. From a letter written on behalf of the Universal House of Justice to an individual, 28 May 1984.

183. From a letter of the Universal House of Justice to a National Spiritual Assembly, 17 June 1987, cited in 'Developing Distinctive Bahá'í Communities: Guidelines for Spiritual Assemblies', a compilation prepared by the Office of Assembly Development of the National Spiritual Assembly of the Bahá'ís of the United States.

184. Shoghi Effendi, *World Order*, p. 203. Emphasis added.

185. Bahá'u'lláh, *Tablets*, pp. 69–70. Emphasis added.

186. ibid. p. 125. Emphasis added.

187. ibid. p. 129.

188. ibid. p. 27.

189. ibid. p. 89.

190. ibid. p. 93.

191. From a letter written on behalf of Shoghi Effendi, 30 November 1930, cited in a letter written on behalf of the Universal House of Justice to an individual, 27 April 1995.

192. Shoghi Effendi, *World Order*, pp. 19–20. Emphasis added.

193. From a letter of Shoghi Effendi, 27 February 1929, in *Compilation*, vol. 1, p. 333, no. 745. Emphasis added.
194. Shoghi Effendi, *God Passes By*, p. 411.
195. See *Messages of the Universal House of Justice 1963–1986*, pp. 269, para. 142.14; and p. 311, and para. 162.37.
196. Shoghi Effendi, *Advent of Divine Justice*, p. 27. Emphasis added.
197. Shoghi Effendi, *Messages to the Bahá'í World*, p. 7. Emphasis added.
198. ibid. pp. 8–9. Emphasis added.
199. ibid. p. 126. Emphasis added.
200. Shoghi Effendi, *God Passes By*, pp. 315–16.
201. Shoghi Effendi, *Messages to the Bahá'í World*, p. 84.
202. From a letter of the Universal House of Justice to the Bahá'ís of the World, April 1964, in *Messages of the Universal House of Justice 1963–1986*, p. 32, para. 14.5.
203. From a letter of the Universal House of Justice to all National Spiritual Assemblies, 4 January 1994.
204. Shoghi Effendi, *Bahá'í Administration*, p. 39. Emphasis added.
205. Shoghi Effendi, *World Order*, p. 148. Emphasis added.
206. Shoghi Effendi, *Bahá'í Administration*, p. 63. Emphasis added.
207. From a letter of Shoghi Effendi, 25 February 1951, in Shoghi Effendi, *Unfolding Destiny*, p. 261. Emphasis added.
208. Shoghi Effendi, *Advent of Divine Justice*, p. 14. Emphasis added.
209. Shoghi Effendi, *Messages to the Bahá'í World*, p. 8. Emphasis added.
210. Shoghi Effendi, *Citadel of Faith*, pp. 94–5.
211. From a letter of Shoghi Effendi to the Bahá'ís of the East, 1924, in *Compilation*, vol. 1, p. 329, no. 741. Emphasis added.
212. Shoghi Effendi, *God Passes By*, pp. 59–60.
213. See Article IX of the By-Laws of the Universal House of Justice, and annotations below.
214. From a letter of the Universal House of Justice to all National Spiritual Assemblies, 30 May 1997.
215. See Article III, Section 2 of the By-Laws and, annotations below.
216. Shoghi Effendi, *Directives from the Guardian*, p. 136. Emphasis added.
217. Bahá'u'lláh, *Kitáb-i-Aqdas*, para. 42. Emphasis added.
218. From a letter of the Universal House of Justice to an

individual, 7 December 1969, in *Messages of the Universal House of Justice 1963–1986*, p. 159, para. 75.14.

219. Bahá'u'lláh, *Kitáb-i-Aqdas*, note 49, p. 121.

220. 'Abdu'l-Bahá, *Selections*, p. 215.

221. Shoghi Effendi, *God Passes By*, p. 371.

222. Shoghi Effendi, *Citadel of Faith*, pp. 94–5 and Shoghi Effendi, *Messages to the Bahá'í World*, pp. 7–8, 151–2.

223. From a letter of the Universal House of Justice to a National Spiritual Assembly, 9 December 1991.

224. From an attachment to a letter written on behalf of the Universal House of Justice to a National Spiritual Assembly, 9 December 1985, in *Lights of Guidance*, pp. 61–2, nos. 216–17.

225. Shoghi Effendi, *World Order*, pp. 22–3. Emphasis added.

226. 'Abdu'l-Bahá, *Will and Testament*, para. 25. Emphasis added.

227. Shoghi Effendi, *Bahá'í Administration*, p. 47.

228. Letter of the Universal House of Justice to an individual, 31 January 1985, in *Messages of the Universal House of Justice 1963–1986*, pp. 655–9.

229. Shoghi Effendi, *Advent of Divine Justice*, p. 22. Emphasis added.

230. From a letter written on behalf of the Universal House of Justice to a National Spiritual Assembly, cited in a compilation on 'Removal of Administrative Rights', 1 January 1989.

231. Bahá'u'lláh, *Kitáb-i-Aqdas*, para. 52.

232. Shoghi Effendi, *God Passes By*, p. 214. Emphasis added.

233. Shoghi Effendi, *Messages to America*, pp. 32–3. Emphasis added.

234. From a letter of Shoghi Effendi to the Bahá'ís of the East, Naw-Rúz 1954, in *Compilation*, vol. 1, p. 341, no. 760.

235. Bahá'u'lláh, *Tablets*, p. 128. Emphasis added.

236. This quotation is from Shoghi Effendi's letter of 8 February 1934 to the Bahá'ís of the West, 'The Dispensation of Bahá'u'lláh', in Shoghi Effendi, *World Order*, p. 153.

5. **Annotations to the By-Laws**

1. Shoghi Effendi, *Messages to the Bahá'í World*, p. 7. Emphasis added.

2. Shoghi Effendi, *Messages to America*, p. 94. Emphasis added.

3. Shoghi Effendi, *Advent of Divine Justice*, p. 63. Emphasis added.

4. Shoghi Effendi, *World Order*, p. 147.

5. ibid. p. 148.
6. ibid. p. 145.
7. ibid. p. 156. Emphasis added.
8. Shoghi Effendi, *God Passes By*, p. 223. Emphasis added.
9. From a letter of the Universal House of Justice to a National Spiritual Assembly, 19 May 1985, in *Lights of Guidance*, pp. 318–19, no. 1072.
10. 'Abdu'l-Bahá, *Will and Testament*, para. 25.
11. Shoghi Effendi, *World Order*, p. 4.
12. 'Abdu'l-Bahá, *Will and Testament*, para. 20.
13. Letter of the Universal House of Justice to the Bahá'ís of the World, 24 June 1968, *Messages of the Universal House of Justice 1963–1986*, p. 131, para. 59 1.
14. From a letter of the Universal House of Justice to a National Spiritual Assembly, 19 May 1994.
15. Shoghi Effendi, *World Order*, p. 144. Emphasis added.
16. Shoghi Effendi, *God Passes By*, p. xv. Emphasis added.
17. Shoghi Effendi, *Messages to America*, p. 79. Emphasis added.
18. ibid. pp. 96–7. Emphasis added.
19. Shoghi Effendi, *Citadel of Faith*, p. 5. Emphasis added.
20. See paragraph 13 of the Declaration of Trust and annotations.
21. Shoghi Effendi, *Advent of Divine Justice*, p. 14. Emphasis added.
22. Shoghi Effendi, *Bahá'í Administration*, p. 90
23. From a letter of the Universal House of Justice to all National Spiritual Assemblies, 4 April 2001, citing Bahá'u'lláh, *Kitáb-i-Aqdas*, para. 1.
24. 'Abdu'l-Bahá, *Will and Testament*, para. 19.
25. Shoghi Effendi, *Bahá'í Administration*, p. 90.
26. Shoghi Effendi, *Directives from the Guardian*, p. 85.
27. Bahá'u'lláh, *Kitáb-i-Aqdas*, para. 30.
28. Shoghi Effendi, *God Passes By*, p. 331.
29. Shoghi Effendi, *Bahá'í Administration*, p. 37.
30. ibid. p. 39.
31. Shoghi Effendi, *God Passes By*, p. 331.
32. Shoghi Effendi, *Bahá'í Administration*, p. 41.
33. The Universal House of Justice, *Four Year Plan*, p. 13.
34. ibid.
35. From a letter written on behalf of the Universal House of Justice to a National Spiritual Assembly, 2 December 1980, in *Lights of Guidance*, p. 5, no. 17.
36. From a letter of the Universal House of Justice to a National

Spiritual Assembly, 12 October 1969, in ibid. p. 6, no. 19.

37. Shoghi Effendi, *Bahá'í Administration*, p. 39.

38. ibid. pp. 37–8.

39. Shoghi Effendi, *God Passes By*, p. 331.

40. See, for example, a letter of the Universal House of Justice to a National Spiritual Assembly, 30 July 1972, in *Lights of Guidance*, p. 42, no. 149.

41. Shoghi Effendi, *Bahá'í Administration*, p. 37.

42. By-Laws of the National Spiritual Assembly, Article VII, Section 3, in *Bahá'í World*, vol. 20, p. 701.

43. From a letter written on behalf of Shoghi Effendi to a National Spiritual Assembly, 11 April 1931, in *Lights of Guidance*, p. 5, no. 17.

44. From a letter written on behalf of Shoghi Effendi to a National Spiritual Assembly, 13 June 1956, in *Messages to the Antipodes*, pp. 411–12.

45. From a letter of the Universal House of Justice to a National Spiritual Assembly, 8 June 1978, in *Lights of Guidance*, p. 7, no. 24. See also a letter written on behalf of Shoghi Effendi to a Local Spiritual Assembly, 28 December 1949, in *Messages to the Antipodes*, p. 277 and a letter written on behalf of Shoghi Effendi to a National Spiritual Assembly, 13 June 1956, in ibid. pp. 411–12.

46. From a letter of the Universal House of Justice to a Bahá'í couple, 25 July 1988.

47. Cited in a memorandum of the Research Department of the Universal House of Justice to the Universal House of Justice, 25 February 2002, attached to an email written on behalf of the Universal House of Justice to the author, 25 February 2002.

48. ibid.

49. Shoghi Effendi, *Bahá'í Administration*, p. 84.

50. ibid. p. 40.

51. Shoghi Effendi, *God Passes By*, pp. 332–3.

52. Shoghi Effendi, *Bahá'í Administration*, p. 40.

53. ibid. pp. 40–1.

54. Shoghi Effendi, *Directives from the Guardian*, p. 50.

55. From a letter written on behalf of Shoghi Effendi to a National Spiritual Assembly, 13 May 1945, in *Messages to the Antipodes*, p. 226.

56. From a letter written on behalf of Shoghi Effendi to a National Spiritual Assembly, 11 June 1934, in *Lights of Guidance*, p. 36, no. 127.

57. Shoghi Effendi, *Bahá'í Administration*, p. 39. Emphasis added.
58. Shoghi Effendi, *God Passes By*, p. 332. Emphasis added.
59. From a letter written on behalf of Shoghi Effendi to an individual, 20 September 1933, in *Lights of Guidance*, p. 36, no. 128.
60. 'Abdu'l-Bahá, *Tablets of the Divine Plan*, p. 74. Emphasis added.
61. See, for example, Shoghi Effendi, *Unfolding Destiny*, p. 368.
62. Shoghi Effendi, *Bahá'í Administration*, pp. 78–80.
63. *National Convention*, December 1992.
64. Shoghi Effendi, *Bahá'í Administration*, pp. 78–80.
65. Rabbaní, *Priceless Pearl*, p. 329.
66. Shoghi Effendi, *Bahá'í Administration*, pp. 143–4. Emphasis added.
67. See Declaration of Trust, p. 6, and annotations above.
68. 'Abdu'l-Bahá, *Selections*, pp. 79–80.
69. Cited in a letter of the Universal House of Justice to the National Spiritual Assembly of New Zealand, 31 May 1988, attached to an email written on behalf of the Universal House of Justice to the author, 13 August 2002.
70. Cited in 'Abdu'l-Bahá, *Paris Talks*, pp. 183–4.
71. Shoghi Effendi, *Messages of Shoghi Effendi to the Indian Subcontinent*, p. 193.
72. Shoghi Effendi, *Directives from the Guardian*, pp. 79–80.
73. ibid. p. 80.
74. From a letter of the Universal House of Justice to the National Spiritual Assembly of New Zealand, 31 May 1988, attached to an email written on behalf of the Universal House of Justice to the author, 13 August 2002.
75. ibid.
76. 'Abdu'l-Bahá, *Will and Testament*, para. 25.
77. ibid. para. 37.
78. Cited in *Messages of the Universal House of Justice 1963–1986*, p. 53, paras. 23.12–14.
79. See a letter of Shoghi Effendi, 29 January 1927, in Shoghi Effendi, *Unfolding Destiny*, p. 62.
80. 'Abdu'l-Bahá, *Tablets*, vol. 1, p. 7.
81. Shoghi Effendi, *Light of Divine Guidance*, vol. 1, p. 182.
82. Shoghi Effendi, *Bahá'í Administration*, p. 80.
83. ibid. p. 79.
84. From a letter written on behalf of Shoghi Effendi to a

National Spiritual Assembly, 12 August 1933, in *Compilation*, vol. 2, p. 101, no. 1455. Emphasis added.

85. From a letter written on behalf of Shoghi Effendi to a National Spiritual Assembly, 18 November 1933, in ibid. p. 103, no. 1456. Emphasis added.
86. From a letter of the Universal House of Justice to all National Spiritual Assemblies, 4 April 2003.
87. Letter of the Universal House of Justice, Riḍván 2003.
88. By-Laws of the National Spiritual Assembly, *Bahá'í World*, vol. 20, p. 702.
89. 'Abdu'l-Bahá, *Will and Testament*, para. 25. Emphasis added.
90. From a letter of the Universal House of Justice to a National Spiritual Assembly, 9 March 1965, in *Messages of the Universal House of Justice 1963–1986*, p. 58, para. 23.24.
91. From a letter of the Universal House of Justice to an individual, 27 May 1966, in ibid. pp. 89–90, para. 35.18.
92. From a letter of the Universal House of Justice to all National Spiritual Assemblies, 15 October 1967, in ibid. p. 155, para. 48.1.
93. Cables of the Universal House of Justice to National Spiritual Assemblies, 15 May 1982, 18 May 1982 and 15 July 1982, in ibid. pp. 541–2 and 548, paras. 326, 327 and 332.
94. 'Abdu'l-Bahá, *Will and Testament*, para. 25.
95. Shoghi Effendi, *World Order*, p. 150.
96. From a letter of the Universal House of Justice to an individual, 7 December 1969, in *Messages of the Universal House of Justice 1963–1986*, pp. 157–8, para. 75.7.
97. From a letter of the Universal House of Justice to an individual, 7 December 1969, in ibid. p. 158, para. 75.10.
98. Cited in a memorandum of the Research Department of the Universal House of Justice to the Universal House of Justice, 25 February 2002, attached to an email written on behalf of the Universal House of Justice to the author, 25 February 2002.
99. Shoghi Effendi, *Bahá'í Administration*, pp. 135–6.
100. ibid. p. 136.
101. Shoghi Effendi, *Light of Divine Guidance*, vol. 1, pp. 67–8.
102. From a letter of Shoghi Effendi to the friends in Persia, 16 January 1932, in *Lights of Guidance*, p. 12, no. 45.
103. From a letter written on behalf of Shoghi Effendi to an

individual, 7 June 1924, in ibid. p. 11, no. 39.

104. From a letter of Shoghi Effendi to the friends in Persia, 16 January 1932, in ibid. p. 12, no. 44.
105. See *Messages of the Universal House of Justice 1963–1986*, p. 208.
106. See *Compilation*, vol. 1, pp. 315–18.
107. Shoghi Effendi, *Bahá'í Administration*, p. 136.
108. Shoghi Effendi, *Light of Divine Guidance*, vol. 1, pp. 68–9.
109. From a letter written on behalf of the Universal House of Justice to a National Spiritual Assembly, 27 July 1981, in *Lights of Guidance*, p. 27, no. 96.
110. From a letter written on behalf of the Universal House of Justice to a National Spiritual Assembly, 18 May 1982, in ibid. p. 25, no. 86.
111. The Universal House of Justice, Declaration of Trust, in *Constitution of the Universal House of Justice*, paras. 9 and 12.
112. From a letter written on behalf of Shoghi Effendi to an individual, 10 July 1942, in *Lights of Guidance*, p. 63, no. 220.
113. From a letter written on behalf of Shoghi Effendi to an individual, 2 October 1935, in ibid. p. 62, no. 218.
114. The Universal House of Justice, *Individual Rights and Freedoms*, para. 19.
115. From a letter written on behalf of Shoghi Effendi to a National Spiritual Assembly, 30 June 1949, in *Lights of Guidance*, pp. 62–3, no. 219.
116. From a letter written on behalf of Shoghi Effendi to an individual, 4 March 1925, in *Compilation*, vol. 3, pp. 55–6, no. 96.
117. Shoghi Effendi, *Directives from the Guardian*, p. 50.
118. From a letter written on behalf of the Universal House of Justice to a National Spiritual Assembly, 22 July 1981, in *Lights of Guidance*, pp. 65–6, no. 230.
119. See Declaration of Trust, paras. 12 and 14, and annotations above.
120. From a letter written on behalf of the Universal House of Justice to a National Spiritual Assembly, 17 July 1979, in *Lights of Guidance*, p. 63, no. 222.
121. From a letter written on behalf of the Universal House of Justice to a National Spiritual Assembly, 1 January 1989.
122. From a letter written on behalf of the Universal House of Justice to a National Spiritual Assembly, 17 June 1975, in *Lights of Guidance*, p. 63, no. 221.
123. Bahá'u'lláh, *Kitáb-i-Aqdas*, note 183, pp. 245–6.

124. 'Abdu'l-Bahá, *Will and Testament*, paras. 17 and 20.
125. ibid. paras. 21–2.
126. From a letter of the Universal House of Justice to an individual, 27 May 1966, in *Messages of the Universal House of Justice 1963–1986*, pp. 89–90, para. 35.18.
127. Cable of the Universal House of Justice to all National Spiritual Assemblies, 21 June 1968, in ibid. p. 130, para. 38.
128. From a letter of the Universal House of Justice to the Bahá'ís of the World, 24 June 1968, in ibid. p. 131, paras. 59.1–2.
129. Letter of the Universal House of Justice to all National Spiritual Assemblies, 24 June 1968, in ibid. pp. 133–4, para. 60.
130. Letter of the Universal House of Justice to the Continental Board of Counsellors and National Spiritual Assemblies, 24 April 1972, in ibid. pp. 214–17, paras. 111.1–111.14.
131. Letter of the Universal House of Justice to all National Spiritual Assemblies, 24 June 1968, in ibid. pp. 133–4, para. 60.
132. Letter of the Universal House of Justice to National Spiritual Assemblies, 10 July 1969, in ibid. p. 149, paras. 70.1–70.4.
133. Letter of the Universal House of Justice to the Bahá'ís of the World, 8 June 1973, in ibid. pp. 246–53, paras. 132.1–132.25.
134. Letter of the Universal House of Justice to all National Spiritual Assemblies, 29 June 1979, in ibid. p. 421, para. 229.
135. Letter of the Universal House of Justice to the Bahá'ís of the World, 3 November 1980, in ibid. pp. 464–6, para. 267.1–267.7.
136. Letter of the Universal House of Justice to the Bahá'ís of the World, 24 October 1985, in ibid. p. 696, para. 439.1.
137. Letter of the Universal House of Justice, 25 May 1986, in *Bahá'í World*, vol. 20, p. 681.
138. Letter of the Universal House of Justice, 25 October 1990, in ibid. p. 686.
139. From a letter of the Universal House of Justice to the Bahá'ís of the World, 24 June 1968, in *Messages of the Universal House of Justice 1963–1986*, p. 132, para. 59.4.
140. The Universal House of Justice, *Institution of the Counsellors*, p. 34.
141. From a letter of the Universal House of Justice to all

National Spiritual Assemblies, 27 March 1978, in *Messages of the Universal House of Justice 1963–1986*, p. 376, para. 206.2.

142. Shoghi Effendi, *Messages to the Bahá'í World*, p. 44.
143. ibid. pp. 58–9. Emphasis added.
144. ibid. p. 63.
145. ibid. p. 128.
146. Cable of the Universal House of Justice to all National Spiritual Assemblies, 21 June 1968, in *Messages of the Universal House of Justice 1963–1986*, p. 130.
147. From a letter of the Universal House of Justice to the Bahá'ís of the World, 24 June 1968, in ibid. p. 132, para. 59.5. See also letter of the Universal House of Justice to the Continental Boards of Counsellors and National Spiritual Assemblies, 1 October 1969, in ibid. pp. 150–3, paras. 72.1–72.11.
148. Letter of the Universal House of Justice to the Bahá'ís of the World, 7 October 1973, in ibid. pp. 255–6, paras. 137.1–137.6.
149. ibid. para. 137.4.
150. *Lights of Guidance*, pp. 328–38, nos. 1103–36.
151. From a letter of the Universal House of Justice to the International Teaching Centre, 4 February 1976, in ibid. p. 328, no. 1106.
152. The Universal House of Justice, *Institution of the Counsellors*, pp. 9–10.
153. From a summary of points prepared by the Universal House of Justice, based on a letter of the Universal House of Justice to a National Spiritual Assembly, 20 May 1970, in *Lights of Guidance*, p. 332, no. 1117.
154. The Universal House of Justice, *Institution of the Counsellors*, p. 10.
155. From a letter of the Universal House of Justice to a National Spiritual Assembly, 25 March 1966, in *Lights of Guidance*, pp. 8–9, no. 29.
156. 'Abdu'l-Bahá, *Will and Testament*, para. 37.
Guidance, p. 36, no. 127.

Appendix II.

1. As published in *Bahá'í World*, vol. 20, pp. 720–3.

Appendix III.

1. As published in *Bahá'í World*, vol. 20, pp. 696–704.

Index